I0815976

Trio of Angolan giraffe

ETOSHA SELF-DRIVE

Routes, Roads & Ratings

Text by **Anja Denker**

Photos by **Anja Denker**

Published by

HPH Publishing

Aerial image of Ekuma river with grasslands and salt deposits interspersed and shaped by wind deflation

Aerial image of flamingo formation over Etosha Pan

Contents

“Only nature is eternal unless we senselessly destroy it. In 50 years, nobody will be interested in the results of the conferences which fill today’s headlines. But 50 years from now, when a lion walks into the red dawn and roars resoundingly, it will mean something to people and quicken their hearts whether they speak English, German, Russian or Swahili. They will stand in quiet awe as, for the first time in their lives, they watch 20 thousand zebras wander across the endless plains.” (Bernhard Grzimek, 1959)

Lion pride at Sueda waterhole

Etosha

African elephant bulls, oryx antelope and springbok at m'Bari waterhole

INTRODUCTION

The flagship national park of Namibia, as well as the country's number one tourist destination, Etosha is the true embodiment of its name, 'Great White Place', and you will be hard-pressed to find a more fitting description of this unique, characteristic and, at times, harsh, spellbinding tract of land.

A place of refuge for an astonishing abundance and variety of wildlife as well as diverse plant communities – characterised by a white salt pan so vast it is visible from space – an important centre of evolution, fascinating geology and shaped by tumultuous historical events, Etosha's fame transcends Namibia's boundaries, and rightly so.

Conjure in your mind a place where you can cast your eyes over an immense expanse so barren and bereft of any form of life, seemingly stretching into eternity.

Imagine then this same expanse filling with water, a shimmering mirage interwoven with undulating hues of pink defining a horizon; that of thousands upon thousands of flamingos having arrived to breed in this former desolate, seemingly barren environment.

These images define Etosha, a place of startling, stark contrasts and equally stark seasonal changes amid dramatic, expansive landscapes. A total of 31 plant communities occur in the park. Despite its flat topography, it is ecologically more complex and diverse than expected. Owing to topography and soil in different areas, some ecozones occur in pockets, which are intricately linked. Woodlands, dwarf-shrub savanna, thornbush savanna, grasslands, saline pans and dolomite hills are testament to the diversity of the habitats, hosting over 114 species of mammals, approximately 412 species of birds, and roughly 112 reptile species, amphibians and invertebrates.

Seasonal changes shape the life patterns of flora and fauna to form a continuous cycle of the ancient rhythm of life. In the dry period, high temperatures sap the energy of most living organisms; water levels sink in most waterholes, and vegetation and grasses wither under the relentless onslaught of the sun's burning rays. Wildlife congregates around the waterholes, and predators have it easy. When, at last, spectacular thunderstorms unleash torrents of rain onto the parched earth, the transformation is swift and dramatic. It heralds the season of plenty; new life begins – from the lush new grass and vegetation seemingly sprouting overnight to the birth of new babies throughout the animal kingdom.

Every season has its unique appeal and no matter what time of the year visitors choose to visit the park, they are likely to be charmed by the signatory's wide open spaces, an abundance of wildlife and the aura of peace and tranquillity you feel when immersed in the healing power of nature.

Like many other national parks, Etosha faces ongoing challenges. Climate and land-use changes, the current scourge of rhino poaching, human-wildlife conflict along some of the park's boundary fences and maintenance of the infrastructure – impacted by the steady stream of mass tourism – all take their toll and require sound management plans and constant monitoring.

The world is changing at an alarming rate. Increasing resource consumption, pressure to convert wildlife habitats into agricultural and urban land, and climate change to a rapidly growing population growth significantly impact our dwindling wildlife. The probable bleak outlook is one where wildlife, forced from their natural habitat, can only eke out an existence in controlled environments like national parks, sanctuaries and corridors.

It is, therefore, imperative that national treasures like Etosha are safeguarded and can continue to act unequivocally as strongholds and places of safety for our wildlife.

Male lion

Female leopard

ACCESS

Etosha can be accessed by land or plane, although most visitors probably choose the former.

FLIGHTS

Fly Namibia offers direct flights from Windhoek to Etosha under its safari flight schedule several days a week, operating directly from **Eros Airport**. Various lodges outside the park also provide **charter flights**, ideal options for those pressed for time or seeking a quick weekend break.

CAR RENTAL

Windhoek's **Hosea Kutako Airport** is the closest international airport, and it is ideal for renting a car directly upon arrival and making your way to Etosha National Park at your own leisurely pace. Access to the park is by road through four access gates, conveniently situated in the south, north, east and west.

Etosha National Park

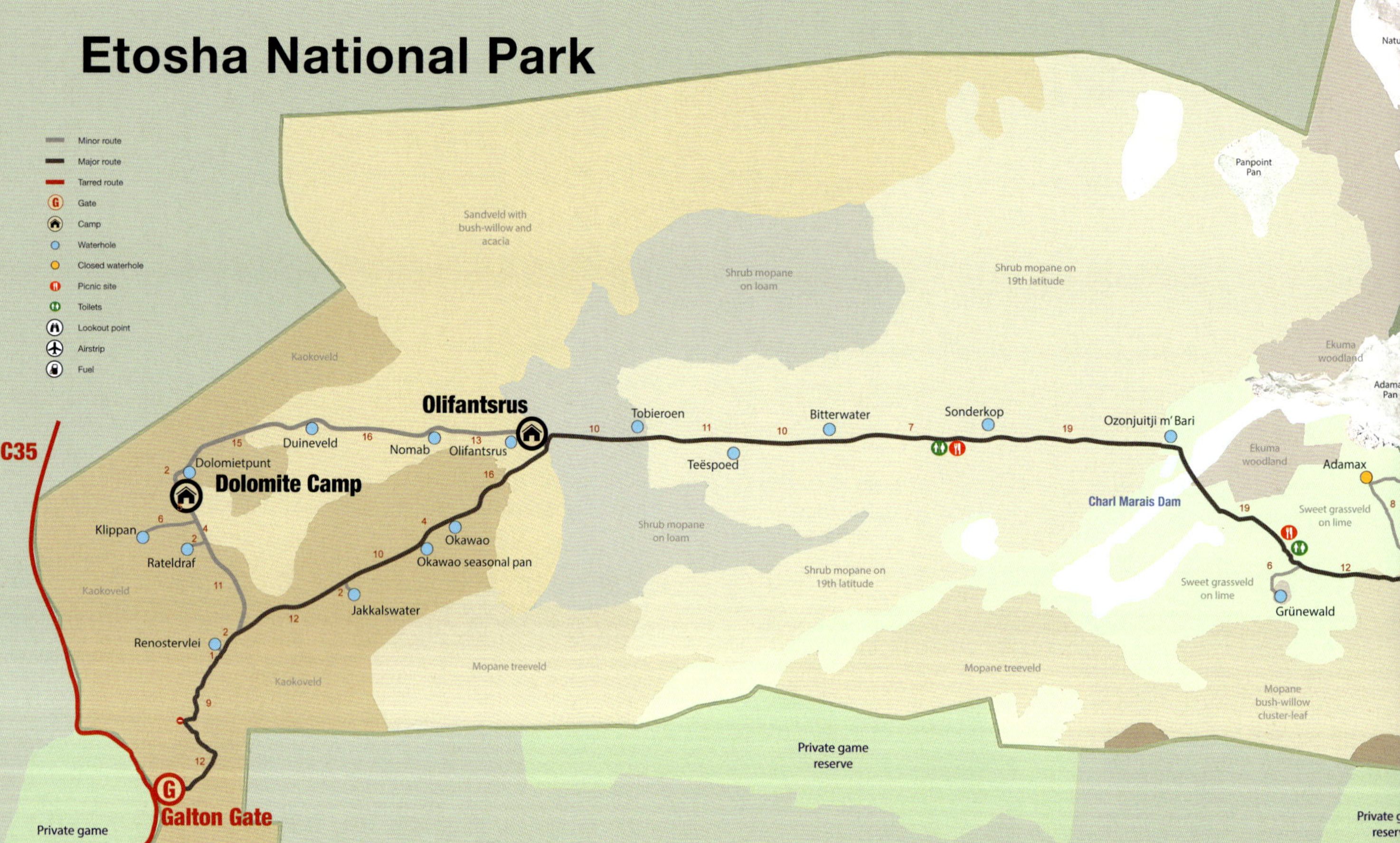

SOUTH

Andersson Gate, named after the early explorer Charles Andersson, one of the first Europeans to reach Etosha, is the park's southern gate that can be accessed from the C38 via Outjo by tar road. The distance to **Okaukuejo Camp** from the gate is 17 km by tar road.

NORTH

The gateway to the north is the **King Nehale LyaMpingana Gate**, named after Nehale Mpingana, king of the Ondonga tribe, who successfully led the 500 men who destroyed the first German Fort at Namutoni in 1904. The northern town of Ondangwa is the closest large town, boasting a small airport. The distance from Ondangwa to King Nehale Gate is 118 km on the B1 tar road. The nearest rest camps in the park from the gate are **Namutoni** at 31.2 km and **Onkoshi** at 30 km.

EAST

Visitors can access the park via the B1 or C38 through the **Von Lindequist Gate**. Tsumeb is the closest town, approximately 103 km from the gate, travelling on tar road. The gate's name is in honour of Dr F von Lindequist, the governor of former German South West Africa, who proclaimed Etosha a game reserve on 22 March 1907. The closest rest camp is **Namutoni**, a mere 11 km stretch of tar road from the gate.

WEST

Galton Gate, named after the explorer Sir Francis Galton, who, together with Charles Andersson, were the first Europeans to record the existence of Etosha in 1851. The gate is the access for the western side of Etosha. The closest town is Kamanjab, 67.8 km away, travelling on the C35 tar road. The location of Dolomite Rest Camp is 43.1 km from Galton Gate, travelling along a scenic gravel road.

NOTE

- All roads in Etosha National Park consist of graded gravel roads, including the main road C38, as well as subsidiary roads leading to various camps and waterholes. The only exceptions are the 18 km stretch of tar road running from Andersson Gate to Okaukuejo Rest Camp and the 12 km tar road from Von Lindequist Gate to Namutoni Rest Camp.
- The conditions of the roads vary throughout the year, depending on the volume of traffic and weather conditions. Heavy to mild corrugation can be encountered in places, and sharp stones may cause a few punctures. Deflating tyre pressure will ensure a more comfortable drive and lessen the impact on the road.

Colours on the map indicate major vegetation zones

- **Adhering to the speed limit, which is 60 km/h, is crucial.** It is advised to **stick to 40 km/h or less**, allowing for more observant travel, with a far better chance of enhancing your wildlife sightings, as well as limiting kicking up excessive fine dust, which is so predominant in Etosha; for instance, when having to apply the brakes suddenly. A slower speed is also less likely to spook the wildlife and birdlife when stopping, allowing you better views and photography opportunities.
- At the time of going to press, a permanent solution to gravel roads was envisaged by the Ministry of Environment, Forestry and Tourism (MEFT) in the form of a low-volume seal road at hotspot tourist attractions in the park, covering an area of 250 km.

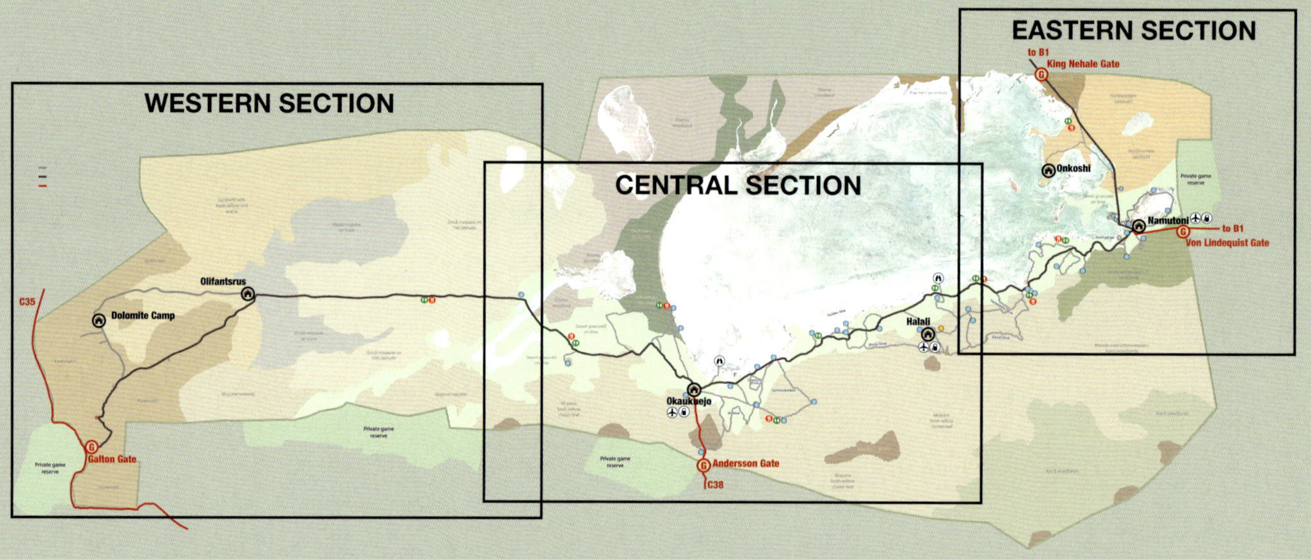

African elephant crossing from Halali plains

REST CAMPS IN ETOSHA

The park boasts five main rest camps and one exclusive camping-only camp, each unique and with a special charm and flair, all managed by Namibia Wildlife Rest camps (NWR).

- **Classic collection:** Namutoni, Halali and Okaukuejo
- **Eco collection:** Dolomite and Onkoshi
- **Adventure collection:** Olifantsrus campsite opened in 2014 and is the first camping resort in the west.
- **New kids on the block:** Onkoshi and Dolomite, opened in September 2008 and June 2011 respectively.

DISTANCES BETWEEN MAIN CAMPS/REST CAMPS

- Okaukuejo to Olifantsrus – 126 km
- Okaukuejo to Dolomite – 173 km
- Okaukuejo to Halali – 68 km
- Okaukuejo to Namutoni – 133 km
- Halali to Namutoni – 73 km
- Namutoni to Onkoshi – 41.5 km

PARK ETIQUETTE AND REGULATIONS

- Familiarise yourself with the rules stipulated on the entry permit handed to you upon arrival at the park entrance gates. This entry permit requires your signature and must be handed in at reception to pay park fees. Upon leaving the park, you must hand in the same entry permit with proof of payment to the gate officials.
- Declare firearms upon arrival at the entrance gates.
- NO drones are permitted.
- NO open vehicles – except game-drive vehicles – no motorcycles, unsealed firearms, pellet guns, bows and arrows, and catapults are permitted.
- Stay in your vehicle at ALL times, except at designated picnic sites and rest camps; keep the doors closed, do not lean out of or sit on windows or climb on top of your vehicle for better views.
- Do not exceed the speed limit of 60 km/h at any given time.
- NO off-road driving.
- Do not litter or feed the animals in the rest camps or the park.
- A valid driver's licence is required.
- Animals have the right of way.
- Do not remove plants, wood or any form of wildlife.
- NO hooting, shouting, loud music or engine revving is allowed, whether in rest camps or the park.
- Do not drink and drive.
- Do not cause a wildfire or toss cigarette butts out of the window.
- Take your litter back to camp.
- Switch your car engines off at waterholes and sightings for the consideration of wildlife and people filming or taking video footage.
- No pets allowed.
- Adhere to the gate times, which open at sunrise and close at sunset.

Black rhino

Accommodation

OKAUKUEJO CAMP

Okaukuejo opened its doors to tourists in 1955 and is the flagship resort of Etosha owing to the iconic and much-famed floodlit waterhole. It can be accessed from the C38 via Outjo through the **Andersson Gate**. It is an excellent option if you arrive in Etosha late or must depart from the park's southern end early in the morning.

The camp also features a landmark **stone tower** built by the German Schutztruppe, a perfect spot for sunset or sunrise shots or to photograph the camp. It surrounds from a bird's eye perspective.

Okaukuejo, the park's administrative headquarters, houses the **Etosha Ecological Institute**, which opened in 1974. It plays a crucial role in ongoing research, and the **museum** there is well worth a visit.

The resort is atmospheric with its beautifully crafted **old stone buildings**, **large trees** and sprawling **green lawns** with **prolific birdlife**. Groundscraper thrush and African hoopoe love to forage on the lawns for worms and other tasty morsels, the diminutive pearl-spotted owlet hunts in broad daylight and sunbirds frequent the little aloe garden near the service station. Okaukuejo is a holiday destination; you don't have to leave camp. Still, you can enjoy endless wildlife meandering to and from the waterhole 24/7.

ACCOMMODATION FACILITIES

- Five luxurious premier double-storey chalets with a balcony overlooking the waterhole. There are two bedrooms with an en suite bathroom, and downstairs are two single beds and queen-size beds upstairs. Lounge area, fridge and tea station.
- Thirty double room chalets overlooking the waterhole with en suite bathrooms, fridge and tea station near the waterhole.
- Two self-catering family chalets with two bedrooms (4 beds), en suite bathroom, kitchenette and braai area.
- Twenty bush chalets (2 beds), bathroom, lounge area, fridge, tea station and braai facilities.
- Forty-five double rooms with en suite bathroom, fridge and tea station.
- Two disabled-access chalets (2 beds), en suite bathroom, fridge and tea station.
- Thirty-seven campsites with power points, water and braai facilities. Ablution blocks provide shower and toilet facilities for campers, as well as facilities for washing dishes.
- Other amenities include a restaurant, pool, bar, kiosk, curio shop and filling station.

Remember to pay your park fees at reception. Okaukuejo and Namutoni are the only camps where you can pay your park fees.

Stone tower at Okaukuejo

Halali Camp

HALALI CAMP

Halali Camp was commissioned in 1967, strategically situated **halfway between Okaukuejo and Namutoni** at the foot of one of the dolomite hills, the signature trademark of the landscape around Halali. The camp nestles among beautiful large old mopane trees and shrubs; it is ideal for ventures in virtually any direction and exploring the many waterholes and scenic drives in proximity.

Thanks to its central location, Halali serves as a convenient and popular stopover for lunch and can get quite busy, but is otherwise quieter than the other camps, with a natural, rustic feel. It is a paradise for bird lovers, with owls being Halali's speciality. **African scops-owl**, **southern white-faced owl**, **barn owl** and **pearl-spotted owlets** can roost in trees around the camp. Look out for noisy **bare-cheeked babblers**, the striking **violet wood-hoopoe**, **Monteiro's hornbill**, and **Carp's tit**, some of the Namibian near-endemics that can be ticked off right on the doorstep of your chalet.

Other critters that make camp life in Halali interesting are the **honey badger**, **scrub hare** and **striped tree squirrels**. Keep your flashlight handy at night and check the trees for **bush babies**.

Taking the short walking trail leading up to the **dolomite hill** in camp is worthwhile, as it supports quite a few '**ghost**' or **moringa trees**, **bird plum**, tall **common corkwood** and a few **Grewia species**. The view from the large dolomite boulders over the waterhole and beyond is very rewarding.

ACCOMMODATION FACILITIES

- Forty double rooms with en suite bathroom, fridge, tea station and large sliding door leading onto a small, shaded veranda.
- Five honeymoon chalets with queen-size beds, en suite bathrooms, a fridge, a tea station and a small private garden with a jacuzzi.
- Four rooms with disabled access (2 beds), en suite bathroom, fridge and tea station.
- Ten bush chalets (2 beds) with bathroom, lounge area, fridge, tea station and braai facilities.
- Ten bush chalets (4 beds) with bathroom, lounge area, fridge, tea station and braai facilities.
- Two self-catering family chalets with two bedrooms (4 beds), en suite bathroom, kitchenette and braai area.
- Fifty-eight campsites have braai facilities, power points and water. The Halali campsite is the largest of the three main camps, nestled under shady mopane trees.
- Five ablution blocks with disability access without laundry area and small kitchen.
- Two ablution blocks with disability access, a laundry area and a small kitchen.
- Other amenities include a restaurant, pool, bar, picnic area, filling station and a small shop selling basics and serving as a curio shop.

The **Moringa waterhole**, named after the signature trees that grow nearby, is one of Halali's best assets and well worth spending a few hours here – expect to be surprised.

NAMUTONI CAMP

Namutoni, the rest camp with probably the most interesting and eventful historical past, officially welcomed visitors in 1957. Visitors can access the easternmost camp through the **Von Lindequist Gate**. Tsumeb is the closest town, approximately 103 km from the gate. Apart from the fact that the landmark old fort, with its striking architecture, holds a massive appeal to visitors, the proximity to Fischer's Pan at the King Nehale waterhole in camp is a big drawcard for birders.

Namutoni has a **regal, quiet, relaxing charm**, with well-tended **green spaces** and **beautiful old trees** and is a testament to the fact that the rainfall in the eastern part of Etosha is higher than in the west. Look out for the **ring-wood tree**, **white seringa**, **Sycamore fig**, **strangler fig**, **bird plum** and **mustard bush** or tree, as well as the signatory tall **fan palms**, also known as **Makalani palms**, a favourite nesting site for palm swifts. For that reason, it is a haven for **waterbirds**. The lush reed beds of the **King Nehale waterhole** support a great variety of birdlife, as does the adjacent Fischer's Pan when holding water. Dining in the open courtyard of the restaurant under a canopy of tall trees, listening to the sounds of nature and gazing up at the expanse of the starry canopy above is a truly unforgettable adventure.

The resident gang of **banded mongooses** entertains the camp, enchanting visitors and offering many photo opportunities. The **proximity of a few waterholes** near the camp is a huge bonus, enabling visitors to use the excellent light and still make it to camp before gate closing times in under 10 minutes.

All rest camps offer free Wi-Fi; the signposted passwords are available at reception and the restaurant.

ACCOMMODATION FACILITIES

- Twenty-four double rooms; open plan bedroom and small lounge area with fridge and tea station, and en suite bathroom.
- Sliding doors open to a small enclosed private seating area in front of the room and the back of the bathroom, with an additional outside shower.
- Twenty bush chalets, spacious open plan bedroom, small lounge area with fridge and tea station, and en suite bathroom. Sliding doors open to a small enclosed private seating area in front and to the back of the bathroom, with an additional outside shower.
- Twenty-five campsites with power points, electricity and braai facilities. The spacious campsite is the only one that boasts grass cover and is nestled under large, shady trees.
- Communal ablution blocks provide shower and toilet facilities for campers and facilities for washing dishes.
- Additional amenities include a restaurant, bar with kiosk, pool, small shop selling basics and serving as a curio shop, filling station and museum (currently under restoration).

Aerial view of Namutoni Camp and King Nehale waterhole

Milky way over Onkoshi Camp

ONKOSHI CAMP

Suppose you seek **true seclusion** in style and **breathtaking scenery**. In that case, Onkoshi offers a more luxurious off-the-beaten-track experience in the park.

Listed under the Eco Portfolio of NWR, this low-impact camp is run almost entirely on solar power and a generator during peak times. At 22:00 until early morning, the power is switched off. The 15 free-standing chalets line the edge of the massive pan, interlinked by an elevated wooden walkway.

The camp has no waterhole but beguiles through the **solitude** and **breathtaking scenery**. During a good rainy season, the pan is likely to hold water and this is an absolute spectacle, drawing various **waterbirds**, including **flamingo**. The unobstructed view over the pan offers the most panoramic and **spectacular sunsets and sunrises**, best viewed or photographed with a sundowner drink in hand on the sunset deck right on the pan, by the pool or the privacy of your balcony. **Oryx** are usually in the vicinity, often lying on the pan; giraffe can be seen browsing on the vegetation around your chalet and **spotted hyena** frequently pass by. On hot summer nights, safely ensconced in your bed under mosquito netting and sliding doors wide open, the deep guttural **roar of a lion** resonating through the night or the plaintive howl of the **black-backed jackal** can be heard, making your getaway at Onkoshi resort near perfect.

ACCOMMODATION FACILITIES

- Fourteen luxurious chalets with spacious lounge area, bathroom including bath and shower, sliding doors opening to outside, additional shower and balcony. Two beds with unobstructed view over the expanse of the pan.
- One honeymoon chalet has a spacious lounge area and bathroom, including a bath and shower, sliding doors opening to the outside, an additional shower and a balcony. Queen bed with unobstructed view over the expanse of the pan.
- Onkoshi is situated on the northernmost side of the park, close to the Andoni plains and **King Nehale LyaMpingana Gate**.
- Additional amenities include a restaurant with a spacious lounge area, bar, outside deck, swimming pool and small curio shop in the reception area. The chalets have no fridge or kettle, but hot water can be obtained from the kitchen for tea and coffee. The lounge area is the best signal to pick up a Wi-Fi signal.

DOLOMITE CAMP

Another low-impact resort listed under the NWR's eco collection, Dolomite Camp, is in western Etosha and is best accessed via the **Galton Gate**, approximately 43km away.

Please note that Dolomite Camp does not accept day visitors; it only accepts booked overnight guests.

On arriving at Dolomite Camp, guests park their vehicles in the shaded parking area at the foot of the hill, where they will be collected with all their belongings by a golf cart or game-drive vehicle and brought to reception.

Magnificent large **star chestnut trees**, **tamboti**, **purple-pod cluster-leaf**, **red bushwillow**, **common paper-bark** and **mopane trees** are some of the natural trees growing on the dolomite ridge, offering a haven for birdlife. Other species to look out for are the **Kaoko pork bush** or **wolftoon**, **butterfly leaf** and **white seringa**. Expect to see one of Namibia's endemics, the striking **Hartlaub's spurfowl**, or the near-endemic **rockrunner** and **white-tailed shrike**, among others.

The camp is unfenced, adding to the thrill of an authentic experience in nature. For this very reason, guests are not allowed to walk about after dark. They will be dropped off by vehicle or escorted to and from the chalet by a staff member. Visitors can spot **rock hyrax** in and around the camp. It is not uncommon to have a **giraffe** clamber up the dolomite slope and browse on some leaves near your chalet. **Chacma baboons** are found only on the western side of Etosha and sometimes make a nuisance of themselves in camp.

ACCOMMODATION FACILITIES

- Seventeen chalets and three deluxe chalets, complete with a small plunge pool, are nestled among the rocky outcrops atop the dolomite mountain ridge.
- Facing either east or west, with unobstructed views over the scenic plains below, you have the distinct feeling of being at one with nature.
- Each chalet has a thatch roof, canvas walls and large panoramic wooden retractable doors leading to a private, elevated wooden deck with seating, ideal for watching a truly unforgettable African sunrise or sunset. En suite bathroom, tea and coffee station and fridge are included.
- Chalets 13 and 14 have a direct bird's-eye view of the waterhole. Still, you can spot the wildlife approaching the waterhole over the plains below from all the chalets.
- Other amenities include a restaurant, guest lounge and bar, fireside boma, two restaurant areas, swimming pool with sunset deck and small curio shop.

Visitors who seek peace and tranquillity will be delighted by the rugged yet luxurious charm of Dolomite Camp. It is off the beaten track in natural, unspoilt wilderness.

On a recent visit to Dolomite, the author had the resident lion pride stroll right across the parking lot just after their return from a game drive. Heading out of camp at first light the following day, they met a black rhino on a stroll to the Dolomite waterhole.

Dolomite point waterhole

African elephant at Olifantsrus waterhole and hide

OLIFANTSRUS CAMPSITE

Olifantsrus is Etosha's **first camping-only facility** listed under the NWR Adventure Collection. Located in western Etosha, this exclusive campsite is between Okaukuejo and Dolomite, and it offers picnic facilities for day visitors until 16:00. Commencing operations in 2014, this small, intimate gem offers several sites near the fence with unhampered wilderness views.

The most incredible feature is the state-of-the-art, two-storey hide jutting out over the Olifantsrus waterhole. You can access the hide via a wooden walkway. The upper level provides seating in a semi-circle of wooden benches next to open hatches overlooking the waterhole. Wooden trays in front of you provide ample space for binoculars, camera equipment or sundowner drinks.

The lower level is truly dramatic, with an extra-strength reflective glass front, allowing you to immerse yourself in a truly unforgettable wildlife encounter by creating the feeling that you are standin right in the waterhole.

A more sobering reminder is contained in the information centre, bearing testament to the culling of 525 elephants between 1983 and 1985, deemed necessary at the time. The elephant skulls and a massive steel structure used to hoist up the elephant carcasses for processing are a haunting reminder of Olifantsrus' controversial past. The Afrikaans 'Olifantsrus' fittingly translates as 'elephants' rest'.

Lying in your tent at night under the canopy of stars, with the glow of campfires flickering and the sounds of the bush lulling you to sleep, you are hard-pressed to find a more intimate and authentic camping adventure than this piece of paradise called Olifantsrus.

ACCOMMODATION FACILITIES

- Ten campsites have five power stands, and power is shared between two campsites.
- Each campsite has a wooded, shaded stand, with mopane trees offering additional shade. The campsite can accommodate a maximum of eight people.
- The communal shower, toilet and kitchen blocks are modern and clean, and there is additional space for doing laundry.
- A small kiosk opposite reception offers refreshments, snacks and is the best area to pick up a Wi-Fi signal.
- Run on solar power and a generator, power is switched off at 22:00 until early morning.
- The camp has a wonderful, intimate feel, surrounded by bushveld, with many sites looking directly into the wilderness.
- The picnic sites have a thatch roof, concrete tables and seating. Several shaded wooden picnic sites are also on offer for day visitors.

Etosha Pan – a brief geomorphological and geological overview

The park lies on the **western escarpment of southern Africa**, immediately east of the Skeleton Coast and northeast and northwest of the Namib and Kalahari deserts, respectively. Only the western part of Etosha is marked by dolomite reliefs and a mountainous landscape and belongs to the Precambrian basement.

Etosha Pan

The Etosha Pan is a large, endorheic* basin, covering an area of approximately **4760 km²** and stretching some **120 km from east to west and 55 km north to south**, at latitude 19° S and longitude 16° E; an area so vast, it is **visible from space**. Although the surface area is markedly flat, the pan is **subtly tilted to the east**, with a gradient difference of about five metres. This tilting sets the pan's gradient to an average of 1:22 400. The **pan covers** about **23% of the park**, with 19 additional smaller pans covering an area of approximately 877 km², or 3.9%. Viewed from a geological aspect, the Cuvelai-Etosha Basin – more correctly called the **Cuvelai Basin** since Etosha is just the lowland culmination of its drainage – is encompassed by the **Ovambo Basin**, which in turn is part of the **Kalahari Basin**.

Climate

The result of a climatic history of alternating dry and wet periods over the last 70 million years has filled the Ovambo Basin with layers of sand, silt and clay, thus lying at an altitude of approximately 1 100 m above sea level. This flat plain constitutes the most significant part of the Etosha National Park.

Geomorphology

Geomorphological studies have shown that the Etosha Pan is not an erosional landform as previously believed but a **relic of a large lake**, termed **Lake Kunene**, which existed most likely until the Late Pliocene. In the intervening period, Lake Etosha became minor and sporadic, which owes its development to diversifying the Kunene River from the Ovambo Basin through intense pluvial phases and tectonic plate activity. Scientists have found a variety of fossils in Etosha Pan, for instance, of semi-aquatic antelope like the sitatunga and tsessebe, as well as pieces of fish fossils belonging to the *Clarias* species, substantiating evidence of perennial lake conditions.

Lake Etosha evolved as an independent entity, scoured by relentless winds, culminating into the dry, flat, immense depression of salt and clay into the modern-day **Etosha Pan**.

Aerial view over Ekuma river draining into Etosha Pan

Flamingo flying over the Ekuma river

We can describe wind erosion as deflation. Typical of arid regions, the Etosha Pan has developed into a **deflation pan**. The present-day floor of this pan consists of 50 m of saline, olive green clay and silt, containing authigenic analcime, monoclinic K-feldspar and glauconite.

An example of the robust and continuous eroding of the wind is the formation of a large, vegetated barchan dune near Andoni, northeastern Etosha. As you approach Andoni from Namutoni, you drive up a slight incline onto the **barchan dune**, and down into the Andoni plains, following the slipface of the dune.

It is hard to imagine that the Etosha Basin was once covered in wind-blown dunes and **resembled the Kalahari**. Still, the red soil on the way is a testament to this.

Most of the time, the pan is a dry, saline desert, with soils mapped as ***calci sodic Solonchaks*** to ***sali calci Solonetzes***, the saltiest, most saline soils in which only a few specialised plants can grow. After good rains or flooding, **salt-loving grasses** like the annual *Sporobolus salsus* and whisk grass grow on the pans.

Perennial grasses and sedges such as prickly brack grass, three salt-loving species of *Sporobolus*, and desert sedge grow on the pan margins. **Woody dwarf shrubs**, namely ink bush and 'blomkoolganna' (*Salsola tuberculata*) also occur on the pan margins.

Ramsar site – a wetland of international importance

During exceptional rainfall, locally known as the **efundja**, surface inflow into the pan is received mainly from the **Cuvelai system** in the northern parts of Namibia and Angola. The pan floods through the **Ekuma River** from the **Omadhiya lakes**, a series of extensive, shallow grassy pans that merge into large bodies of water during periods of flooding. The pan receives occasional inflow from the **Omuramba Owambo**, which drains into **Fischer's Pan** at Namutoni. On the pan's surface, traces can be seen of an ancient watercourse originating from the southwestern part of the pan near Wolfsnes, running eastwards towards Springbokfontein and Okerfontein. During the rainy season, this watercourse can fill to a depth of 60 cm.

Etosha Pan becomes a **shallow wetland paradise when flooded**, where huge flocks of lesser and greater flamingo, pelicans and other waterbirds arrive to feed and breed.

Five groups of wetland systems occur in Namibia, with the Etosha Pan belonging to the **Lacustrine system**, a **standing** or **lentic open water system** with little or no vegetation such as lakes, sinkholes, pans and dams. On 19 June 1995, the Etosha Pan became a Ramsar site, the only inland **Ramsar site**** in Namibia and a wetland of international importance.

*__Endorheic__ – A lake or body of water that doesn't drain towards the ocean. The local topography prevents these lakes from eventually draining towards the sea via rivers. Endorheic lakes are typically found far inland and are most common in desert regions. The primary water loss from these lakes occurs through evaporation and seepage.

**__Ramsar site__ – A wetland site designated as internationally important, especially as a Waterfowl Habitat under the Ramsar Convention. This intergovernmental treaty provides the framework for international cooperation in conserving wetland habitats, established in 1975 by UNESCO. Such a site refers to a wetland of international significance in ecology, botany, zoology, limnology or hydrology.

ROUTES AND ROADS

Camelthorn trees en route to Klippan waterhole

WESTERN ETOSHA

Routes in the western block – from Galton Gate, Dolomite Camp and Olifantsrus

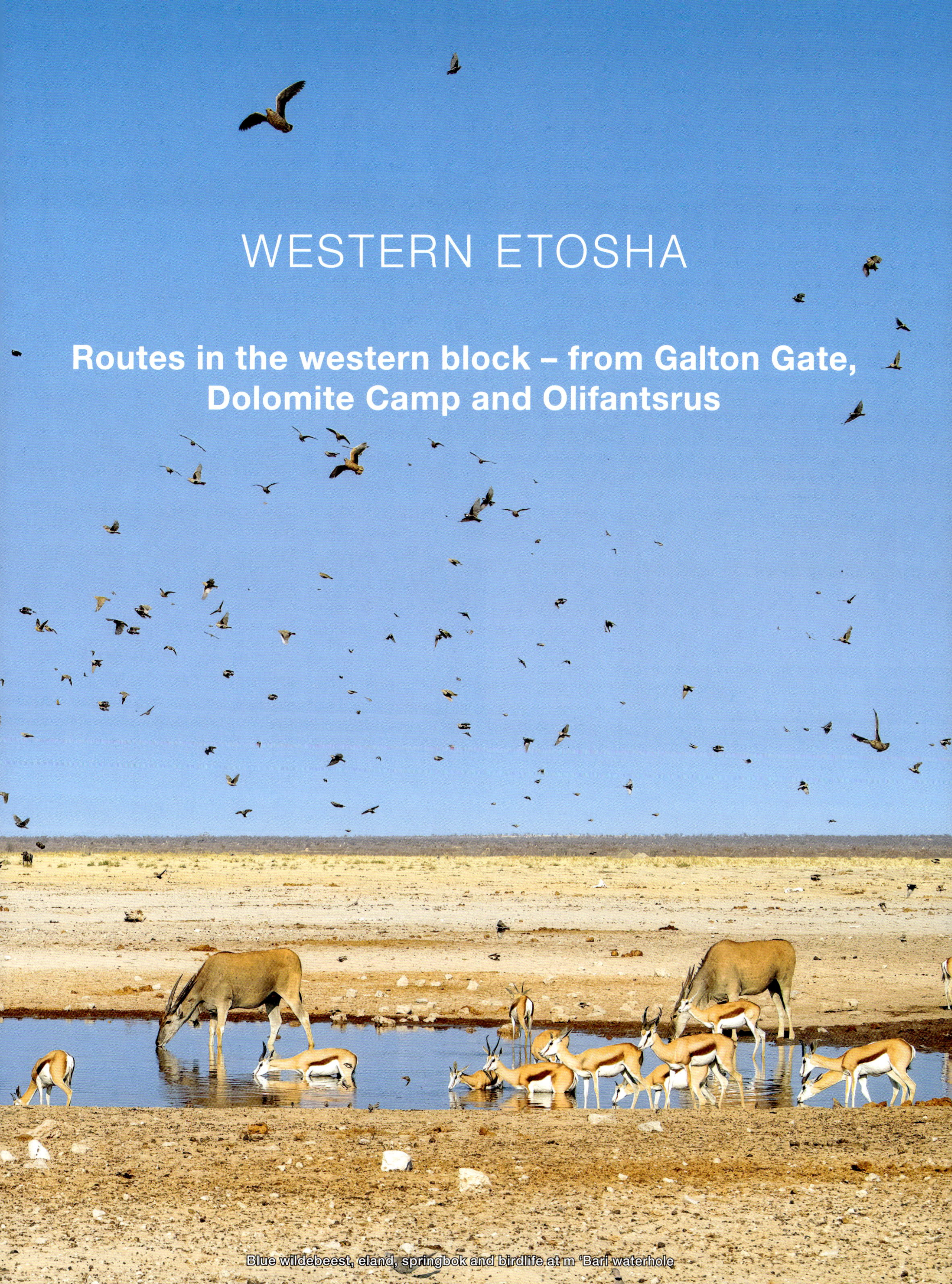

Blue wildebeest, eland, springbok and birdlife at m 'Bari waterhole

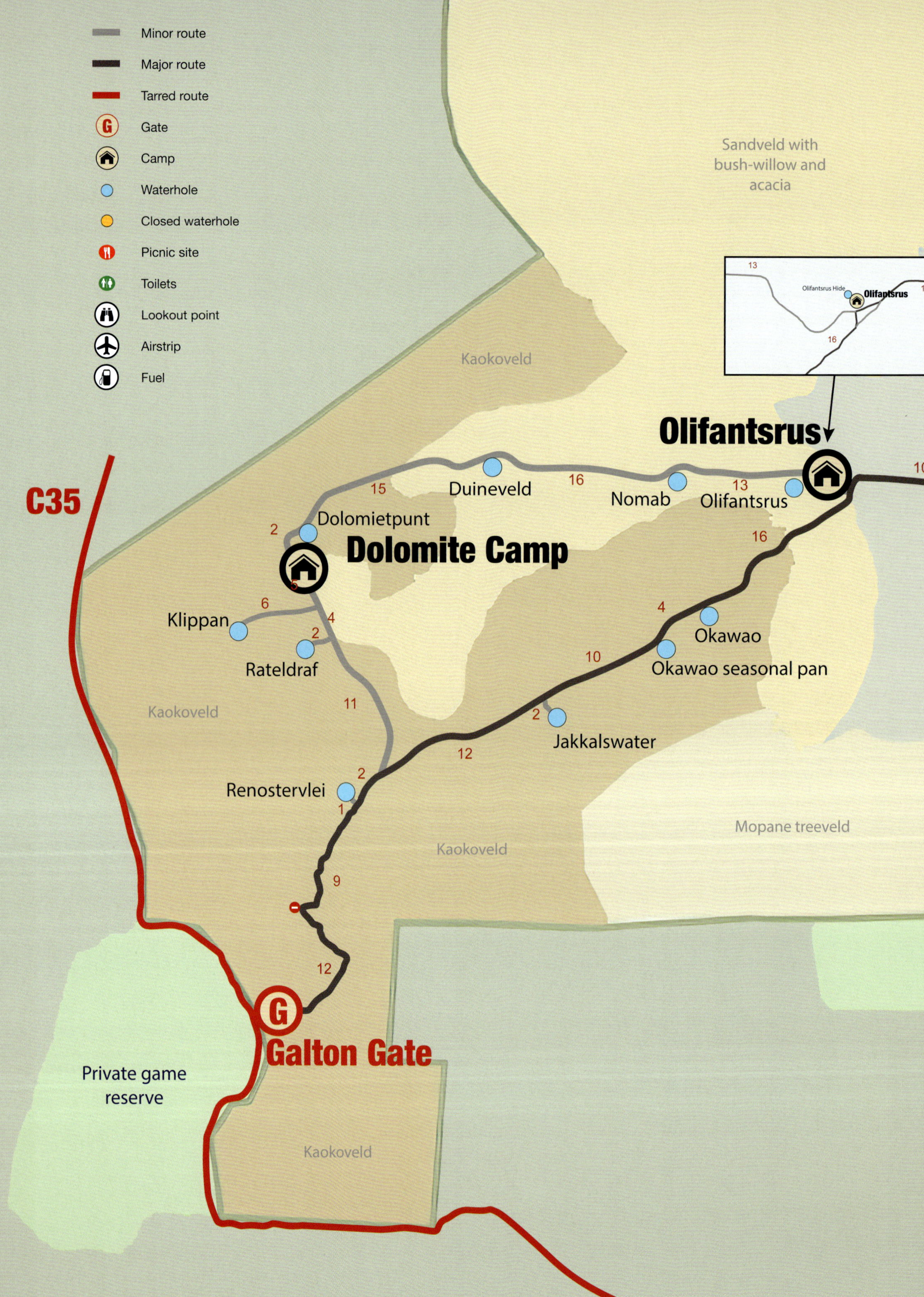
Minor route
Major route
Tarred route
Gate
Camp
Waterhole
Closed waterhole
Picnic site
Toilets
Lookout point
Airstrip
Fuel
Sandveld with bush-willow and acacia
Kaokoveld
Olifantsrus Hide
Olifantsrus
Olifantsrus
C35
Duineveld
Nomab
Olifantsrus
Dolomietpunt
Dolomite Camp
Klippan
Rateldraf
Okawao
Okawao seasonal pan
Kaokoveld
Jakkalswater
Renostervlei
Mopane treeveld
Kaokoveld
Galton Gate
Private game reserve
Kaokoveld

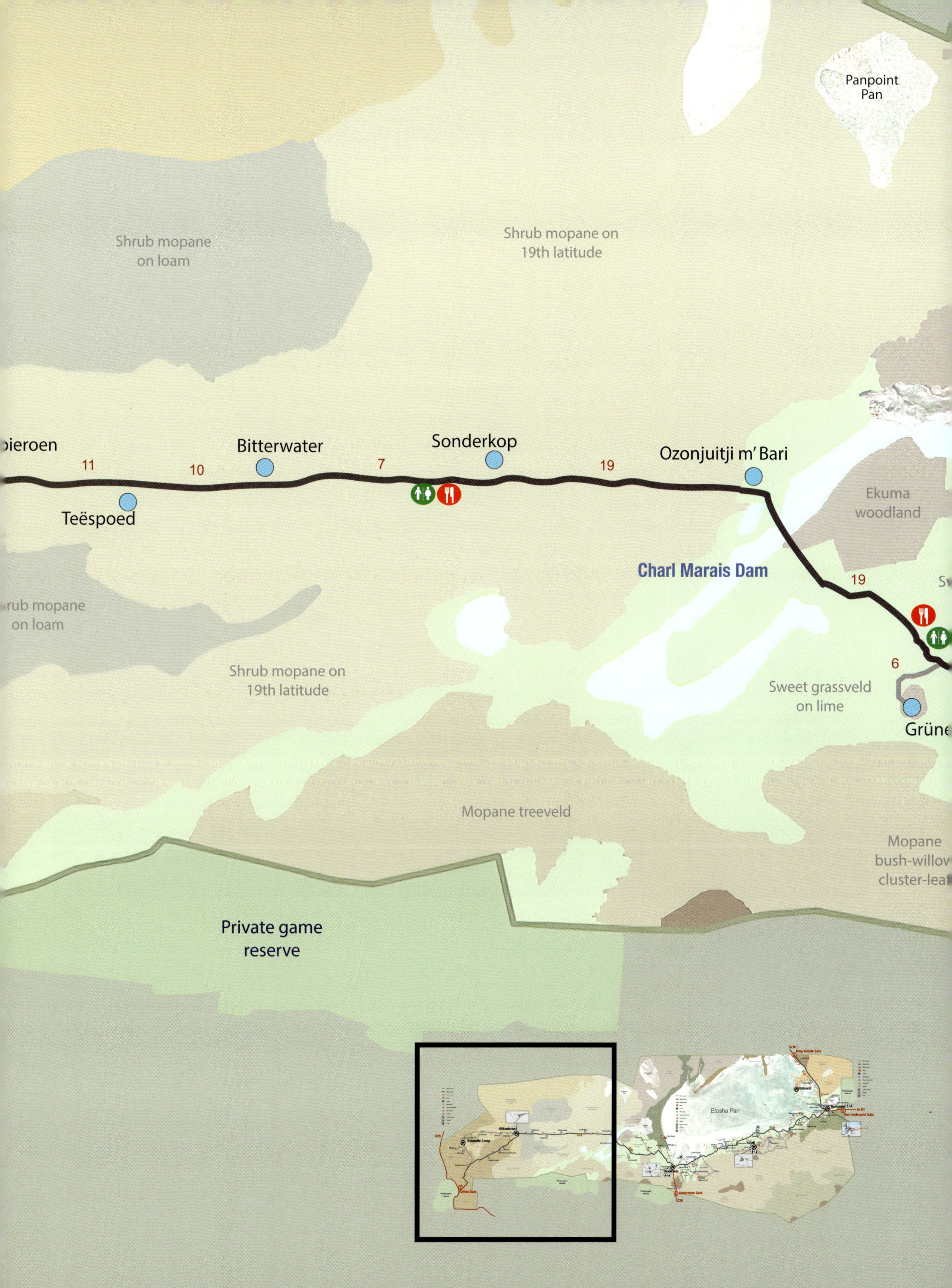
Panpoint Pan
Shrub mopane on loam
Shrub mopane on 19th latitude
ieroen
11
10
Bitterwater
7
Sonderkop
19
Ozonjuitji m' Bari
Teëspoed
Ekuma woodland
Charl Marais Dam
19
rub mopane on loam
Shrub mopane on 19th latitude
6
Sweet grassveld on lime
Grüne
Mopane treeveld
Mopane bush-willov cluster-lea
Private game reserve
Etosha Pan

Red hartebeest

Western Etosha can be compared to an unpolished gem – markedly different from the eastern side – and offers a startlingly different landscape. Unique, with a special charm and appeal, the rugged, undulating terrain is characterised by the **predominantly red soil** and **craggy hills** formed by **dolomite** and **limestone slabs**. This side of the park tends to be less crowded and entices more solitude than its famous eastern counterpart.

The western part of Etosha has different ecozones to the eastern and central parts. It is mainly a mixture of **shrub mopane woodland** and **sandy acacia shrubland on red Kalahari-like sand**, of which **tree mopane** and **shrub mopane**, **purple-pod cluster-leaf** and **red bushwillow** are the most common.

Previously restricted to the general public and self-drives and open only to safari outfitters, the park welcomed visitors through the **Galton entrance gate** for the first time in 2011. Visitors can access the western side via the **main road from Okaukuejo**; the distance from Okaukuejo Camp to Dolomite Camp measures approximately 173 km. Not having been exposed to a large influx of people before, the wildlife has adapted quite well to the surge of more visitors to this part of the world.

Extensive attention is devoted to **upgrading the roads** on the western side, widening them and simultaneously minimising corrugation. Nearly all waterholes currently in use are **boreholes that run on solar power**.

Male lion

Galton Gate to Dolomite Camp

Via Renostervlei (p. 135) and Rateldraf (p. 134) waterholes

- 50 km
- Hilly with dolomite inselbergs, red soil
- Kaokoveld – *Renostervlei mopane/russet bushwillow/ Herero sesame-bush shrubland*
- Herero sesame-bush; russet bushwillow
- Pale chanting goshawk; Gabar goshawk; crowned lapwing; lark-like buntings
- Hartmann's mountain zebra; black-faced impala

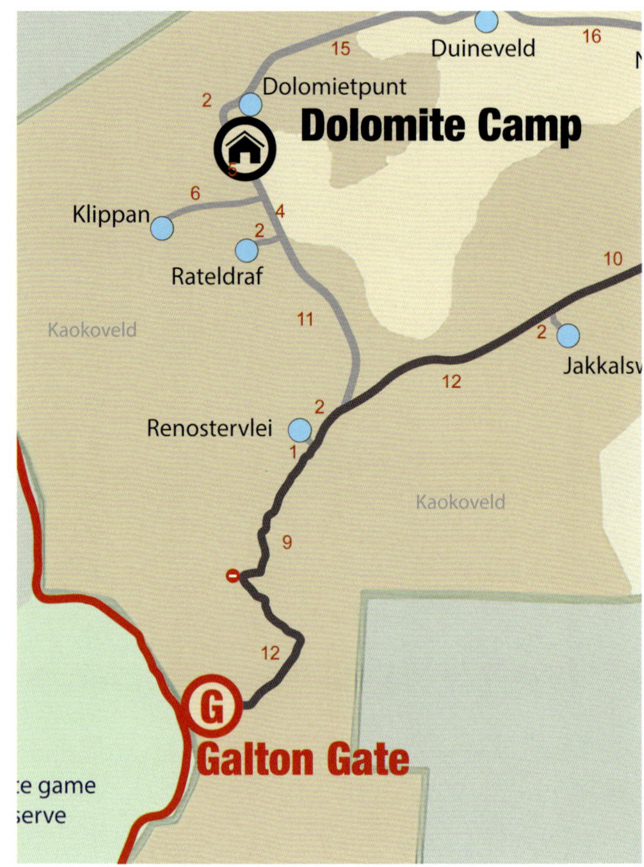

Most visitors to the park's western side are overnight guests at Dolomite Camp and thus go straight to the camp or Olifantsrus campsite. A few exceptions would be game-drive vehicles from the nearby Hobatere Lodge, entering Galton Gate with day visitors. The route to Dolomite Camp passes through a few ecozones or landscapes. It is a wonderful introduction to the rugged western region of the park compared to its predominantly flat and sprawling eastern cousin.

A scenic gravel road winds its way from the gate through gently sloping terrain, starting with Otjovasandu's hilly **mopane savanna**, as the western part has the only points of natural elevation in the park, except for the dolomite hills near Halali. The vegetation is typical **shrub mopane** interspersed with **purple-pod cluster-leaf**, **russet bushwillow** and single **smelly shepherd's tree** specimens.

The **Herero sesame bush**, a several-stemmed shrub or tree and Namibian near endemic, is a conspicuous feature as you approach Renostervlei. The shiny, fat trunks store moisture and are topped by stiff, erect branches with small, dark grey-green leaves. When in bloom, it sports lovely, elegant yellow trumpet-shaped flowers.

Kaokoveld is the primary vegetation community with a smaller sub-division titled ***Renostervlei mopane/russet bushwillow/Herero sesame bush shrubland***. Stunted shrub mopane is a predominant feature on red soil near Rateldraf. **Keep an eye out for elephants** as they favour the foliage of the mopane lining the roadside**,** offering an element of surprise when they suddenly appear out of nowhere and materialise next to your vehicle. **Giraffes** favour the area and are often seen on the lower slopes of the dolomite hills lining the main road.

The gravel road is usually in good condition, with minor corrugation. Extensive road maintenance has recently been conducted in the western part of the park.

Depending on the sightings and how long you intend to stop, this drive should be ideal for an afternoon drive from Galton Gate to Dolomite, taking approximately two to three hours.

Black-chested snake eagle

Mopane or *Colophospermum mopane*

Mopane constitutes about 80% of the vegetation of Etosha in the form of stands of **tall, well-formed trees**, for instance, in the area around Halali, as well as **shrub mopane**. It is not uncommon for expanses of shrub mopane to grow near much larger tree mopane, and suggested causes range from frost damage, fire, damage by elephants and root restriction owing to soil type. The **butterfly-shaped leaves** are signatory. During the rainy season, mopane vegetation hosts innumerable fat larvae of the **emperor moth *(Gonimbrasia belina),*** commonly called **mopane worms**. African people consider them a delicacy when roasted or dried. A serving of 100 g provides 76% of a human's daily protein requirement. Mopane forms new leaves from about August and flowers from December to March.

Leopard under mopane tree

Galton Gate to Olifantsrus Camp

via Renostervlei (p. 135), Jakkalswater (p. 125), Okawao (p. 128) and Okawao Pan (p. 128)

- 67 km
- Seasonal pan at Okawao
- Kaokoveld – *sandy cluster-leaf/acacia shrubland*
- Gemsbok bean; skew-leafed elephant root; Bushman's poison; *Gossypium triphyllum*
- Raptors; plains birds; sandgrouse; lapwings
- Damara dik-dik; red hartebeest; lion; giraffe

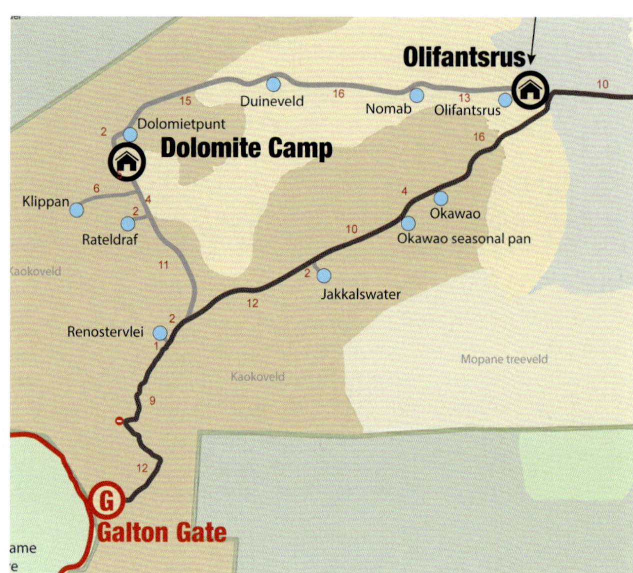

Entering Galton Gate, with bookings in place for Olifantsrus Camp, this stretch of road is approximately 20 km longer than that to Dolomite, with three waterholes and one seasonal pan en route worth visiting. All waterholes and the seasonal pan, except for Jakkalswater, are near the road.

Again, emphasis must be placed on the fact that the gravel roads in western Etosha have been widened and improved substantially. The road from Galton Gate to Olifantsrus is no exception. It is in good condition, barring minor corrugation, depending on the amount of vehicle traffic experienced.

Look out for the diminutive near-endemic **Damara dik-dik** near the Renostervlei waterhole. They usually browse on mopane- and russet bushwillow shrubs that line the roadside. The red- and russet bushwillow members of the ***Combretum*** family, with their distinctive four-winged fruit, attract browsers like **giraffe** and **kudu**.

Red hartebeest and Burchell's zebra

Driving towards Jakkalswater, the primary plant community is a short stretch of ***sandy cluster-leaf/Acacia shrubland***, with the area opening considerably. Plains and isolated trees, like camelthorn and red umbrella-thorn, sometimes occur in denser thickets, interspersed with purple-pod cluster-leaf and mopane, opening up to **Kaokoveld.**

Look out for the common **gemsbok bean,** a scrambling legume growing from a large tuberous root beside the roadside between Jakkalswater and Okawao. In flower, the tiny purple flowers eventually give way to pea-like pods. Conspicuous is the **skew-leaved elephant root**, a deciduous large woody tree or shrub with an underground rhizome or tuber particularly sought after by elephants.

Close to the seasonal pan of Okawao and Okawao waterhole, striking taller **purple-pod cluster-leaf** trees are prolific. They are components of **tall shrub savanna** and an impressive and glorious sight when the two-winged seeds change into their brilliant wine-red to purple colours. **Giraffes** are usually seen near these trees as they are partial to the young shoots and flowers.

A few kilometres before Olifantsrus, **roadside borrow pits** can be encountered next to the roadside, as well as depressions and shallow pans. It is a scenic, open stretch of road with a few red and white termite mounds. **Burchell's zebra**, **springbok** and **blue wildebeest** usually favour this area.

Dolomite Camp to Duineveld

Via Dolomite Point waterhole (p. 124)

- 36 km return
- Red Kalahari soil; open plains
- Western sandveld – *sandy cluster-leaf/acacia shrubland*
- Herero sesame-bush; smelly shepherd's tree; trumpet thorn; stekelbossie; forked geigeria
- Vultures; raptors; lapwings
- Rhino; lion; elephant; oryx

Travelling in the northerly direction and then turning in the easterly direction, Duineveld waterhole would be a good destination for an afternoon drive. On leaving camp, the road takes you past Dolomite Point waterhole, defined as **sweet grassveld on lime**, with thickets of **water thorn acacia** lining the road near the access road to the waterhole.

Expect to see the usual herbivores approaching and leaving the waterhole from all directions, particularly **springbok**, **blue wildebeest** and **zebra**. A short stretch leads through ***mopane/red bushwillow/Herero sesame-bush bushveld***. The first part of the drive heads through more impenetrable shrub, hampering visibility. Thickets of **trumpet thorn**, **shrub mopane** and **red bushwillow** are prominent. Stately examples of the **Herero sesame bush** and the **smelly shepherd's tree** are found intermittently.

The landscape is monotonous, especially in the dry season, with little wildlife seen along the first stretch. The author did have a recent astonishing sighting of three cheetahs crossing the road in front of their vehicle, a testament to the fact that anything is possible!

Smaller shrubs that provide splashes of colour next to the roadside are **forked geigeria**, an annual herb and Namibian endemic sporting bright yellow flowers, and the **stekelbossie**, with its pinkish-white flowers covering large areas of alkaline soil in the park.

The scenery changes dramatically in the last four kilometres before reaching Duineveld. The primary vegetation zone is **western sandveld**, subdivided into ***sandy cluster-leaf/ thorn tree shrubland.*** Beautiful and scenic open plains stretch on either side of the road, characterised by red Kalahari soil, shallow to moderately deep and **camelthorn**, **red umbrella-thorn** and **silver cluster-leaf** and **mopane** are some of the dominant tree species.

Near the access road leading to Duineveld, as well as the fringes of the open plains, shrub mopanes and clusters of larger mopane trees are closely grouped. Drive slowly and scan the area for **lions**, often found resting under the larger mopane trees near the access road to the waterhole.

The afternoon excursion is especially worthwhile for spending time at the **Duineveld waterhole**. It is a highly productive waterhole, drawing massive herds of herbivores, especially both zebra species and blue wildebeest. You can reasonably expect surprise sightings. The open plains provide excellent visibility for watching animal behaviour, which can be highly entertaining, especially among zebra.

Returning from Duineveld, you have a realistic chance of observing **rhinos** or lions at the waterhole, as they are more active towards the cooler hours of the day, especially in the heat of summer.

Burchell's zebra

Dolomite Camp to Klippan Waterhole

Via Dolomite Point (p. 124) waterhole

- 26.5 km return
- Vast plains; dolomite ridges; elevated landscape
- Kaokoveld – *Kowares Sand Mopane Veld*
- Camelthorn trees; skew-leaved elephant root; red umbrella-thorn; mopane; purple-pod cluster-leaf
- Ludwig's bustard; vultures; eagles
- Klipspringer; chacma baboon; rock hyrax

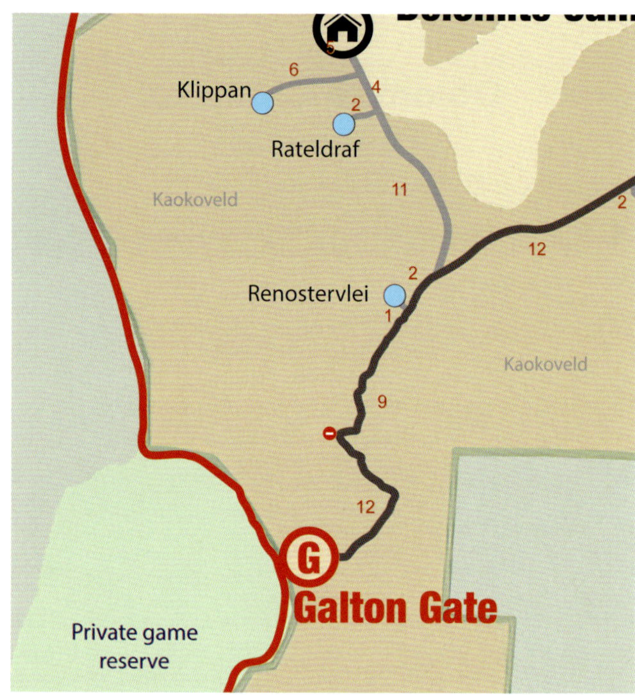

This short route is perfect for a late afternoon excursion from camp. As you drive out, consider turning right first and briefly checking in at **Dolomite Point waterhole** to see if anything exciting is on its way to the waterhole. The immense plains afford good visibility, especially in winter when the vegetation cover is sparse. **Wild sage** is in abundance on the plains and next to the roadside, as well as **water thorn acacia**, sometimes growing in dense thickets.

Heading south towards Klippan, **dolomite ridges** lie to the left of the road, some forms of relief characteristic of the elevated landscape of parts of western Etosha. It might be rewarding to stop for a while and scan the ridges and slopes with binoculars in search of **klipspringer**, **chacma baboon**, **rock hyrax** or **leopard**, as it is their ideal habitat. The former three species are found only in the park's western section and are not that commonly seen, so consider yourself lucky if you can spot one.

The gravel road is in good condition. Previously, it was possible to continue from Klippan in the westerly direction to Kowares. However, this is no longer possible and the loop road is closed to visitors.

Black rhino

African wild cat

Dolomite Camp to Olifantsrus Camp

Via Dolomite Point (p. 124), Duineveld (p. 124) and Nomab (p. 127) waterholes

 90 km return

 Vast plains; state-of-the-art viewing hide

 Kaokoveld and dry western sandveld

 Smelly shepherd's tree

 Vultures; Burchell's and Namaqua sandgrouse; seedeaters; secretarybird; Kori bustard

 Elephant; Hartmann's mountain zebra; Burchell's zebra; oryx; rhino; lion; hyena; black-backed jackal; terrapin

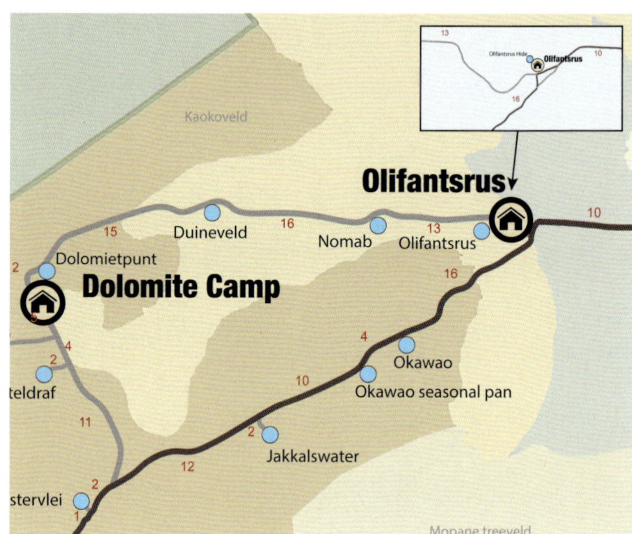

A good option for a morning drive from Dolomite Camp would be to go further east after **Duineveld** and stop at the expansive and very productive **Nomab waterhole** before proceeding to Olifantsrus Camp for a pleasant mid-morning to early lunch picnic stop, depending on sightings and time at hand.

You could turn this into a whole day event, so plan to include a lunch pack, which Dolomite Camp will gladly prepare for you. You can buy refreshments at the small kiosk at Olifantsrus but be sure to take enough water. The cool state-of-the-art hide overlooking the waterhole should offer plenty of entertainment, and the information centre with visuals and information that provides insight and background on the controversial elephant culling operation is also worth a visit.

Shaded picnic sites are open for day visitors until 16:00 and are an ideal spot for brunch or late lunch.

The road is generally in good condition, with minor corrugation in places.

Springbok at Olifantsrus waterhole

Steenbok

Female Hartlaub's spurfowl

Dolomite Camp to Dolomite Circle Route

Dolomite Point (p. 124), Duineveld (p. 124), Nomab (p. 127), Olifantsrus (p. 130), Okawao (p. 128), Okawao Pan (p. 128), Jakkalswater (p. 125), Rateldraf (p. 134), Klippan (p. 126) waterholes and back to Dolomite Camp

- 129.6 km
- Dolomite hills
- Kaokoveld; dry western sandveld
- Bushman's poison; red umbrella-thorn; mopane; purple-pod cluster-leaf
- Vultures; raptors; plains birds; key species of the west – Monteiro's hornbill, Hartlaub's francolin, white-tailed shrike, rockrunner, great sparrow, Rüppell's parrot and bare-cheeked babbler
- Masses of herbivores at places

A good alternative for a full-day excursion from Dolomite Camp would be to continue from Olifantsrus to Okawao, Okawao Pan, Jakkalswater, Rateldraf, Klippan, and back to Dolomite Camp.

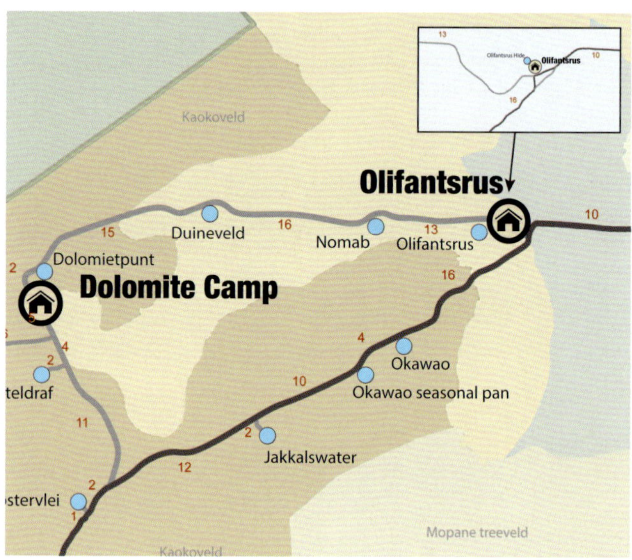

The whole route is scenically diverse, traversing at least **five vegetation zones**, with comfortable and easy driving. Wildlife encounters should be varied and abundant, with the route incorporating **nine different waterholes**, including the **Dolomite Point** waterhole. Be flexible and structure your day according to sightings en route and at different waterholes and the suggested lunch break at Olifantsrus Camp.

African elephant herd

Male lion

Olifantsrus Camp to Nomab waterhole

To Nomab (p. 127) and back

24 km return

Scenic; calcrete rocks; red sands; termite mounds

Kaokoveld; dry western sandveld – *sandy shrub mopaneveld*

Bushman's poison plant; mopane

Abdim's stork; Kori bustard; ostrich; vultures

Herds of antelopes; rhino; elephant; oryx

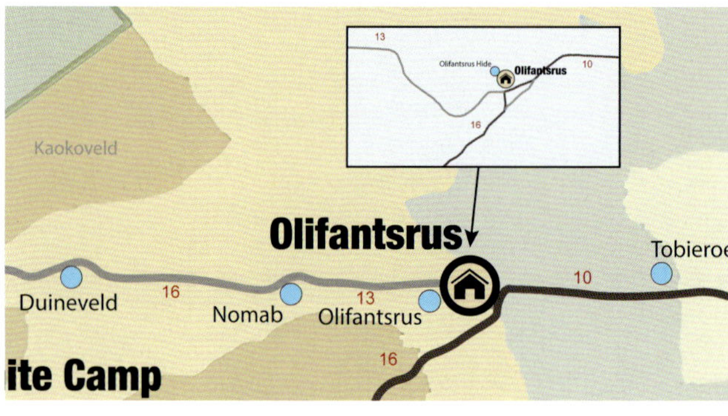

This short and scenic route would make an ideal afternoon excursion from Olifantsrus, so choose your favourite sundowner drink and head in the westerly direction towards the **Nomab** waterhole. This drive should evoke a feeling of peace and tranquillity as you revel in the scenic beauty of nature. The light is particularly favourable in the afternoon, highlighting the contrast between the deep red Kalahari soil, some lush green vegetation and the brilliant blue sky.

Expect to find the **usual herbivores**, such as springbok, red hartebeest, steenbok, blue wildebeest, Burchell's zebra, giraffe and kudu, peacefully grazing in small clusters near the roadside or further away on open plains dotted with **shrub mopane** and **acacia**.

A **rhino** might appear and sightings of **black-backed jackals**, always on the trot, are usually safe bets.

This stretch of road is also good for catching a glimpse of the striking **Bushman's poison plant**; their brilliant pink blooms are a perfect foil against the large, elongated, lush green leaves. Sometimes, they grow in the shade of other trees close to the roadside.

Nomab lies south of the main road, and the afternoon light is perfect for photography. When the park welcomes its summer migrants, **Abdim's storks** arrive in great numbers. They are partial to Nomab, probably because of the vast, open plains surrounding the waterhole, which enable them to congregate here in large numbers.

The **Kori bustard** and ostrich are usually around, as well as **white-backed** or **lappet-faced vultures**. **Elephants** might appear, so enjoy your sundowner and absorb the ambience of the picturesque surroundings and any form of wildlife that approaches the waterhole.

The road is generally in a relatively good condition.

Black-winged stilt and elephant tracks

Smelly shepherd's tree

Fruit, smelly shepherd's tree

Gemsbok bean and skew-leaved elephant root

Olifantsrus to Ozonjuitji m'Bari

Via Tobieroen (p. 138), Teëspoed (p. 138), Bitterwater (inactive), Duiwelsvuur (inactive), Sonderkop (p. 136) to Ozonjuitji m'Bari (p. 132) waterhole

- 136 km return
- Loam soils
- Shrub mopane veld
- Mopane; wool bush; trumpet thorn; sickle bush; silky bushman grass
- Pale chanting goshawk; tawny eagle, bateleur
- Brown hyena; lion; African wild cat; honey badger; elephant; eland; oryx

Plan half a day for this excursion, leaving camp as soon as the gates open. The route takes you in the easterly direction along the 19th latitude, **past three active waterholes**, before reaching an exciting and productive waterhole on the western side, Ozonjuitj m'Bari.

Shrub mopane is predominant for large stretches along the 19th latitude in the form of short, stunted shrub mopane and trees on loamy soil. Other shrubs found include the **trumpet thorn**, **wool-bush** and **sickle-bush**. A prominent species in the herbaceous layer is the **silky Bushman grass**, a palatable, tufted perennial grass and one of the most palatable grazing grasses in the region.

While the landscape's flatness, largely covered by **shrub mopane**, might appear monotonous and impact visibility owing to dense vegetation lining the road, there are some open areas and interesting features to break the monotony. This area features small depressions characterised by their soils, which belong to the soil family of the Arcadia form. These soils are highly fertile and have a solid soil structure. Grasses tend to cover these depressions.

Open expanses with good visibility surround the **Tobieroen** and **Teëspoed** waterholes. Next to the roadside, a few **road-side borrow pits** are visible. They are usually filled with water during the rainy season and frequented by wildlife.

Termite mounds, all mini-ecosystems, are scattered throughout large areas of western Etosha, with colours varying from greyish white to darker grey or rich red, depending on the soil type. Please pay close attention to termite mounds; **cheetahs** use them as vantage points for spotting prey and as markers by depositing their scat. Cheetahs are also sometimes observed lying in the shade at the base of termite mounds. A few bird species perch on termite mounds, like the **lilac-breasted roller**, **pale chanting goshawk** and **Swainson's spurfowl**. Keep a lookout for **elephants** on the stretch of road between Tobieroen and Teëspoed because they often occur in the area.

Thicker **shrub mopane** dominates the area after Teëspoed, Bitterwater and Duiwelsvuur. This almost 30 km stretch of road

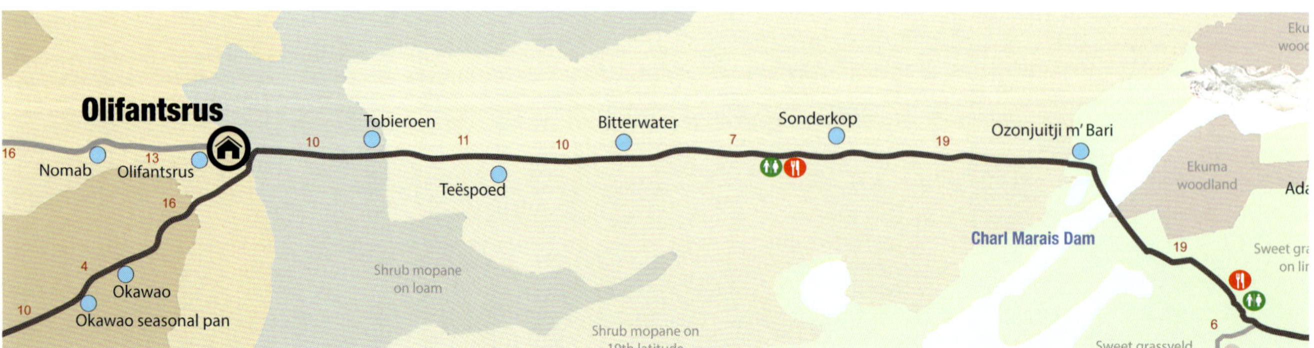

Angolan giraffe, oryx, sprinbok and birdlife at m'Bari waterhole

up to **Sonderkop** is relatively quiet, especially in the dry season; the most significant restrictive factor for game distribution is access to permanent water sources. However, the author recently enjoyed a sighting of a **brown hyena**, **African wild cat** and **honey badger**, proof that nature is unpredictable and anything can happen when you least expect it.

A short stop at the **picnic site** 2.5 km before the Sonderkop waterhole is a good idea since this is the only rest stop on this route to m'Bari.

Sonderkop is a welcome change in scenery; the waterhole and surrounding area is frequently a hive of activity with abundant wildlife, especially in the dry season. An expanse of open territory surrounds the waterhole, with a large concentration of termite mounds characterising the scenery. The picture will change considerably in the rainy season as extensive grass covers the bare plain. Free-standing large mopane trees grow within a few metres from the road, with denser clusters occurring on the further fringes of the plains beyond.

Sonderkop is a **stronghold for lions;** visitors frequently report sightings of these charismatic large cats. When they don't hog the waterhole for themselves, lions love to lounge next to the water tanks on the edge of the parking area or under the shade of large mopane trees, keeping the thirsty game at bay.

The last 18 km to m'Bari meander through dense shrub mopane veld, often limiting visibility to a few metres from the road. Look out for **a honey badger** that can sometimes be seen foraging, often accompanied by an opportunistic **pale chanting goshawk** hovering nearby, waiting to relieve the honey badger of his spoils. The badgers are vigorous and prolific foragers and diggers, flushing prey like rodents and reptiles from underground refuges and shrubs; the goshawks closely stick to the badgers, waiting for an easy meal.

Short, stunted **shrub mopane** and thickets of **water thorn acacia** are prominent within a few kilometres of the access road leading to the **m'Bari** waterhole. Expect to see many **springbok** mingling among the thickets, nibbling on the leaves and flowers of the water thorn.

Large herds of plains game herald the proximity of the waterhole, approaching on well-worn game paths from all directions. Be on the lookout for the resident **lion pride**.

It is a place where most game found in the park congregate during the dry season. It is a perfect spot to observe the shy **eland** that often approach in large numbers. The largest concentration of game is found from mid-morning onwards, with a steady stream of thirsty wildlife travelling from far and wide. **Elephants** monopolise the waterhole around midday and early afternoon.

Travelling this route is worthwhile for spending quality time at Sonderkop and m'Bari, particularly in the dry season – you will not be disappointed. However, with the onset of the rains, wildlife spreads and activity at the waterholes diminishes.

CENTRAL ETOSHA

Routes in the central block – from Andersson Gate, Okaukuejo and Halali

Lioness, kori bustard and ostrich at Okondeka

Pan
Minor route
Major route
Tarred route
Gate
Camp
Waterhole
Closed waterhole
Picnic site
Toilets
Lookout point
Airstrip
Fuel
Okondeka duneveld
Ekuma woodland
Adamax Pan
Ekuma woodland
Okondeka duneveld
Okondeka
Adamax
Sweet grassveld on lime
Leeubron
Natco
Wolfsnes
Grünewald
Ondongab
Kapupuhedi
Pan
Diamond drive
Nebrownii
Gemsbokvlak
Okaukuejo
Okaukuejo
Gaseb
Gemsbokvlakt
W-drive
Olifantsbad
Mopane bush-willow cluster-leaf
Ombika
Private game reserve
Andersson Gate
C38

Etosha Pan
Okerfontein
Springbok
Batia
Goas
Hartebeest Drive
Noniams
Eland Drive
Helio
Halali
Moringa
Nuamses
Rietfontein
Golden Mile
Salvadora
Sueda
Charitsaub
Rhino Drive
Aus
Helio Hills
Mopane bush-willow cluster-leaf
Mopane treeveld
Mopane bush-willow cluster-leaf
Etosha Pan

Morning drive from Andersson Gate

Circular Drive

Via Ombika (p. 164), Gemsbokvlakte (p. 146), and Nebrownii (p. 157), Okaukuejo (p. 160) to Andersson Gate

- 66 km return
- Scenic; open plains; grassland
- Sweet grassveld on lime; eastern karst woodlands – *mopane treeveld; mopane/red bushwillow/ purple-pod cluster-leaf bushveld*
- Mopane; red bushwillow; purple-pod cluster-leaf
- Raptors; plains birds; grassland birds; birds in trees
- Lion; hyena; black rhino; cheetah; 'ghost' elephant; Cape fox; aardwolf; black-backed jackal

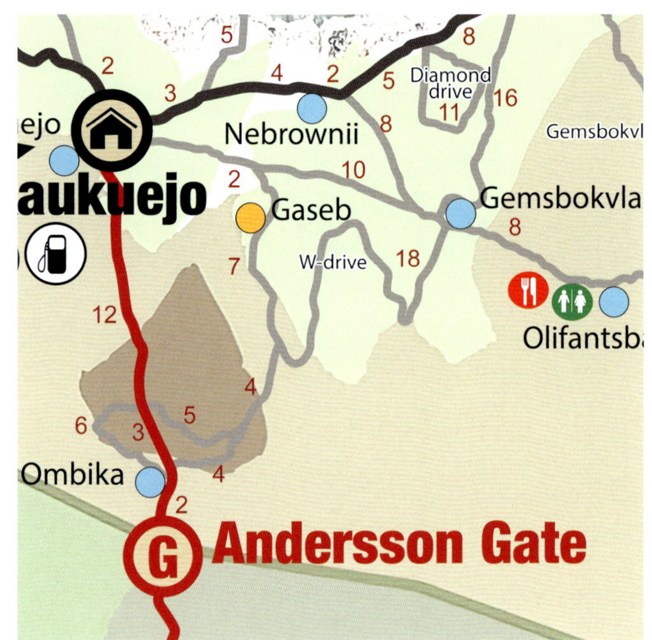

This route is a perfect option for a half-day drive. Enter from outside via the Andersson Gate at first light and intend to spend the whole morning in the park. Start on the western side at the **Ombika** waterhole before proceeding on the scenic detour.

Look out for **lions** regularly patrolling their territory. They can often be found near the waterhole at the break of day, with **spotted hyenas** never far away. **Black rhinos** also favour the waterhole in the early morning and again towards late afternoon.

After travelling on the eastern loop of the detour for five kilometres, the road to the left eventually accesses part of **W-drive**. The 19km long route takes you to the **Gemsbokvlakte waterhole**.

This route is really productive for encounters with **cheetah** in the morning, as they favour the expansive plains in places, especially near Gemsbokvlakte. Visitors often report **Cape fox** and **aardwolf** along this stretch and find **black-backed jackal** dens near the road. Depending on sightings and the speed at which you travel, you will probably reach Gemsbokvlakte around mid-morning, which should be abuzz with an abundance and variety of wildlife. The entertainment value should be high and is bound to keep you enthralled.

The seven-kilometre gravel road is the shortest route to **Nebrownii**. Access the road one kilometre west of Gemsbokvlakte, which will take you directly to the main road. Expansive grasslands border on both sides and plains game, usually **springbok** and **Burchell's zebra**, are found milling about.

Nebrownii waterhole is particularly active around noon, with good chances of **elephant** and **rhino** at the waterhole. They favour the mud wallow behind the waterhole, following their daily beauty regimen and coating themselves with the **white clay** so predominant in the area. You may see magnificent specimens of the iconic 'white' or 'ghost' elephants here. The seven-kilometre stretch back to Okaukuejo tends to be corrugated.

Remember to pay your park fees at Okaukuejo before exiting through Andersson Gate.

Lioness hunting Burchell's zebra

From Andersson Gate or from Okaukuejo
Sundowner Drive

Ombika (p. 164)

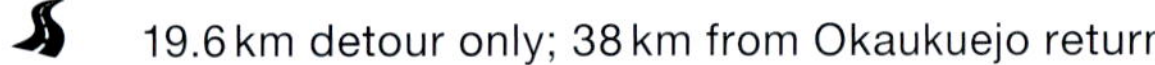

- 19.6 km detour only; 38 km from Okaukuejo return
- Termite mounds
- Mopane treeveld; karstveld turf pans
- Red and russet bushwillow; purple-pod cluster-leaf; shepherd's tree; trumpet thorn; lavender croton; cork-bush
- Red-billed spurfowl; helmeted guineafowl; ostrich; Kori bustard
- Lion; black rhino; giraffe; kudu; oryx; Burchell's zebra; black-faced impala; steenbok

Immature ostrich

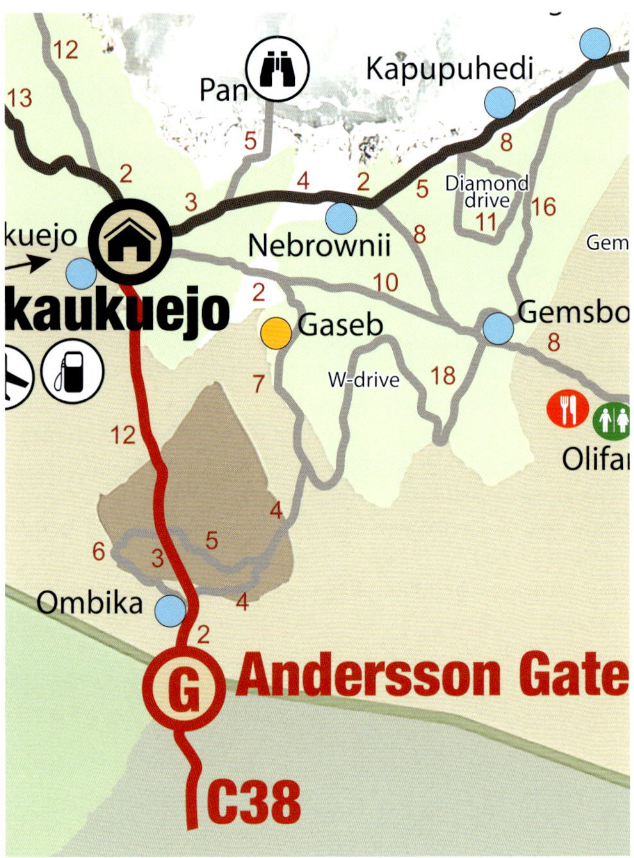

Day visitor drive

A viable option for day visitors wanting to again enter the park in the **afternoon** for a shorter game drive is to experience the ambience of the **Ombika detour**, starting on the eastern section of the loop. The detour is very scenic in the afternoon light, and many plains game spread out on the adjacent plains, painting a beautiful picture. The gate entrance is just under two kilometres from the Ombika waterhole, allowing you to enjoy the excellent light to maximum effect and enough time to exit the park in under 10 minutes.

Drive from Okaukuejo

Leave the camp and drive the tar road south. Find the detour on both the tar road's left and right sides, with the entrance to both sides at the turn-off to the **Ombika** waterhole. It meanders through a predominantly mopane landscape and once again joins with the tar road leading to Okaukuejo camp. Both loops are well worth taking and ideal for a late afternoon or early morning foray from camp.

The Ombika detour

The western side of the loop leads through **mopane treeveld**, mixed with **red bushwillow**, **russet bushwillow** and **purple-pod cluster-leaf**. Single specimens of **shepherd's tree** grow intermittently. Open plains with seasonal **palatable grasses on limestone soil** attract browsers and grazers. **Giraffe**, **kudu**, **oryx**, **Burchell's zebra**, **black-faced impala** and **steenbok** favour the area. You have a perfect chance of catching a glimpse of a pride of **lions** that regularly patrol their territories, as well as **rhino**, **elephant**, **hyena** and **black-backed jackal.**

Trumpet thorn, **lavender croton**, and **corkbush** line the road in places, their white and lilac-coloured blooms provide splashes of colour when flowering. The vegetation on the eastern loop is much like the western section, but there are denser mopane shrubs, especially the part closest to Andersson Gate. The first stretch is particularly scenic, opening to sprawling open plains and depressions, sparsely dotted with **grey termite mounds** and isolated, **larger mopane** and **bushwillow** trees.

A few small turf pans also occur along this detour, and the vegetation zone is called **karstveld turf pans**. The black clay is deeply cracked and fissured in the dry season, becoming impassable in the rainy season. Tall **turf grass** grows along the roadside in places, a sign of disturbed soil, and **wether love grass**, as well as **foxtail buffalo grass**, are some of the palatable grasses growing on both sides of the detour. **Flood-plain acacias** are also found on the eastern side of the detour, favouring turf pan soil and along the tar road leading to Okaukuejo.

Look out for **red-billed spurfowl** and **helmeted guinea-fowl** near the roadside. **Fork-tailed drongo** and two of Etosha's most significant bird species – the **ostrich** and omni-present **Kori bustard** – favour this area.

The road is generally in good condition throughout the detour, without too much corrugation or many rough patches.

Female kudu feeding on purple-pod cluster-leaf

From Andersson Gate

Day Visitor, Day Drive

Andersson Gate via Ombika (p. 164) and W-drive to Gemsbokvlakte (p. 146), Aus (p. 142), Olifantsbad (p. 162), Kapupuhedi (p. 152), Diamond drive, Nebrownii (p. 157), Okaukuejo (p. 160), Gaseb (p. 144) and Ombika detour and waterhole (p. 164)

86 km morning, 37 km afternoon

Grassland plains; mopane with red bushwillow and purple-pod cluster-leaf

Sweet grassveld on lime; mopane treeveld

Mopane; red and russet bushwillow; purple-pod cluster-leaf; shepherd's tree; trumpet thorn; lavender croton; cork-bush

Birds of prey; grassland birds; plains birds

Lion; cheetah; leopard; rhino; aardwolf; bat-eared fox; brown hyena; black-backed jackal; kudu; black-faced impala; elephant; giraffe; blue wildebeest; eland; oryx; Burchell's zebra; springbok

This route is recommended if you are a **day visitor** entering through Andersson Gate and intend to spend a **whole day**, including a lunch break at Okaukuejo Camp in the park. Pack snacks and refreshments, especially water, before starting your day trip. Also, think of packing your swimming costume for a dip in the pool at Okaukuejo, as it is an ideal stopover for lunch.

You can proceed to the **Gemsbokvlakte waterhole** by accessing the eastern loop of the Ombika detour, which joins up with the **W-drive** and heads northeasterly.

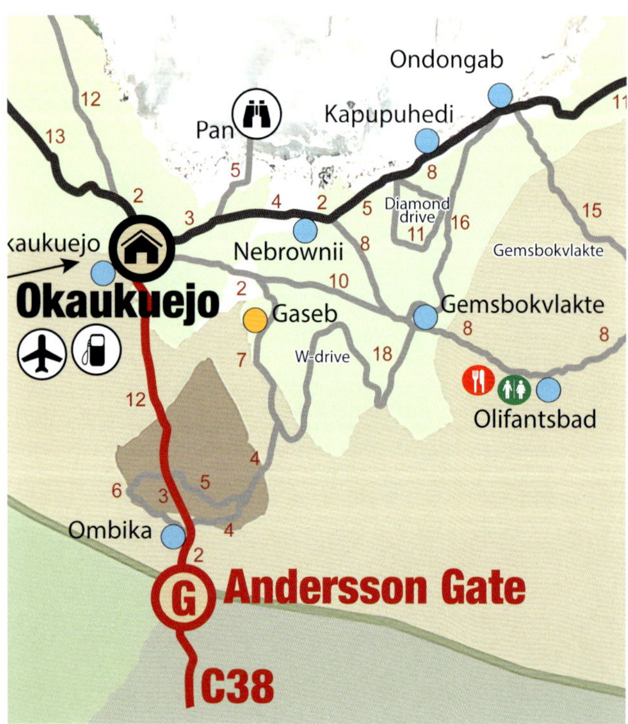

Brown hyena

On this stretch of road, early mornings are always good for sightings of predators or possible encounters of the more nocturnal species like **aardwolf**, **bat-eared fox** and **brown hyena**, so drive slowly, turn down your windows, and listen to the sounds of nature.

Gemsbokvlakte is the first waterhole on your way, and with some luck, you might see lions there. Be sure to stop at **Olifantsbad Picnic Site** for a coffee and restroom break, as it is the only picnic site on your route until you reach Okaukuejo. **Aus** waterhole should be productive for game viewing around mid-morning, and you are most likely to see **kudu**, **black-faced impala** and elephants at the waterhole.

Kapupuhedi waterhole is a seasonal waterhole that is active only in the rainy season but affords exceptional views of the pan. The **Diamond Drive** loop should be productive, with good sightings of plains game like **blue wildebeest**, **Burchell's zebra**, **springbok** and **oryx,** which mill around and can comfortably access the nearby waterholes of Nebrownii and Gemsbokvlakte. **White rhino** are also likely.

Nebrownii waterhole is highly productive at midday and worth stopping here for a while before making your way to Okaukuejo. You can spend at least three comfortable hours fortifying yourself with lunch at the restaurant and around the pool area. Be sure to **visit the Okaukuejo waterhole**, which is usually a hive of activity all day, especially in the dry season.

You can purchase souvenirs at the small **curio shop** and visit the **Etosha Ecological Institute Museum**, which is always worth a visit. Acquaint yourself with birdlife in camp; it is plentiful and varied. The round, landmark **stone tower** just outside the restaurant offers an excellent photographic opportunity from a high vantage point, as the panoramic views over Okaukuejo and its surroundings are exceptional.

The **Gaseb route** is a popular afternoon drive, and there is always something to see. The road will join up with the eastern loop of the **Ombika detour**; keep on the right for five kilometres before joining up with the western section of the loop, which will take you to the **Ombika waterhole**. Sundowners are a good idea, and you will end the day with your favourite beverage in hand, filled with a feeling of deep contentment and toasting to an exciting day filled with good sightings before exiting through Andersson Gate.

Remember to pay your park fees at the office before returning to Andersson Gate on your afternoon drive.

Male oryx

Andersson Gate or Okaukuejo Camp to W-Drive

The famous drive between Ombika Loop and Gemsbokvlakte

- 27.5 km
- Short-grass flats; dwarf-shrub savanna
- Sweet grassveld on lime; mopane treeveld
- Petal-bush; saltbush; corkbush; water thorn acacia; red umbrella-thorn
- Raptors; plains birds
- Black rhino; apex predators; plains game

You can access this drive from the **eastern Ombika loop** or **Gaseb Drive**. From the south (i.e. Andersson Gate), a four-kilometre access road on the east side of the Ombika detour joins up with a drive that **resembles the letter W** on a map of Etosha, hence the name of the 27.5 km **W-Drive**.

Open and sprawling calcrete-surfaced short-grass flats with short shrubs, all components of **dwarf-shrub savanna**, consisting mainly of **petal-bush, saltbush and cork bush**, fringed by **mopane bushveld**, prevail. A few islands consisting of thornbush, mostly **water thorn acacia** or **red umbrella-thorn** interspersed with **trumpet thorn**, are visible on the plains and along the roadside. The '**stekelbos**', a bushy perennial herb with pale pink flowers, is a significant component in the dwarf-shrub savanna.

The whole area is beautiful in the rainy season, as large pools of water collect in shallow depressions next to the roadside, yielding incredible sightings of predators and raptors drinking from these pools. The area around W-drive is **exceptionally productive for encounters with lions**, as these apex predators usually follow the large herds of **Burchell's zebra** that utilise the excellent grazing available on the vast, expansive plains. There are good chances of spotting **black rhino**, usually in the early morning or late afternoon.

Cheetahs are more common on the right side of W-drive, where the road leads to Gemsbokvlakte – the southern part of the W, to be exact. You can expect to see **Cape foxes** and **aardwolves** in this area and **black-backed jackals** often den near the road.

The road is generally in good condition, but as with most gravel roads in Etosha, minor corrugation can occur in places. A few potholes and depressions tend to hold water in the rainy season. If driven slowly and carefully, it is safe for any sedan car, even in wet conditions.

You can incorporate parts of this drive in a morning or afternoon drive, accessed from various points and navigated in various route combinations, shortened and lengthened according to personal preferences.

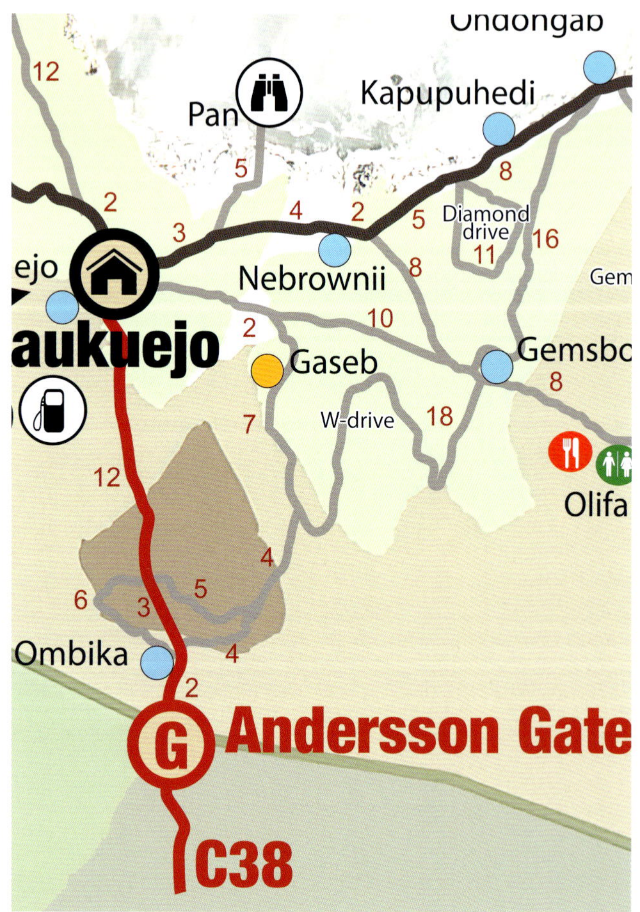

Black-backed jackal interaction

Greater kestrel on trumpet thorn

Okaukuejo Camp to Pan Drive

Popular short detour without waterhole

- 5.5 km
- Panoramic views of pan
- Sweet grassveld on lime
- Water thorn acacia; desert sedge grass
- Scaly-feathered finch; some lark species
- Burchell's zebra; blue wildebeest; springbok

Situated just under nine kilometres northeast of Okaukuejo, this is one of the **scenic lookout points** at the edge of the pan. Exiting Okaukuejo in an easterly direction and driving for just over three kilometres, the turn-off to the five-and-a-half-kilometre access road is on your left.

Water thorn acacia thickets line the road in places, and the usual **plains game** will likely be encountered in the vicinity, especially **Burchell's zebra, blue wildebeest** and **springbok**. Halophytic grasses and thick stands of desert sedge fringe the pan edges and the verges of the parking lot. It is a relatively quiet stretch of road but you should include it purely for the panoramic views of the main pan, which are always spectacular. More wildlife congregates in the area when seasonal water is available in some depressions on the pan but the road is sometimes closed in the rainy season, as it gets soggy and muddy.

Owing to its proximity to Okaukuejo, it can easily be included in a morning or afternoon excursion from camp.

Aerial view of Pan point

Okaukuejo Camp to Diamond Drive

Popular detour out of the main road 3 km from Kapupuhedi (p. 152)

- 11 km
- Dwarf shrub savanna; Ondundozonanandana Mountains
- Sweet grassveld on lime
- Water thorn acacia; trumpet thorn; saltbush; wool bush; petal-bush; horse bush
- Amur falcon; Abdim's stork
- Lion; Burchell's zebra; wildebeest; white rhino; springbok, bat-eared fox

Driving along the main road from Okaukuejo Camp towards Namutoni, approximately four kilometres after the Nebrownii waterhole, you reach an inconspicuous turn-off, signposted as a cul-de-sac. This road leads to a delightful loop, **Diamond Drive**, aptly named after the design of the detour, which resembles the shape of a diamond when looking at your GPS or map of Etosha.

The vegetation zone is **sweet grassveld on lime,** and the road meanders through **dwarf shrub savanna** with dense thickets of **water thorn acacia** lining parts of the road, interspersed with **trumpet thorn**, **saltbush**, **wool bush**, **petal-bush** and **horse bush**. Towards half of the 11 km detour, the thickets open up and afford great views over the adjacent plains, as far as Okaukuejo and the **Ondundozonanandana Mountains**, a low dolomite mountain range lying west of Andersson Gate. Translated into English, the name means 'mountain where the boy took the calves'.

According to legend, a boy who herded calves at the foot of the mountain never returned, as he and his animals fell prey to a leopard. Hence, this mountain range is also known as **Leopard Hills**.

A lone, sprawling **buffalo-thorn** (wag-'n-bietjie) bush breaks the flatness of the landscape, which is covered with dense **saltbush**. The smooth, brown berries of the buffalo-thorn are edible and eaten by squirrels, birds, rats and mice, while dik-dik, springbok, kudu and giraffes browse on the leaves. Traditionally, a good substitute for coffee is made from chopped and roasted roots, although the taste is slightly bitter.

This area has the highest concentration of **Amur falcons** in Etosha, also known as the eastern red-footed kestrel. These insectivorous migrants hunt from a perch or hover, feeding mainly on termites, beetles, locusts, grasshoppers and bees. The whole area is also a stronghold for **Abdim's stork**, another migratory species prolific in Etosha during the rainy season.

The dense dwarf shrub offers ideal concealment opportunities for **lions** as they wait for the large herds of **zebra** and **wildebeest** that graze the plains. You will have an excellent chance of spotting **white rhino** and large herds of **springbok** browsing on the dwarf shrubs covering the plains. You may even be lucky to spot **bat-eared foxes** in the early morning or late afternoon.

This quiet, scenic detour tends to be 'off the beaten track' and is ideal for a **short, late afternoon excursion from camp**, ideally combined with a stop at Nebrownii waterhole. Suppose you plan a more extended excursion for the morning or even a half-day outing, you can combine it with a visit to Gemsbokvlakte, W-drive, Aus and Olifantsbad, with the picnic site at Olifantsbad, an ideal stopover for a mid-morning break.

White rhino

Okaukuejo Camp to Gemsbokvlakte and Loop

Via turn-off to Gaseb closed waterhole (p. 144), Gemsbokvlakte (p. 146), Olifantsbad (p. 162), Aus (p. 142), Ondangab (p. 164), Gemsbokvlakte (p. 146)

- 15 km to Gemsbokvlakte; loop leading back to Gemsbokvlakte 42 km
- Open plains; dwarf shrub savanna
- Eastern karst woodlands; sweet grassveld on lime
- Saltbush; mopane; purple-pod cluster-leaf
- Plains birds; raptors
- Lion; leopard; Burchell's zebra; blue wildebeest; oryx; springbok; elephant

This extensive Gemsbokvlakte loop is a productive route, and it is recommended for a morning drive from Okaukuejo.

You can reach the **Gemsbokvlakte area** and the **waterhole** from several different points. One of them is the turn-off signposted **Gaseb**, a few metres to the right after exiting camp in the easterly direction. This 15 km stretch of gravel road runs parallel to the main road and takes you to the Gemsbokvlakte. Ignoring the right turn-off to the W-drive, further on the turn-off to the left will take you directly to the **Gemsbokvlakte waterhole**.

The vegetation is much the same as that described for **W-drive**, with open plains and components of **dwarf shrub savanna**. The **saltbush**, a many-stemmed grey shrub, is one of the significant components of the dwarf shrub savanna and is dominant on the surrounding plains up to Ondongab. The visibility is excellent, especially for the last few kilometres before reaching the waterhole at Gemsbokvlakte.

Expect to see the usual plains game grazing in the area. From mid-morning onwards, large processions of **Burchell's zebra**, **wildebeest**, **oryx** and **springbok** make their way along well-worn animal tracks towards the waterhole from all directions, especially in the dry season.

After stopping at the waterhole, take the eight-kilometre gravel road to **Olifantsbad.** It winds through **mopane tree-veld** and **shrubs** on **calcrete soil** and **rocks**. Imposing

Male lions at Gemsbokvlakte waterhole

Yellow-billed hornbill

specimens of old, single-stemmed, high-branching mopane trees line the roadside as you approach the waterhole. Sunlight filters through their dense canopies, dappling the road with lights and shadows. Look out for **lions** that love to recline in the shade of the trees and for **leopards**.

Olifantsbad is one of the park's most productive waterholes. It is well worth spending time in the area and feasting your eyes on the wildlife that frequents the waterhole. You can stretch your legs and take a break at the nearby **picnic site**. Toilet facilities are simple.

Exiting the waterhole and carrying on for the next eight kilometres towards **Aus**, the scenery changes slightly, giving way to denser **shrub mopane** and less visibility on either side of the road. Drive slowly and be vigilant for **elephants** that might surprise you by suddenly stepping out onto the road from the dense vegetation, as well as small groups of **black-faced impala** and **Burchell's zebra** that like to block the road in places. **Helmeted guineafowl** are abundant in the area, often foraging next to the road's verges or haphazardly zigzagging across it. Look out for yellow-billed and African-grey **hornbills** perching on shrubs or trees or chasing tasty morsels beside the roadside.

The turn-off to **Aus** waterhole to your right takes you to a medium-sized parking area fringed by mopane shrubs.

The area surrounding the **Aus** waterhole is an ideal habitat for large herds of **black-faced impala.** It is one of the best places to see them browsing on the mopane leaves next to the roadside and wandering to and from the waterhole. The ambience is peaceful and tranquil, guaranteed to put anyone in a relaxed mood; appreciate the scenery.

The 15 km stretch between the **Aus** waterhole and the main road where **Ondongab** is accessed requires careful navigation for the first part. A few potholes and shallow depressions in the calcrete surface of the gravel road will let you in for a bit of a bumpy ride in places and slight corrugation; therefore, the advice is to drive slowly. The depressions get waterlogged in the rainy season. Always be cautious and take it easy, as it is difficult to gauge the exact depth of the depressions. Two or three road borrow pits that may hold water seasonally occur.

A few grey-coloured **termite mounds** are visible next to the roadside in places, which play an essential part in the ecosystem, and birds are fond of perching on them. Be on the lookout for birdlife in the form of **lilac-breasted rollers**, **fork-tailed drongos**, **hornbills**, **red-billed spurfowl** and smaller raptors like **Gabar goshawk** and **black-winged kite**.

The significant vegetation community in the whole area is described as **eastern karst woodlands**, with mixed bushveld consisting of **mopane shrub**, **red bushwillow** and **purple-pod cluster-leaf**, limiting visibility in places. After a few kilometres, the scenery changes, opening up to sprawling **grassland**, and better road conditions prevail. It is a much quieter stretch of road with less wildlife but one unusual or surprise sighting can alter that perception. As the road exits, joining up with the C38 main road, the access to the **Ondongab waterhole** is signposted directly opposite.

Turning directly to your left on the main road, a scenic 15 km road will take you back to the **Gemsbokvlakte waterhole**, completing the loop. You will likely see a greater variety and larger game densities along this road. This area is more open, with unhampered views over the surrounding plains interspersed with areas of **thornbush savanna**, attracting both browsers and grazers. The side of the road towards the pan features a **dwarf-shrub savanna**, with **petal-bush**, **salt-bush**, **wool bush** and **horse-bush**. **Springboks** are fond of these dwarf shrubs; you may see large herds in the area.

Thick stands of **trumpet thorns** occur extensively in the area, especially near the Gemsbokvlakte waterhole. **Burchell's zebra** and **springbok** eat the leaves, **rhinos** nibble the branches, and **kudu** are particularly fond of the large, white, trumpet-shaped flowers.

Gregarious **ground squirrels** live in colonies near the roadside in multi-entranced warrens. It pays to spend a few minutes in their company, as they are great entertainers and their interactions are fascinating to watch. They prefer open terrain with sparse bush cover and often use their tails as umbrellas for sunshades.

With such high game densities in the area, predators follow suit, and the entire area around Gemsbokvlate is a perfect area to look for **lions**. They usually move between Nebrownii waterhole, Okaukuejo waterhole and Gemsbokvlakte. Your other options include taking the main road back towards Okaukuejo and visiting Nebrownii waterhole en route back to camp.

Okaukuejo Camp to Okondeka Waterhole

Option A

Via Wolfsnes (p. 171) to Okondeka (p. 162)

- 45 km
- Blue sky; expansive plains; white pan
- Tall grassveld communities; dwarf shrub savanna
- Saltbush; desert sedge grass; Kalahari acacia
- Ostrich; plains birds
- Lion pride; zebra; springbok; blue wildebeest; oryx; bat-eared fox; scrub hare; African wild cat; spotted hyena

This delightful route is ideal for an **afternoon excursion**. After exiting camp, turn northwest. The first stretch takes you through typical **Etosha grassland** and **dwarf shrubland**, bordering the saline desert on the pan side to the right.

Expect several **plains game** to mill around, going to and from the Okaukuejo waterhole. **Zebra**, **springbok**, **blue wildebeest** and **ostrich** are abundant.

You will pass the small Okaukuejo airstrip to your right and head towards **Wolfsnes**, where a seasonal seepage is at the pan's edge. As far as the eye can see, the sprawling, open plains to both sides of the road are bound to evoke a sense of freedom and wonderment. The **saltbush**, a significant component of dwarf shrub savanna, is particularly noticeable.

Cape fox

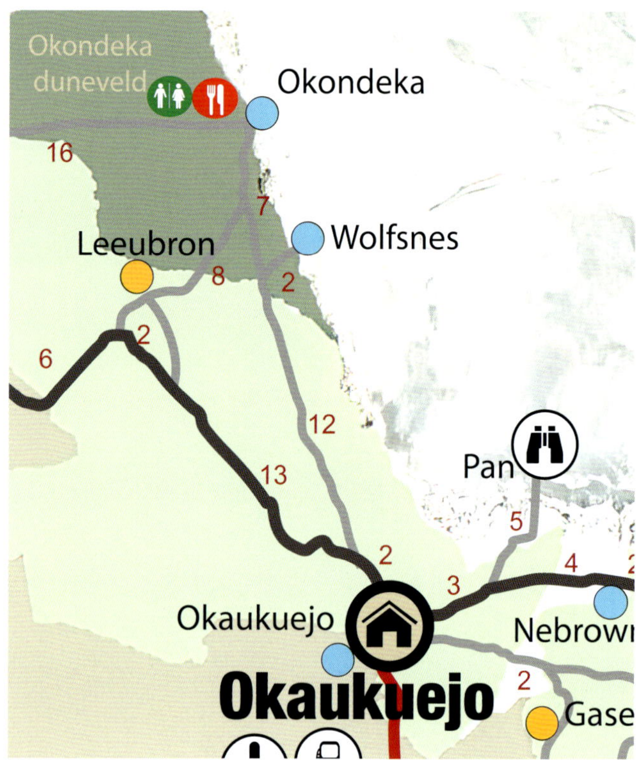

Although the vegetation might seem sparse in the dry season, the scenery is still very appealing.

Just before the access road to Wolfsnes on your left, two tall **Kalahari acacias** flank the main road, an incongruous sight in the otherwise flat landscape. Look out for a variety of bird species sheltering in the trees.

The approximately two-kilometre access road to Wolfsnes is worth a quick visit. Sometimes, smaller mammals like ground squirrels are active next to the roadside. Look for **bat-eared foxes**, which often have dens near the main road. From late afternoon onwards, there is a good chance of catching a glimpse of them.

The last two or three kilometres before Okondeka will take your breath away. The lush green **desert sedge grass** fringing the spring, interspersed with golden grass, the white expanse of the white pan, and the mostly blue sky, is a feast for the eye. Many animals, especially in the dry season, are bound to be near the waterhole.

You will likely have an incredible sighting of the Okondeka **lion pride** or some of its members. The **Okondeka duneveld** offers great concealment opportunities for these predators in the form of grassy hummocks lining the west of the pan and dense sedges surrounding the waterhole.

It is an ideal area for a sundowner while soaking up the breathtaking scenery before heading back to camp in the golden glow of the late afternoon. Allocate a bit of extra time along the way, as the light is truly spectacular for photography and fantastic sightings in the form of **scrub hare**, **African wild cat**, **spotted hyena**, **Cape- and bat-eared foxes** are very likely.

The road is usually in good condition, barring slight corrugation in places.

Male blue wildebeest

Okaukuejo Camp to Okondeka Waterhole
Option B

Via Okondeka (p. 162), Adamax (p. 142), Natco (p. 156) and Leeubron (p. 154) Loop

72 km

Pan views

Sweet grassveld on lime; tall grassveld communities

Water thorn acacia; blackthorn; wool-bush; silver bush; *Monechma tonsum*

Ostrich

Cape fox; aardwolf; brown hyena; typical wildlife

You can easily transform the afternoon drive from Okaukuejo to Okondeka into a longer drive for the **morning**. Carry on from Okondeka, head towards **Adamax**, **Natco** and **Leeubron,** and then leisurely make your way back to Okaukuejo via the main road.

Cape fox pup

This stretch would be particularly productive in the rainy season, as the waterholes of **Adamax**, **Natco** and **Leeubron are inactive**. During the rainy season, however, depressions in the area hold water and good grazing, with the significant vegetation community described as **sweet grassveld on lime** drawing vast herds of plains game, which also give birth during this season.

These extensive grasslands border the southern and southwestern edge of the pan, extending westwards towards Leeubron, all the way to the 'Enchanted Forest'. Examples of vegetation on the edges of these plains are thickets of **water thorn acacia**, **blackthorn acacia** and typical dwarf shrubs like **wool-bush**, **petal-bush** and ***Monechma tonsum*** (no common name), a many-stemmed light bluish dwarf shrub. Ostriches feed on the leaves and shoots. The dominant grasses are **eight-day grass**, so named because it takes only eight days to germinate, grow and produce seeds, and **wether love grass**, a perennial sub-climax and relatively palatable grass.

Predators follow the prey and exciting sightings are likely. You may encounter most of the park's wildlife. Expect the former only during the rainy season; the dry season is less productive and will paint a bleaker picture when the plains are bare and without grasses.

The 16 km route from Okondeka is particularly productive. Look for **Cape fox dens** close to the road, **aardwolves** often seen, and a **brown hyena** den south of the main road.

Young male springbok

Okaukuejo Camp to Ozonjuitji m'Bari, Sprokieswoud and Grünewald

Via Leeubron (p. 154) and back via Sprokieswoud and Grünewald (p. 149)

- 120 km
- Grootvlakte; Charl Marais Dam
- Mopane savanna on calcrete; sweet grassveld on lime
- Moringa trees; wether love grass; nine-awned grass; eight-day grass; Kalahari gold
- Temminck's courser; eastern clapper lark
- Excellent game viewing; herds of herbivores; most top predators

This route is suggested as a **half-day excursion** from Okaukuejo Camp if you have a few days to explore waterholes and routes in the area. If pressed for time, focus on exploring the region closer to camp. Arrange for a breakfast pack or cater for enough snacks and drinks. The distance to m'Bari is approximately 54 km, but spending time here warrants travelling all this way. M'Bari is **one of the park's most exciting and productive waterholes**, especially in the dry season, as it is the only waterhole west of Okaukuejo and Okondeka that holds water during that time. The predominant vegetation en route is typical **mopane savanna on calcrete**, with shallow soil.

It is advisable to visit the **picnic site** at the entrance opposite the access road to Sprokieswoud before continuing your excursion to m'Bari, as it is the last opportunity to stretch your legs or use the ablution facilities. Along this stretch of road, you can see **Temminck's courser** and the medium-sized **eastern clapper lark**.

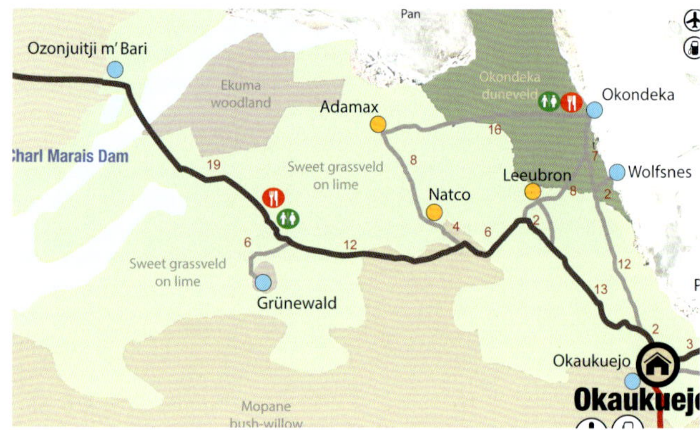

Thick mopane shrubs line the road in places as you approach **Charl Marais Dam**. Look out for the simple-leaved rhigozum or **Kalahari gold** along the route. It is a shrub or multi-stemmed small tree that is eye-catching and beautiful when flowering, as it bears a profusion of golden-yellow flowers soon after the first rains. The dam holds water seasonally and draws an abundance of wildlife and birdlife.

The road leads over the dam wall to a slight incline at the top, with a small, elevated parking area on either side of the road overlooking the dam and surrounding plains. You may not exit your car at this point but it is worthwhile to scan the area with your binoculars, absorb the tranquil atmosphere, and enjoy the view over the dam and surrounding plains.

The access road to **the m'Bari waterhole** is just a few metres to your right, directly after the road signposted 'No entry'. Thickets of **water thorn acacia** line the road, and typical **shrub mopane** vegetation dominates the area west of the m'Bari waterhole. The vegetation is stunted and not more than one to two metres tall.

On your way back to Okaukuejo, it is worthwhile to briefly explore the short six-kilometre detour to **Grünewald** if only to observe the **moringa trees** of the **Sprokieswoud**. Feast your eyes on the beautiful specimens of large, single-stemmed **mopane trees** of Grünewald that grow along the road in

White-backed vulture displaying

White-backed vultures, black-backed jackals and spotted hyena on Burchell's zebra carcass

places. Grünewald translated means 'Green Forest'. On your way, you will see expansive views of the sprawling plains of **Grootvlakte**, which extend to Charl Marais Dam.

Grootvlakte means 'great plain' in Afrikaans, as it is one of the most extensive plains in the park, approximately 400 km^2 in size, forming the most significant single component of the vegetation type classified as **sweet grassveld on lime**. Frequently occurring grasses are the perennial **wether love grass**, **nine-awned grass** and **eight-day grass**. Components of **dwarf-shrub savanna** are low-lying shrubs like **horse-bush**, which are dominant on Grootvlakte, as well as **wool bush** and **petal-bush**. Herbivores like **Burchell's zebra**, **wildebeest** and **springbok** congregate in large herds during summer rainfall. People previously saw large herds of **eland** here, but they no longer occur following their decline throughout Etosha. It is a vast, open plain of scenic beauty and well worth a visit in the rainy season. The area tends to appear dry and bleak in the dry season, with a noticeable absence of large herds of game.

Directly translated from Afrikaans, Sprokieswoud means 'Fairy-tale Forest' or 'Enchanted Forest', which refers to the bizarre shapes of the **African moringa** or **ghost trees**. The forest is approximately 38 km west of Okaukuejo and immediately east of Grootvlakte, extending for about one square kilometre. These remarkable trees usually occur on rocky hillsides, but **growing on a flat plain** is an **unusual phenomenon** yet to be scientifically explained. Elephants, giraffes and springbok feed on their fruit and leaves. Sadly, many moringa trees have fallen victim to elephants, easily pushing them over to get the moisture-holding, pulpy fibre in the trunks. The once magnificent forest is now a shadow of its former self, especially in the dry period. The park management had to fence off the remaining moringa trees to protect them against these giant pachyderms. The author recommends visiting this area during the rainy season when more wildlife will frequent the area, and the moringa trees begin to bloom at the beginning of November and continue up to May, producing slender sprays of small, fragrant, creamy white flowers. Elephants, giraffes and springbok eat the flowers and leaves.

Some stretches of the gravel road along the 19th latitude tend to be badly corrugated at times but extensive roadworks are currently underway in the park, especially the western side.

Okaukuejo (or Halali) to the Golden Mile

Scenic detour along the pan

Via Homob (p. 151), Sueda (p. 170), Charitsaub (p. 143) and Salvadora (p. 168) waterholes

- 40 + 15 + 40 km direct from Okaukuejo
- Scenic; pan view, picnic site; artesian spring; sprawling plain; undulating grassland
- Saline desert habitat; sweet grassveld on lime
- Halophytic grasses; ink bush; Kalahari acacia; desert sedge; mopane aloes
- Ostrich; blue crane; small raptors
- Black rhino; cheetah; lion; springbok; oryx; Burchell's zebra; wildebeest

Approaching from Okaukuejo direction west to the east

Travelling along the C38 from Okaukuejo and taking a left-turn two kilometres after the turn-off to the picnic site, also on your left, heralds the start of a scenic nine-kilometre detour meandering along the fringes of the pan. It encompasses **three of Etosha's most productive and iconic waterholes** and breathtaking and diverse scenery, usually hosting a diversity and abundance of wildlife, thus referred to by some as the 'Golden Mile'.

Pay a visit to **Homob waterhole** on your way. The 3.4 km access road leads over some uneven areas of hard calcrete stones and shallow potholes, which hold water in the rainy season. **Mopane treeveld** is characteristic of the region, and beautiful, tall, stately and widely spaced mopane trees and purple-pod cluster-leaf line a significant part of the road and afford good visibility on either side. It is a picturesque setting, adequately compensating for the slight bumpy ride. You might be lucky to see the **territorial leopard** patrolling his territory en route to the waterhole. **Homob is a very active waterhole**, good for exciting and unexpected sightings and worth visiting. Stopping at the **picnic site** situated conveniently two kilometres after exciting Homob and before embarking on the Golden Mile Detour is advisable.

The first four-kilometre stretch of the detour affords glimpses of the saline desert habitat of the pan to the left, with mixed shrubland to your right. Look out for a **scenic lookout on the left**, not signposted, but visible and ideal for panoramic photographs of the vast expanse of the pan. **It is not permissible to get out here**. The mixed shrub gives way to open plains on the right as you get close to the contact spring of **Sueda.** As you approach the turn-off to Sueda, look out for a rocky outcrop on your right, hosting a small colony of mopane aloes. They are unusual and **banded mongooses** are frequently seen perched on the rocks near the aloes.

Look out for **black rhinos**, **cheetahs** and **lions**. Lionesses sometimes hide their cubs in concealed nooks along the elevated calcrete ridges along the edge of the pan, so it pays to drive slowly and carefully study your surroundings. You might be able to see lions walking along the pan towards the Homob waterhole when they patrol their territory.

Cheetahs favour the open terrain and grasslands as they make reasonable hunting grounds for running down their prey. **Salt-loving** or **halophytic grasses** like **prickly brack grass** growing on the brackish soil dominate the vegetation on the pan side. The **ink bush,** a low spreading, many-stemmed shrub with tiny green fleshy leaves, which turn a bright reddish pink at certain times of the year, covers considerable stretches along the Sueda, Charitsaub and Salvadora route, creating intermittent eye-catching, pretty carpets of colour.

Exiting the access road from Sueda and taking a left turn, vast, open grasslands stretch on either side of the one-kilometre gravel road leading to the **artesian spring of Charitsaub** on the right-hand side. A **Kalahari acacia** marks the turn-off to the short access road to the right, leading to an elevated parking area overlooking the spring.

Thick stands of **desert sedges** often yield an unexpected sighting of a predator lying in ambush for herbivores approaching to drink. After good rains, the sprawling plain surrounding the **Charitsaub** waterhole hosts thousands of springbok, oryx, Burchell's zebra and wildebeest.

The short, one-kilometre stretch between Charitsaub and Salvadora features expanses of particularly tall, undulating **grasslands** that are prominent just after the first rains have fallen, with the **ink bush** also conspicuous. The vista from

the Salvadora parking lot is breathtaking, and you can easily spend a few hours with binoculars in hand, soaking up the views and scenic atmosphere, gazing over the backdrop of the pan dotted with specks of wildlife.

Look out for **ostriches**, as they are often breeding on the pan. Ostrich nests have been found on raised ground, even as far as 10 km from the edge of the pan, surrounded by water when the pan does hold water, to escape predators. When nutritious grasses cover the adjacent plains, the Salvadora contact spring, with its palatable water, draws masses of herbivores from mid-morning onwards.

Like Charitsaub, dense **desert sedge thickets** surround the spring. Many surprise sightings of **lions** or even **leopards** concealing themselves in the thickets, successfully ambushing prey, have been recorded. Look out for **blue cranes** near Charitsaub and Salvadora during the rainy season and through winter until August. A breeding pair often chooses this area to raise their chicks.

A further two kilometres after exiting Salvadora to the left, you reach the junction where the detour joins the main road C38.

Cheetah

Approaching from Halali

31 km one way, 62 km return. An alternative route back to camp via the main road 27 km

This route is a beautiful morning drive and an obvious choice for all visitors to Etosha, as it leads through one of the most scenic places in Etosha. Leaving Halali Camp and heading westwards toward Okaukuejo, travelling about 13 km along the main road before taking a right turn, takes you to the start of what is known as the Golden Mile.

Exiting Sueda, turning to your right and driving a few metres, look for a rocky outcrop on your left. Mopane **aloes** and **banded mongooses** are frequently seen perched on the rocks close to the aloes. The **picnic site** is two kilometres away, with the main road to the right, ideal for a short mid-morning break. Be sure to turn in at Homob waterhole, the access road a mere two kilometres from the picnic site. **The detour to Homob will add another 10.4 km to the route.**

The way back to camp via the main road is four kilometres shorter but less scenic than the route along the pan. Whichever way you choose, depending on sightings, make sure you still allocate enough time for a stop at **Rietfontein waterhole** on the way back to camp. It is usually a hive of activity from mid-morning onwards and is always worth your while. During the rainy season, when water is freely available, and wildlife is not bound by waterholes, driving for more extended stretches is the better option as you can enjoy incredible and unexpected sightings virtually anywhere.

Banded mongoose and mopane aloe

Male lion coalition

Halali Camp to Rietfontein Detour and Picnic Site

Via Rietfontein waterhole (p. 166), detour pan side and detour south side

- 56 km + 15 km
- Picnic site; mixed shrubveld; open plains
- Mopane treeveld; sweet grassveld on lime
- Water thorn acacia; wild sage; cork-bush; saltbush
- European roller; secretarybird; larks; coursers; small raptors; sandgrouse.
- Black rhino; lion; spotted hyena; leopard; bat-eared fox; honey badger; Burchell's zebra; springbok; wildebeest; yellow mongoose

This detour, situated on both sides of the main road and looking like an **elongated figure of eight** on the map, would be a good choice for a **morning drive**. It includes spending time at **Rietfontein waterhole**, a productive spot for action-packed wildlife sightings.

Male lion

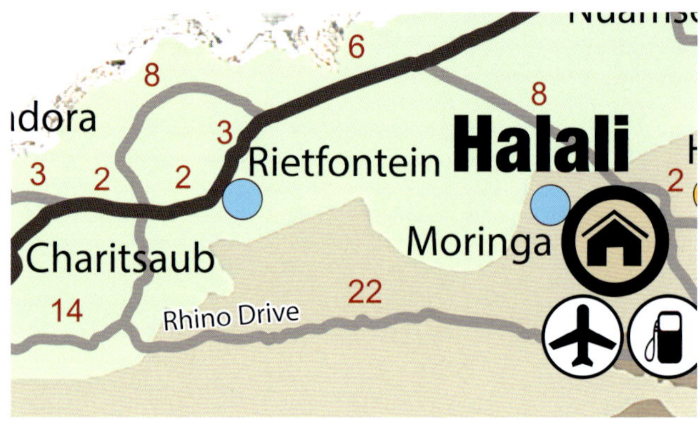

Leaving camp and heading in a westerly direction, the eight-kilometre access road suits **black rhinos**, which often browse on the branches of **water thorn acacia**. Joining up with the C38 main road and turning towards Rietfontein, sprawling and picturesque **plains** line the main road on both sides. **Wild sage** grows abundantly, and other components of dwarf shrub savanna, like the **saltbush**, grow closer to the detour. Look out for **bat-eared foxes** and **honey badgers** along this stretch in the early morning. If you are lucky, you might encounter **lions** walking on the road. After six kilometres, you can access the nine-kilometre detour to the pan to your right.

Consider heading towards the **Rietfontein waterhole** first before navigating the other half of the detour. As it is an active waterhole, drawing many animals, the prospects are usually good for an unusual or surprise sighting.

Water thorn acacia thickets line the road, interspersed with **trumpet thorn and corkbush**. The conspicuous, showy mauve (occasionally white) flowers of the corkbush add a dash of colour from October to January. Still, the bark and leaves contain the poison rotenone, used as a fish poison.

The vegetation zone is typically **sweet grassveld on lime,** with **mopane treeveld** prominently in the centre of the detour, further away from the roadside. Visibility is good, especially in the winter months, with glimpses of the pan in the distance in places.

Many herbivores such as **springbok**, **zebra** and **wildebeest** are attracted to the area when palatable grasses start sprouting and covering the plains during and after the rainy season. Springbok are particularly partial to the leaves and flowers of the water thorn acacia. Predators, notably **lions**, follow the abundant herds, and opportunistic **spotted hyenas** frequent the area.

The whole area is superb for sighting the elusive **leopard**; you might be lucky and have an exceptional sighting, with many a springbok kill made near the detour and Rietfontein waterhole. The detour is also a firm favourite with the **black rhino**, and you may see one browsing in the area, especially on the **water thorn acacia thickets** in the early morning or late afternoon. The migratory colourful **European roller** is usually around, perched on shrubs by the roadside, foraging for insects. **Secretarybirds** can sometimes be seen quite comfortably from the roadside, roosting and nesting in trees. Look out for the yellow mongoose's isolated dens, often near the roadside.

Springbok

The entrance to the southern loop lies directly opposite the exit of the first loop, on the other side of the main road. Looking at the map, both halves of the detour resemble an elongated figure of eight.

Ground squirrels have extensive colonies next to the roadside towards the beginning of the detour. These gregarious, diurnal creatures are proper little ecosystem engineers, industriously digging large burrow systems, their refuge from extreme temperatures, and a quick escape route from predators and raptors. Females with their young usually live close to the burrows, while males live in different burrow systems, moving from colony to colony. They can provide hours of entertainment when interacting with each other and are rewarding subjects to photograph.

The vegetation is much the same as the pan-side detour, with **mopane treeveld** dominant on the southeastern side of the road. Towards the second half of the detour, dense thickets of **trumpet thorn** line the roadside in places, obscuring visibility before opening again to grassland. This part of the detour hosts fewer grazers owing to the thicker shrub. Smaller concentrations of plains game are found on this loop, especially on the north side of the road, as the area borders open grassland. It does yield good sightings, though, particularly of smaller mammals like the **African wild cat** and the **yellow-** and **banded mongoose**. You may find any of them near the concrete signposts at the road entrances. It is also a productive road for birdlife and yields good sightings of **larks**, **coursers**, **small raptors** and **sandgrouse**.

The road is usually in excellent condition, and the early morning and late afternoon light are best suited for photography. Upon completing the second detour, it is advisable to head 7.5 km west on the main road towards the **picnic site** for a brief break, the only facility in the area other than Halali Camp. **Including the picnic site** in your route will add another **15 km.** Depending on your time and sightings, you might visit **Homob waterhole** nearby, **adding an extra 10.4 km to the trip.**

Heading back on the main road towards Rietfontein waterhole takes you through **mixed shrubveld** and **open plains** on either side; look out for the usual plains game. Just before you turn towards the Rietfontein waterhole, **mopane treeveld** lines the road with beautiful large, single-stemmed mopane trees with spreading canopies. **White calcrete rock** and **soil** are prominent, and they are also around the waterhole. Scan your surroundings closely, as the area is exceedingly good for leopard sightings.

A steady stream of wildlife usually approaches the waterhole from mid-morning onwards, drawing huge herds of **Burchell's zebra**. Most other game found in Etosha frequent this waterhole at different times of the day, and it pays to spend a long time here. You can even return in the afternoon for sundowners, as you have a good chance of seeing leopard, black rhino and lion.

Halali Camp to Etosha Lookout and Nuamses

Halali plains seepages (p. 150), Nuamses waterhole (p. 159)

50 km

Twin hills of Helio; seepages on Halali plains

Sweet grassveld on lime; mopane treeveld

Water thorn acacia; Juncus sedges

Predators; rhino; African wild cat; cheetah; black-faced impala; kudu

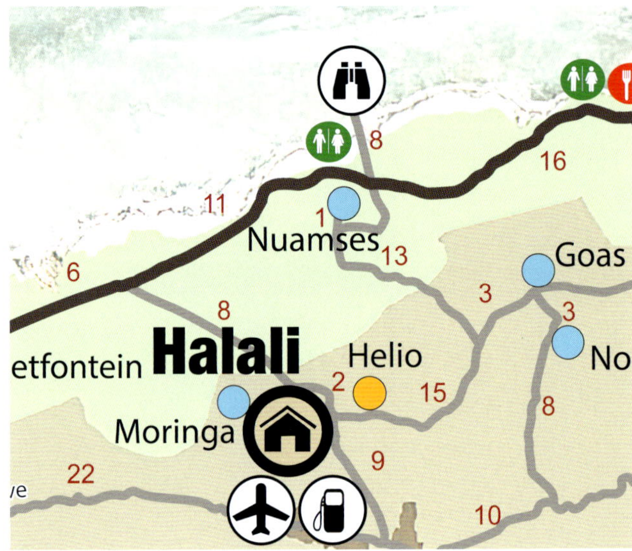

Owing to the resort's central location, you are spoilt for choice when contemplating routes for game drives from Halali Camp. There are many options virtually in all directions.

A good recommendation for an afternoon foray from camp is a visit to the **Etosha Lookout**. Heading out from camp on the eight-kilometre access road in the northwesterly direction and taking a right turn towards the east on the main road will set you well on the way on another picturesque drive, with glimpses of the pan on your left and **open grassland plains** of Halali on your right, with its signatory **twin hills** distinctly visible in the distance.

Watch for the **Halali plains seepages** on the pan side after passing through a thicket of **water thorn acacia**. Dark green vegetation consisting of **Juncus sedges** marks the area around the edges of the seeps. Large processions of game usually make their way to and from the water. Look out for **rhinos** and **predators**, as well as **African wild cat**.

Turning left onto the three-kilometre access road, which takes you all the way out onto the pan, the vast expanse opens, particularly beautiful in the golden glow of the afternoon sun. The same stage is set for a completely different kind of beauty when the rains arrive: moody blue-black thunderclouds rolling across the salt pan and the heavens opening, releasing torrential sheets of rain, with parts of the pan rapidly filling up with water.

During the dry season, the access road enables you to drive to a circular area onto the fringes of the pan, where you may **alight from your vehicle**. It is an excellent photographic opportunity, which many visitors make use of. Dry, cracked white clay covering the surface of the bare expanse stretching out as far as the eye can see is a spectacle. You may spot

Lioness

Aerial view of Etosha lookout

Burchell's zebra, **springbok**, **blue wildebeest**, **spotted hyena**, **black-backed jackal** or **ostrich** crossing the pan at places and, if you are lucky, the ultimate prize of **a lion**, too. These are, of course, **fantastic photo opportunities**, greatly sought after by many wildlife photographers.

When heading back towards the main road, pay attention to your immediate surroundings, especially to the left of the road. The number of animals in the vicinity indicates a water source on the plains. The water source is not accessible to the public and is barely visible from the road, but you might be lucky to have a special sighting in the area.

The first four kilometres of the route to Nuamses waterhole can also yield exciting sights. **Cheetahs**, **rhinos**, **elephants**, and **most plains game** regularly visit the open expanses owing to permanent water in the vicinity.

Another spring, which is not accessible to visitors or visible, is situated on the right side. This short stretch of road has a few dips and depressions, which fill up with water in the rainy season. The road is sometimes closed owing to unavoidable conditions.

Be careful when turning right towards **Nuamses waterhole**. Drive slowly as the road's hard, uneven, calcrete surface tends to be badly corrugated. Fortunately, it is just a short stretch of approximately 1.5 km. However, the scenery makes up for the slight discomfort, traversing through a particularly charming **mopane treeveld**.

Mostly tall, widely spaced, single-stemmed mopane trees line both sides of the road, the golden sunlight filtering through the canopies creating a dreamlike, peaceful atmosphere. This is a **black-faced impala** area, with **kudu** also favouring this habitat. The mopane vegetation dominates the whole region, especially beautiful in autumn when the leaves turn from vibrant green to russet, red, and golden brown shades.

Nuamses is a unique and quaint waterhole, particularly beautiful in the afternoon. The parking area is relatively small but usually not greatly frequented by much vehicle traffic, and it is an ideal location for a quiet sundowner.

A **leopard** may surprise you, while **elephants** regularly use the waterhole as their giant bathtub, usually between mid-morning and early afternoon.

Allocate at least 45 minutes for the return trip, as some parts of the eight-kilometre road require slow driving until you reach the turn-off to Halali. The last 10 kilometres back to camp is easy driving, once again taking you past the **twin hills of Helio** on your right.

Routes from Halali Camp to Hartebeest Drive

via Goas waterhole (p. 148)

- 68 km
- Twin hills of Helio; picnic site
- Mopane/red bushwillow/purple-pod cluster-leaf bushveld
- African moringa; Grewia species; bird plum; sickle-bush; common Commiphora
- African hawk-eagle; ostrich; African hoopoe
- Leopard; black-faced impala; black rhino; elephant; red hartebeest; blue wildebeest; springbok; Burchell's zebra

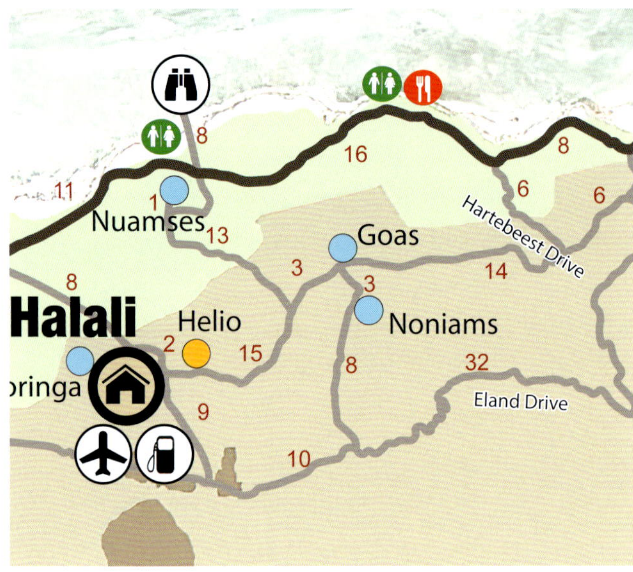

There are quite a few scenic routes from Halali Camp. Combining an excursion to **Hartebeest Drive** with a stop at **Goas waterhole** on your route would be a good option for the afternoon, especially in summer when the gates close later, allowing for more time.

Female leopard

If you turn easterly from camp, the road meanders through typical bushveld, with **mopane**, **red bushwillow** and **purple-pod cluster-leaf** dominating the scenery.

Pass the distinct cone-like dolomite **twin hills of Helio** on your left, named after the heliograph station located on top in times of German military presence. The **ghost** or **African moringa trees** dominate the hillsides, their **white trunks** visible from a distance. **Grewia species, bird plum, sickle-bush and common commiphora**, grow here. This habitat is ideal for **leopards**, **black-faced impalas**, **black rhinos** and **elephants.** Look out for **African hawk eagles**, which prefer to nest along the hill slopes, building large nests composed of sticks placed high up in a tree.

Various herbivores may browse or graze close to both sides of the road, especially as you approach the access road leading to **the Goas waterhole**. Large elephant breeding herds are often found in the area since they favour the large, open area surrounding the Goas waterhole. Drive slowly and give way to **Burchell's zebra**, **black-faced impala** and other herbivores that frequently cross the road. Look out for the striking **African hoopoe**, often darting between the mopane trees in pursuit of insects.

Visibility is good along most of the road, with widely spaced, taller mopane trees and open plains to the left side of the road.

Hartebeest Drive, named after the **red hartebeest** frequenting this area, is a scenic, triangular-shaped detour linking the Goas Road to the main road leading to Springbokfontein. The first stretch of road meanders along a sprawling plain on your left and mopane treeveld on your right. This part is atmospheric and tranquil, with few other vehicles on the road. It is a good area for encountering **leopards** and **black and white rhinos**. The elevation point is highest towards the end of the drive before it joins up with the C38 main road, affording good views over the plains to your left. The vast expanse of the pan is visible ahead, with a **natural seepage ahead directly next to the main road.** The seepage is easy to spot, lined with dense desert sedge grass. It is a prime position for predators to conceal themselves and lie in wait for the abundant game in the area, often crossing the road towards the pan side to drink at the number of seepages in the area.

Scanning the area closely with binoculars might reward you with a decent sighting. As you head east on the main road towards Namutoni, glimpses of the pan are visible to your left in places. Game is usually present along this stretch of road: **springbok**, **ostrich**, **red hartebeest**, **Burchell's zebra** and **blue wildebeest**.

A nearby **picnic site** is conveniently located as you reach the turn-off to your right, which leads to Eland Drive and Goas. It is an 18-kilometre stretch back to Goas and a relatively quiet stretch of road, especially the seven kilometres before the access road back to Hartebeest Drive. However, remember this is prime leopard habitat, so scan the area closely. Some birds to look out for are the **African hoopoe, common scimitarbill, purple roller** and **hornbill species.**

The road is usually in good condition, and the corrugation level depends on the traffic and weather. During the rainy season, some road parts tend to get waterlogged.

Depending on sightings, you should enjoy a leisurely sundowner at Goas. Towards dusk, it is particularly scenic, radiates a tranquil atmosphere, and offers a surprise when you least expect it.

Spotted hyena at seepage near Hartebeest drive

Halali Camp to Rhino Drive and Rietfontein

via Noniams (p. 158)

75 km for the morning or
53 km for the afternoon option

Open plains; mopane trees and shrub

Mopane/red bushwillow/purple-pod cluster-leaf bushveld

Mopane; sickle bush

Pale chanting goshawk

Black-faced impala; Burchell's zebra; kudu; steenbok; small animals; predators

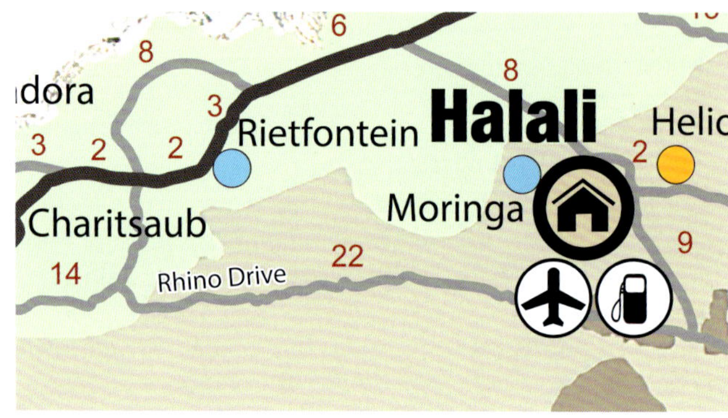

MORNING OPTION

This route would be a good option for a leisurely **morning drive**. First, you would **head east** from camp, enabling you to experience the charm and scenic beauty of the region around Halali. The **access road to Noniams** is signposted to your right just before you reach Goas waterhole.

Although the seasonal spring became dormant in the long dry period of Etosha around 1981, it carries water in the rainy season, and a variety of wildlife still frequents the area even during the dry season, probably because of the proximity of **Goas** waterhole as a permanent source of water. The immediate vicinity of the waterhole is an excellent area to view **black-faced impala**, **zebra**, **kudu** and **steenbok**.

Tall, widely spaced, single-stemmed **mopane trees** are a beautiful feature and create an atmosphere of peace and tranquillity. Thickets of **mopane shrub** and **sickle-bush** are also found along the roadside, with the sickle-bush seemingly particularly affected in the dry winter months, looking dry, drab and sad. It is a lovely **flowering shrub** sporting conspicuous two-coloured, pendulous spikes. It consists of a mauve to pale pink section (sterile flowers) with a bright yellow tip (fertile flowers), usually from November to January. Dik-dik, kudu and eland favour the curly, twisted pods with a high protein content, while rhino and giraffe browse the leaves and shoots.

Access **Rhino Drive** to your right and **Eland Drive** to your left as you reach the junction.

The vegetation zone, as a whole, is described as **mopane/ red bushwillow/purple-pod cluster-leaf bushveld**. Dense shrubs and grasses line the roadside, with extensive open plains. The gravel road is narrow in places, especially in the first section of the drive, with a few corrugated areas and hard calcrete stone in places. **Black rhinos** are often sighted on Rhino Drive, as are the usual browsers and grazers. As you head towards the end of Rhino Drive, near Rietfontein, you may find **lions** walking along the road, and there is a good chance of spotting **a leopard**. Although some people maintain they have not seen much on Rhino Drive, please don't miss it. You will always find something special: either a **pale-chanting goshawk** with lizard kill, a **leopard tortoise**, **yellow mongooses** playing near a den, a **flap-neck chameleon** slowly rocking across the road or a **spotted hyena** on the move to the nearest waterhole. If a special sighting awaits you, you will probably have it primarily for yourself, which is a bonus.

Time your drive so that you will be in **Rietfontein** mid-morning. This time is guaranteed to be the busiest and most entertaining period of the day, well up to lunchtime.

AFTERNOON OPTION

A slightly different option approaching Rhino Drive and better suited for an **afternoon drive** would be **omitting Noniams** by exiting camp, heading east and, after three kilometres, taking the right turn onto the seven-kilometre access road that takes you straight onto **Rhino Drive**. The length of the drive is approximately 53 km in total. The late afternoon is an opportune time to be keeping vigil at Rietfontein waterhole as you have a good chance of special sightings in the form of leopard, black rhino and lion in the golden glow of the late afternoon light, ideally suited for photography purposes.

Flap-necked chameleon

Black rhino

Halali Camp to Batia and Springbokfontein

Via Goas (p. 148), Nuamses (p. 159), Batia (p. 175), Springbokfontein (p. 190), plains seepages

80 km; 2.5 km extra if including Nuamses

Scenic and panoramic route; Helio hills; picnic site; seepages

Sweet grassveld on lime; mopane treeveld

Halophytic grass; desert sedges

Grey hornbill; African hoopoe; waterbirds

Predators; black-faced impala

This route is an ideal **half-day outing**, taking a scenic route along the pan and incorporating **four waterholes** on your route. Request a breakfast pack and head out at first light, taking the easterly route towards **Goas**. Look out for **rhinos** and **leopards** near **Helio Hills**; both are active early in the day.

Stop at **Goas** waterhole, a productive waterhole virtually all day. Sightings of **spotted hyenas** and **lions** are best in the early morning, with good chances of a lion pride reclining near the water. Leisurely head in the direction of **Hartebeest Drive**. Pay close attention to the immediate vicinity of the roadside, as sightings of **leopard** are frequent and regular.

Passing the turn-off to Hartebeest Drive on your left and later the turn-off to Eland Drive to your right, the last four kilometres until the road joins the main road can be relatively quiet, without the immense concentration and variety of game, but the scenery more than makes up for it, with beautiful **tree mopane** on either side of the road.

Look out for **grey hornbills** and the **African hoopoe**, frequently seen on this stretch of road. **Black-faced impalas** usually frequent the area. Also, keep scanning the area for leopards. **Cheetahs** are sometimes observed on the plains to the right, near the turn-off to Eland Drive.

The **picnic site** is on your right and ideal for a quick break to stretch your legs before heading towards **Springbokfontein** and **Batia**. Springbokfontein is a strong **springwater spring** but it is more copious and larger than Batia. The spring lies north and south of the main road and is a strong freshwater spring drainage line, extending along the edge of the central pan, which projects narrowly to Batia.

The whole area is **panoramic**, with premium viewing opportunities. In times of prolific rainfall, the pan on both sides of the main road carries water for a while and attracts several wetland birds like **flamingos** and an array of **waders**, **ducks** and **geese**. Look out for **wood sandpiper**, **common greenshank**, **little stint** and **Cape teal**. These paradise conditions, however, are temporary, and in the dry winter months, the pan is a barren, white expanse with fringes of **halophytic grass**.

The immediate vicinity of Springbokfontein and the access road leading to Batia are covered with thickets of dense, green **desert sedges** all year round. **Predators** are often encountered in the area. **Lions** regularly patrol their territory, and territorial **leopards** can conceal themselves well in the dense sedges and wait for prey opportunities. The surrounding plains are ideal hunting grounds for **cheetahs**, and **spotted hyenas** often use the culverts beside the roadside to sleep and escape the day's heat.

The access road to **Batia** is slightly elevated, affording excellent views over the pan and surrounding plains. **Small seepages** on the right side of the road leading to Batia attract several species of wildlife, including **elephants**. It is an excellent location to sit in your car and scan the surroundings, mainly early to mid-morning.

Especially during the drier months, an endless procession of wildlife can be seen trekking towards the springs and the edge of the pan, where natural seeps occur.

Dense sedges obscure the actual spring at Batia**,** and visibility could be better, although it is just a few metres from the road. It is challenging to watch predators at this spot unless they are near the parking lot, but it is a **scenic spot,** and the rest of the area is very open.

African elephant

After rainfall, shallow clay depressions along the roadside hold water for a long time and **blacksmith lapwings** sometimes have their nests nearby. Also, look for **three-banded plovers**, **chestnut-banded plovers** and other small waders. They are used to vehicle traffic, and the scenery is picturesque and ideal for photographing birds from a close angle.

As you head back along the main road toward Nuamses and Goas, prepare to be enchanted by this **scenic route meandering alongside the pan**.

Again, natural seepages occur at the pan's edge and, although not visible from the road, indicate the wildlife traffic approaching from the plains on the left, particularly from mid-morning onwards. A wide variety of wildlife should cross your path, with a significant probability of an unusual or exciting sighting. **Cheetahs** sometimes lie in wait for springbok when they make their way to the springs; lions follow the zebra and wildebeest; sightings of **leopards** are frequently reported; **rhinos** and **elephants** travel to the springs for their daily beauty treatment in the form of mud packs, and birdlife is varied and plenty.

You are also heading for the **best picnic site** in the park, conveniently situated at the pan's edge, shaded by large mopane trees. An additional thatched area provides shade; there is a concrete table and seating, and clean restrooms with running water most of the time. **Information tables** provide insight and interesting facts.

You can also **walk to the pan's edge** and take photographs, especially if some form of wildlife is moving across the pan. However, don't move further than the fringes of the parking lot and exercise great caution, as the area is not fenced.

The **following 11 km**, until you reach the access road leading to Nuamses, are **equally scenic**, with the road turning further away from the pan. The area is open to the right, with denser shrubs and woodland to the left. Both Nuamses and Goas should be productive towards lunchtime; depending on sightings and your schedule, visiting both or one of the waterholes on your way back to camp would be worthwhile. Goas usually draws large herds of elephants during this time of day, while Nuamses tends to be good for leopards, kudu and black-faced impalas, as well as elephants, but in smaller numbers.

The road is usually in good condition, except for the short stretch to Nuamses and parts of the access road leading back to Goas and the main road.

Halali Camp to Eland Drive

via Goas (p. 148) and Noniams (p. 158)

88 km

Picnic site; scenic – especially in autumn

Sweet grassveld on lime; mopane treeveld

Red bushwillow; wether love grass

Spurfowl; guineafowl; hornbills

Large predators; black rhino; black-faced impala and kudu

This would be a good route for a **half-day outing**. Before heading out, arrange for breakfast packs and enough liquids to be consumed at a scenic spot or **Goas waterhole**. It is recommended to head out at first light from camp in the easterly direction towards Goas waterhole.

Coupled with the possibility of good wildlife sightings and experiencing the charm and solitude of roads less travelled, this route, mostly off the beaten track, will appeal to you. Checking in at **Goas waterhole** as early as possible is always worthwhile to anticipate an extraordinary wildlife encounter before making your way towards **Eland Drive**. Early mornings are always promising for sightings of the large carnivores, especially in the hotter months when temperatures are quick to rise.

Drive with the windows open and listen to the sounds of the bush. The warning call of **spurfowl** or **helmeted guineafowl** often alerts to the presence of a predator.

Before you enter Eland Drive, make a quick stop at the **picnic site** close by, as this is the only opportunity for a quick break on this stretch of road.

Soak up the beautiful, tranquil scenery, keeping your eyes open for special sightings. The route offers a particular charm in spring and autumn when the leaves of the stately mopane trees sport a lovely coppery, golden-yellow hue or deep russet-red to orange-pink hues, respectively.

Swainson's spurfowl

Pay careful attention to the road and drive slowly, especially towards the second half. You should navigate extremely skillfully around deep ditches and crags, which are deceptive and even dangerous in the rainy season. In times of heavy rainfall, the whole drive is closed periodically as it tends to get waterlogged and muddy. However, it is an enchanting drive and, if navigated slowly and carefully, enjoyable in dry conditions.

As the entrance to Goas waterhole is diagonally across the main road as you exit Eland Drive on the road leading past the **seasonal waterhole of Noniams**, plan to spend another hour or so at **Goas**, as the waterhole should be teeming with wildlife from mid-morning onwards. When Noniams holds water in good rain seasons, it also pays to stop here for a while. It offers a more intimate and secluded experience than Goas, with less vehicle traffic and not the abundance of wildlife, but nonetheless good sightings of predators, black rhino, black-faced impala and kudu.

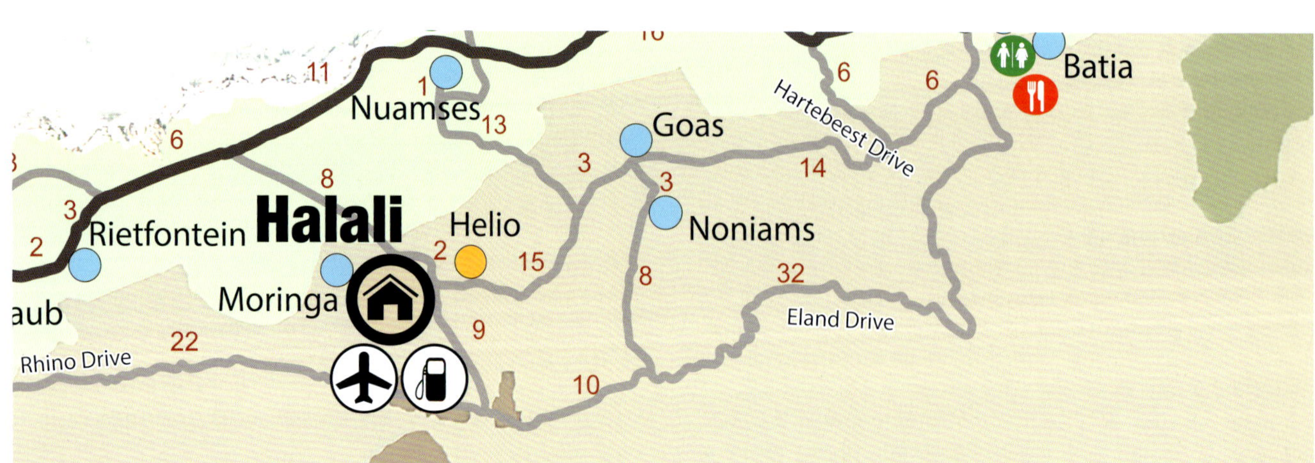

Black-faced impala

EASTERN ETOSHA

Routes in the eastern block – from Von Lindequist Gate, Namutoni and King Nehale LyaMpingana Gate

Angolan giraffe bull

Poachers' peninsula
Etosha Pan
Golden Mile
Homob
Sueda
Salvadora
Charitsaub
Rietfontein
Halali
Moringa
Helio
Nuamses
Goas
Noniams
Hartebeest Drive
Eland Drive
Rhino Drive

o B1
King Nehale Gate
Andoniveld
Andoni
Northeastern sandveld
Stinkwater
Onkoshi
Northeastern sandveld
Tsumcor
Aroe
Sweet grassveld on lime
Fischer's Pan
Twee Palms
Private game reserve
Groot Okevi
King Nehale
Namutoni
Klein Okevi
to B1
Koinachas
Doringdraai
kerfontein
Klein Namutoni
Von Lindequist Gate
Chudop
Ngobib
Kalkheuwel
Bush-willow/tamboti woodland
Springbokfontein
Batia
Marula associations/eastern Karst woodlands
Minor route
Major route
Tarred route
Gate
Camp
Waterhole
Closed waterhole
Picnic site
Toilets
Lookout point
Airstrip
Fuel
Twee Palms
Fischer's Pan
Groot Okevi
Klein Okevi
King Nehale
Namutoni
Von Lindequist Gate
Koinachas
Doringdraai
Klein Namutoni
Dikdik Drive
Chudop

Day visitors from Von Lindequist Gate to Andoni, Fischer's Pan and Klein Namutoni

Via Klein Okevi (p. 180), Groot Okevi (p. 180), Tsumcor (p. 193), Andoni waterhole and loop (p. 174), Stinkwater (p. 192), Fischer's Pan (p. 178), Aroe (p. 175), Twee Palms (p. 194) and Klein Namutoni (p. 185)

- Approximately 140 km, depending on the choice of routes and waterholes
- Expansive plains; scenic landscapes
- Sweet grassveld on lime; sandveld; eastern karst woodlands
- White bauhinia; sickle bush; worm-cure albizia; makalani palms; cork-bush; trumpet thorn; tall common corkwood; lavender fever berry; floodplain acacia
- Wetland birds; flamingo; blue crane and general birdlife
- Eland; warthog; plains game and predators

If you plan a day's outing in the park, the above route would be suitable for exploring Etosha's scenic places and the probability of productive wildlife sightings. Day visitors should plan to have lunch at Namutoni and think of packing a swimming costume and enough food and drink for a mid-morning breakfast snack. The restaurant offers lunches but there is also a picnic area, shaded by broad-canopied trees opposite the camping site, which is well suited for self-catering purposes.

Upon entering the park or leaving the camp, head north towards Tsumcor. Be sure to stop at the waterholes of **Klein** and **Groot Okevi**, saving **the Klein Namutoni** waterhole for later in the afternoon.

Tsumcor waterhole is usually productive all day, drawing an abundance and a variety of game from mid-morning onwards and peaking around noon. The **white bauhinia** is an attractive tree or big woody shrub found only in the **sandveld** area around Tsumcor. Flowering between December and February, the showy white flowers have five crinkly petals. **Eland** favours the leaves and young shoots, while **warthogs** forage and dig out the roots.

There are **two options** for reaching the **Andoni plains**: the scenic and open **Stinkwater route along the edge of the pan**, which is one kilometre longer; or the **main road**, which also produces good encounters with wildlife and features beautiful, large trees next to the roadsides.

Plan a mid-morning break at the **picnic site** shortly before reaching the Andoni plains. Anticipate to see various **plains game** and **elephants** as they make their way to the waterhole. In times of good rain, water is abundant in depressions next to the roadside or on the vast, **expansive plains** on either side of the main road. Whichever route you choose to travel to Andoni, make sure you navigate back using the alternative way.

Depending on your schedule and sightings, choose which waterholes you wish to stop at for a timely **lunch break at Namutoni**.

As with all the main camps, there are plenty of options to keep you comfortable, relaxed and enthused while in camp. The location of the restaurant is next to a shady, open courtyard near a sparkling blue swimming pool, accessible to day visitors. **Banded mongoose**, **tree-** and **ground squirrels**, and **birdlife** often entertain visitors. Big, stately trees have identification tags near the restaurant, chalets and the old historic Fort building. **King Nehale waterhole** also beckons with its various wetland birds and other game species.

The small curio shop offers ice cream and other refreshments, and it would be a good idea to stock up on your supplies if you intend to have a sundowner at Klein Namutoni waterhole on your way out.

Please remember to pay your park fees at the office.

You can access **Fischer's Pan loop** from two sides: turning left as you exit Namutoni or from the causeway off the main road as you head north. You will pass the **Twee Palm waterhole** and, depending on time and sightings, incorporate the **Aroe waterhole** into your route. It is a particularly pleasing drive in the afternoon and rounding off your day with a sundowner at Klein Namutoni waterhole would be a good choice and a fitting end to a hopefully eventful and exciting day in the park.

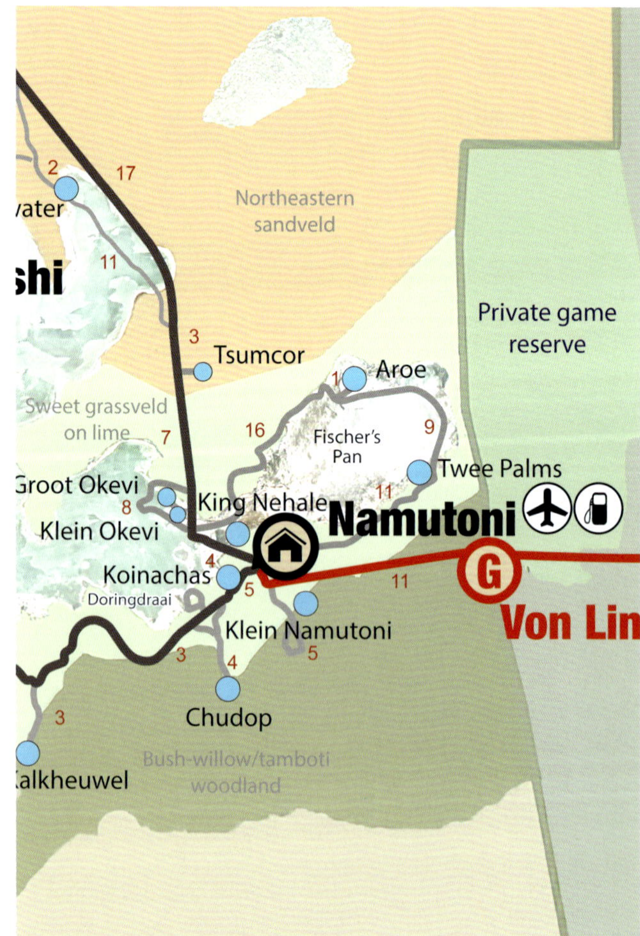

Lion cubs on termite mound

Short day drive from Von Lindequist Gate or Namutoni to Klein Namutoni and Dik-Dik Drive

Via Klein Namutoni (p. 185)

34 km Von Lindequist Gate; 16 km Namutoni

 Mixed bushveld

 Eastern karst woodlands; marula associations

 Purple-pod cluster-leaf; marula; leadwood; tamboti

 Vultures; marabou stork; tawny eagle; hornbills

 Elephant; leopard; spotted hyena; Damara dik-dik; giraffe; leopard

This delightful route is a great choice for an afternoon outing for day visitors to Etosha.

Approaching Etosha on the eastern side through the Von Lindequist Gate, you cannot help but notice the beautiful **marula tree** to the left of the entrance. This tree indicates the vegetation zone as **marula association on calcrete soils.**

The first 10 km of the road is tarred up to Namutoni Camp and leads through predominantly **eastern woodland** and **mixed bushveld**. Most of the area is on calcrete. Some tall specimens of **purple-pod cluster-leaf** occur in places. People tend to speed on this road but please adhere to the speed limit as a variety of game occurs in the area and frequently crosses the road. Look out for **elephant** and **leopard**. After travelling on the road for approximately 10 km, you will see Namutoni Camp ahead, with the access road to **Klein Namutoni waterhole** situated just after the bend on your left.

The first short stretch of the access road has fine, powdery soil. Take care to drive slowly. Also, look out for **Damara dik-diks**, which love to forage on the shrubs near the roadside. Notice the stately examples of **leadwood trees** on your right as you near the access road to Klein Namutoni waterhole to the left.

Klein Namutoni is always a wonderful welcome and introduction to Etosha, as it hosts abundant birdlife and wildlife; the larger carnivores, like lions, enjoy the early morning hours. Spotted **hyenas** have a den near the main road and are frequently seen in early to mid-morning and late afternoon.

It is one of the best areas to see **giraffes**, often approaching the waterhole from the road to Dik-Dik Drive. Interesting behaviour known as **osteophagia** is sometimes displayed by giraffes when they pick up a bone, roll it around with their tongue, seemingly sucking on it. By doing so, they are trying to maintain their **calcium and phosphorus ratio**. They get calcium from the foliage consumed, but phosphorus is not readily available, especially in winter. Bones are an ideal source of this nutrient and other minerals.

Elephants approach from late afternoon to early dusk, and most other game quenches their thirst here all day. **Vultures, marabou storks and tawny eagles** are indicators of a kill somewhere in the dense woodlands that are a signatory of the area.

Angolan giraffe at Klein Namutoni waterhole

Damara dik-dik female and calf

As you exit the waterhole, look out for the **hyena den** on the right side of the road, approximately 50 m away from the access road towards Dik-Dik Drive. It is quite an active den.

This stretch of road is particularly busy and carries an endless procession of game to and from the waterhole. It is worth driving slowly and scanning the area closely for **dik-dik** and **leopard**. Yellow- and red-billed **hornbills** are often seen foraging on the ground for insects.

Entering **Dik Dik Drive** on the right, keep to the left as it is a one-way road and maintain a maximum speed of 20 km/h. Many dense shrubs and bushes offer good concealment opportunities for the **dik-dik**. In the afternoon, the sunlight filtering through the thick, leafy canopies of tall trees is gorgeous, adding to the ethereal charm of this enchanting loop.

Named after the diminutive and **near-endemic Damara dik-dik**, this loop or detour circles a section of **purple-pod cluster-leaf and tamboti woodland** on stony ground. Look out for the **smelly shepherd's tree** and a few tall **bird plum trees**. The dense understorey of bush and shrub thickets includes **croton species** (attractive small shrubs with silvery green leaves), blue **sour-plum** and a few **Grewia species**, offering ideal concealment and camouflage for the Damara dik-dik.

The **Kalahari apple-leaf** tree is also conspicuous when flowering, with masses of small, violet, pea-shaped flowers. **Dik-dik** feed on the flowers as soon as they fall to the ground. **Black-faced impala** forage on the pods and **eland** feed on the leaves.

Klein Namutoni is a wonderful **leopard** area. Look out for **spotted hyenas** since they have their dens in the area and are around with their pups. Their dens are recessed holes in the ground surrounded by calcrete rocks and ridges. **Giraffes** frequent this picturesque drive, as do black-faced impala and kudu. **Crimson-breasted shrikes** provide a brilliant dash of colour as they forage for food in the undergrowth. **Cardinal woodpecker**, **red-** and **yellow-billed hornbill**, **grey go-away birds**, **black-faced babbler, long-billed crombec** and **Swainson's spurfowl** are a few of the bird species encountered, as well as seedeaters like the **rattling cisticola**, **green-winged pytilia** and **blue- and violet-eared waxbill**.

Head out on this enchanting loop at first light or in the golden glow of the late afternoon, as the dik-diks often nibble on the foliage of shrubs lining the side of the road during those times. Take the drive slowly and quietly. Your reward will be an excellent opportunity to get close to these dainty and diminutive antelope without scaring them.

Round off the afternoon by stopping at Klein Namutoni waterhole. Spotted hyenas habitually take a late afternoon bath, and elephants usually appear from the dense woodlands behind the waterhole to slake their thirst.

Allow enough time for the 10 km route back to the exit gate without breaking the speed limit. On this stretch of road, keep looking for dik-dik.

Remember to pay your park fees at the office in Namutoni before exiting the park.

Namutoni Camp to Fischer's Pan Loop

Including Twee Palms (p. 194), Aroe (p. 175) and Klein Okevi (p. 180)

38.7 km

Termite mounds; spectacular pan views

Open plains; tall perennial grasses; dense bushveld

Sickle bush; worm-cure albizia; makalani palms; corkwood; trumpet thorn

Waterbirds; lilac-breasted roller; bee-eater; hornbills; drongos; blue crane

Cheetah; eland; lion; elephant; black rhino; warthog; aardwolf; African wild cat

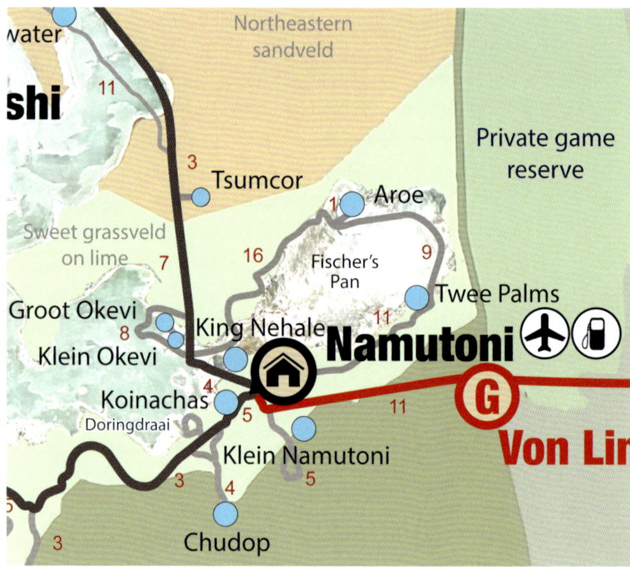

This route would be ideal for a **late afternoon drive** from Namutoni. Turning left at the camp gates takes you to the panoramic loop circling **Fischer's Pan**. Open plains stretch out before you.

One of the unique features noticeable on the loop is the **termite mounds**, especially on the first half of the drive. The plains are ideal **cheetah** territory, and these sprinters often use the mounds as vantage points and territorial markers. Many visitors have witnessed the exciting sight of a cheetah hunt; the vast, flat plains of the pan are ideal cheetah hunting grounds and perfectly suited for running down their prey.

Plenty of **springbok**, a cheetah's favourite prey animal, are found in the area. Springbok are both browsers and grazers. They browse in the dry season and switch to grazing after the first rains have fallen and new grass has sprouted.

After prolific rainfall, prominent, isolated parts of the pan are covered in **tall**, **perennial grasses**, hosting large **herds of herbivores**. An incongruous sight and landmark close to **the Twee Palms waterhole** is the cluster of tall real fan or **makalani palms**, 13 in total, which occur only in the eastern parts of Etosha. Thickets of **sickle-bush** also grow in the area. Unfortunately, the two signatory Makalani palms heralding the Twee Palms waterhole have fallen and are no more.

After passing the turn-off to Twee Palms waterhole, the road dissects the pan, passing dry, cracked clay on the surface

Female cheetah and cub

Female cheetah

on either side. This sight normally greets visitors until prolific rains have fallen, particularly in winter. The scene then changes dramatically; the pan holds water on both sides and you can feast your eyes on myriad **waterbirds** stalking the shimmering expanse. Expect to see great white pelicans; flamingos; storks, egrets and herons; pied avocet; black-winged stilts; Cape- and red-billed teals; knob-billed ducks; Cape shovelers and Egyptian geese.

Another unusual and incongruous sight is the ostriches that can sometimes be seen treading water. The **northern half** of Fischer's Pan features a more **dense, impenetrable mixed bushveld** on the side of the road away from the pan. **Worm-cure albizia** are plentiful, especially near the turn-off to Aroe waterhole.

Aroe is incredibly productive during the rainy season when the ***Omuramba Omuthyia*** – a seasonal flooding watercourse named after **camelthorn trees** growing along its bank – carries water. With its beautiful mauve and sometimes white flowers, corkwood lines the road in places, as does **trumpet thorn**. The pan side affords beautiful views with rolling grasslands. Be vigilant for **lion**, **cheetah**, **elephant** and **black rhino**. Fischer's Pan is also one of the best places to see **warthog**, as there are many smaller mud wallows around. You may also be treated to good sightings of **aardwolf** and **an African wild cat** on the northern side of the pan.

There are plenty of lilac-breasted rollers, European- and swallow-tailed bee-eaters, African-grey-, red- and yellow-billed hornbills, fork-tailed drongos and a variety of smaller seed-eaters. If you are lucky, it is also one of the best places to spot at least one pair of **blue cranes** with chicks.

The last stretch on the left before joining up with the main road is breathtaking when water fills the pan and draws numerous **wetland birds**, including **pelicans** and large colonies of **flamingos**. The shimmering expanse of water becomes infused with the pink hues of these beauties. The light is spectacular towards late afternoon, enhancing the soft pastel shades created by the flamingos. During winter, this stretch is dry.

Klein Okevi is less than half a kilometre from the exit of Fischer's Pan Loop. What better way to end a scenic drive than with a spectacular wildlife sighting towards late afternoon? It is an ideal sundowner spot, enabling you to utilise good light for a maximum time before returning to camp in under 10 minutes.

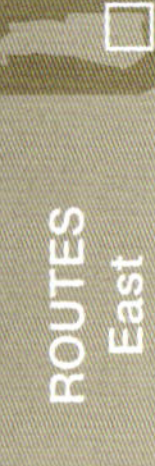

Namutoni Camp to Andoni flats

Via Klein- and Groot Okevi (p. 180), Tsumcor (p. 193), Andoni (p. 174) and Stinkwater (p. 192)

85 km

Picnic site; sightings of warthog and sand acacia

Northeastern sandveld; Andoniveld

Purple-pod cluster-leaf; Kalahari apple-leaf; camelthorn; white bauhinia; common Commiphora; tall common corkwood; the rare sand acacia

White-backed vulture; lilac-breasted roller; Verreaux's eagle owl

Elephant; giraffe; rhino; bat-eared fox; warthog; bullfrog; antelope

The route to Andoni Flats is an ideal route for a **half-day outing**. Arrange for a breakfast pack; or if you are camping, pack a few snacks and drinks and travel in the northern direction towards Andoni, making your way along the main road.

It is always a good idea to stop at **Klein-** and **Groot Okevi** on the way as predators are frequently spotted close to the road quite early. The vegetation zone is described as **northeastern sandveld**, and the abrupt change in vegetation is noticeable a short way after the turn-off to the Groot Okevi waterhole. The mixed tree and shrub savanna here is supported by sands varying in colour and consistency.

The most dominant tree here is the **purple-pod cluster-leaf,** with particularly tall and beautiful specimens growing well up to 6–8 m in the tallest and densest patches, interspersed with **Kalahari apple-leaf, camel-thorn** and **white bauhinia.** Also conspicuous are the isolated and tall species of the **common Commiphora**, known as **tall common corkwood**. The Afrikaans name is 'kanniedood', referring to the tree's hardiness and ability to root from a stump. It is fairly recognisable by its straight, dark green, smooth trunk, covered with papery yellowish brown peeling bark. They reach heights of between 2–10 m, with leaves growing on short, spiny branchlets. Elephants favour the branches and dig up the moisture-laden roots in the dry season. Look out for **white-backed vultures**, regularly breeding in the tall, purple-pod cluster-leaf trees.

There is also a dense understorey of smaller trees, bushes and shrubs, including the sickle-bush, at least two **Croton species**, and **Grewia species**. In some places, the woodland gives way to scrub, with **red umbrella thorn acacia** and **silver cluster-leaf** as dominants.

Pay particular attention to the roadsides near **Tsumcor**. Elephant, **giraffe** and **kudu** often browse near the roadside, dwarfed and well concealed under the canopies of the larger trees and dense vegetation. Wildlife crosses the road frequently during their pilgrimages to the waterhole, and it is crucial to **reduce speed** and pay close attention to your surroundings.

Tsumcor is a great waterhole for early morning sightings of **lions** or **leopards** and the busiest time for a variety of wildlife from mid-morning onwards.

A small, fenced scenic **picnic site** is situated to the left, just before the Andoni plains open in front of you. It is ideal for stretching the legs or a mid-morning coffee break. The area is shaded and nestled under tall trees, with seating at a concrete table and benches.

Look immediately to your left as you enter the expansive plains. A significant depression holds water seasonally, and a variety of game, especially elephant and giraffe, like to drink there. You can continue along the main road towards the **Andoni waterhole** or take a **scenic detour** by taking a right turn.

The slight detour is **incredibly productive** in the rainy season, as several small, deep depressions along the detour retain water and attract a variety of birdlife and wildlife, creating good opportunities for surprise encounters. The right side of the road is fringed with **mixed tree-** and **shrubveld** and is dense in places. Look out for the primarily nocturnal **bat-eared fox** on this stretch; they are often active in the early hours of the morning or towards late afternoon and play an essential role in termite control, a significant part of their diet. They also feed on dung beetles, insects and arthropods. Much of their water intake is derived from the body fluids of the insects they consume. They have such a refined sense of hearing that they hear beetle larvae hatching from dung balls.

This stretch of road hosts many striking, colourful, **lilac-breasted rollers**. They often perch on trees and shrubs lining the roadside and termite mounds before swooping down in their hunt for insects.

Look for the single sprawling **sand acacia**, a many-stemmed shrub on the left along this detour. Sand acacias are **rare** in Etosha, with a few specimens growing along the edge of the pan north of Namutoni.

As you approach **Andoni waterhole**, look out for **warthogs**, usually found in the vicinity. The area offers good places for mud wallows after the rains. The area around Andoni and the north side of Fischer's Pan is one of the **park's most productive places to see warthogs**.

As you head back along the main road, vast grasslands stretch along both sides, classified as **Andoniveld.** This vegetation is dominated by an almost mono-specific stand of the perennial course **salt grass**. Burchell's **zebra**, **giraffe**, **blue wildebeest** and **oryx** usually graze on the plains. After the first heavy rainfall, **African bullfrogs**, also known as giant bullfrogs, can be found in shallow depressions along the road or places that hold water for a few weeks.

The picturesque **Stinkwater detour**, which runs parallel to the main road along the pan, is the more scenic option for the return route back to camp. It affords the feeling of almost driving on the pan, with the road meandering close to the pan's edge in places. It should be rated as one of the **park's most atmospheric stretches of road**. It is one kilometre longer than the main road, and you can access Onkoshi Camp directly from here.

Look out for **Verreaux's eagle owl** along the first stretch, which leads through woodland with a few particularly tall and stately trees. **Spotted eagle owls are** also sometimes observed here. The **Kori bustard** is conspicuous in the area, often seen in small groups of up to five individuals.

Stinkwater is a seasonal, natural spring that becomes dormant in the dry season and consists of a series of small, muddy seeps in proximity to each other on the pan side. **Rhino**, **giraffe**, **antelope**, **elephant** and **predators** frequent these muddy pools when they hold water. **Honey badgers** and **black-backed jackals** are often on the trot in the area, too. Be particularly vigilant for elephants along this stretch of road. They have the unnerving habit of suddenly materialising from the dense woodland beside the roadside, virtually invisible until they are right next to your car.

Depending on your schedule and sightings, you can stop by a few waterholes en route as soon as you are back on the main road. **Tsumcor** attracts the shy eland, and herds of elephant visit at midday. **Groot** and **Klein Okevi** are equally good prospects.

Aerial view of Andoni waterhole

Namutoni Camp to Northern Pan Loop

Encompassing Edge of Pan Detour, Klein Okevi and Groot Okevi (p.180)

- 22 km
- King Nehale Warriors' Memorial
- Sweetveld on lime; mixed bushveld
- Trumpet thorn; false umbrella-thorn; African lovegrass; foxtail buffalo grass
- Western cattle egret; wetland birds
- Blue wildebeest; caracal; African wild cat; black and white rhino; lion; elephant, kudu

This picturesque route, which meanders along the pan for eight kilometres and passes **Klein** and **Groot Okevi** waterholes, is ideal for a relaxing **late afternoon** drive.

As you head in the northeasterly direction, the **King Nehale waterhole** – with its dense bed of reeds – will be to the right and several **herbivores** are usually near the waterhole, either grazing or coming to and from the waterhole. The waterhole is an excellent area to observe the inter-species relationship between **western cattle egrets** and **blue wildebeest**. As with buffalo, a symbiotic relationship exists between the egret and wildebeest. The birds perch on the wildebeest, picking off and ridding the wildebeest of parasites in this manner. Still, they mainly follow closely in the animals' wake as they feed on the insects disturbed when the wildebeest moves to browse. This interaction can create some rewarding photographic opportunities.

Western cattle egret on blue wildebeest

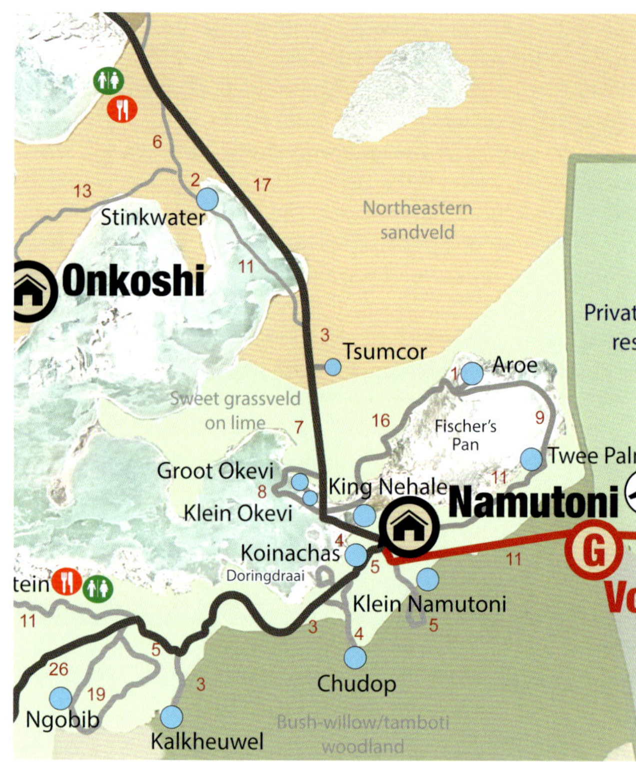

Immediately to the left, opposite the King Nehale waterhole, is a **memorial** commemorating the battle of **Amutoni Iyomanenge** on 28 January 1904, led by King Nehale against German soldiers at Etosha.

Travelling further on the main road, **Fischer's Pan** stretches out on the right side and the primary pan is to your left. When the pan holds water, it's worthwhile stopping by the causeway and observing the sheer variety and abundance of **wetland birds** assembled here; the light is favourable in the late afternoon.

Shortly after the causeway, a right turn takes you on the **Fischer's Pan Loop**, with the left turn directly opposite leading to a superb **eight-kilometre detour along the edge of the pan**, with uninterrupted views of its broad expanse. It is a highly productive stretch, **with sweet grassveld on lime** bordering the pan. It offers good grazing for the herbivores; with mixed bushveld to the right attracting browsers and grazers, and predators following them.

Caracal have frequently been reported from this area, as well as **African wild cats**. Many animals usually cross the road from the pan side, going to **Klein Okevi** and **Groot Okevi** waterholes, which lie parallel to the right on the right, well concealed by dense shrubs and bushes. It's a productive area for **black** and **white rhino**, which are active early morning and again late afternoon. **Kudu** favour the area, as do **giraffes.**

Termite mounds dot the landscape, adding to the area's scenic beauty. Two elevation areas en route offer views over the pan and its surroundings, presenting great opportunities for panoramic landscape shots of the pan.

Lions sometimes walk on the road in the early morning. Towards the final part of the drive, approximately the last two kilometres, the road turns away from the pan as it joins the main road, and visibility is obscured by thickets of shrubs and bushes lining the road. Be especially vigilant for **elephant, rhino** and **other wildlife** that may surprise you. The **trumpet thorn** is predominant here.

Turn right on the main road and to the right again onto the access road to **Groot Okevi**. Keep an eye out for **elephants,** which can have the habit of appearing in front of you as you navigate the bends in the road, dodging a few deeper depressions and uneven parts of the road in places. Groot and Klein Okevi are good sundowner options, each quite different in habitat and appeal.

The vegetation at Groot Okevi is dense, with the waterhole **in a slight depression,** surrounded by woodland in the form of thick shrubs and larger trees. This is particularly appealing because when a predator makes a surprise appearance, it creates great excitement. It also appears out of nowhere unless alarm calls of nearby birds or game give it away. The whole area has a quiet, secluded feel, which is part of its charm.

Klein Okevi, on the other hand, is open, the parking lot is close to the waterhole, and the ambience is scenic. African wild cats, lions, caracals, elephants and rhinos regularly frequent this waterhole. Both waterholes would be excellent choices in pristine nature to round off the atmospheric route, leaving you relaxed and at peace with the world as you head back to camp.

Female cheetah along pan's edge

Namutoni Camp to Okerfontein

Via Koinachas (p. 186), Chudop (p. 176) and Kalkheuwel (p. 181)
Okerfontein (p. 188) Springbokfontein (p. 190) and Batia (p. 175)

- 107 km
- Spectacular scenery
- Eastern karst woodland; sweet grass on lime
- Purple-pod cluster-leaf; tamboti; flowering herbs/shrubs; ink-bush
- Shaft-tailed- and paradise whydah; lilac-breasted roller; European bee-eater; fork-tailed drongo; pale chanting goshawk; plains birds
- Leopard; lion; cheetah; springbok; Damara dik-dik; red hartebeest

This diverse route is ideal for a **half-day drive**. It encompasses many waterholes, promising productive and prolific wildlife sightings. It is scenically **one of the most picturesque routes** in the far eastern region of the park. Arrange for a breakfast or lunch pack, or if camping, provide enough food and drinks and leave camp as soon as the gates open.

Many waterholes around Namutoni are near the camp, with **Koinachas** a mere kilometre away and the first waterhole en route. Visitors frequently report seeing **leopards**. As the waterhole is located next to the road, it's logical to quickly check and see whether anything exciting is happening there.

Male red-hartebeest

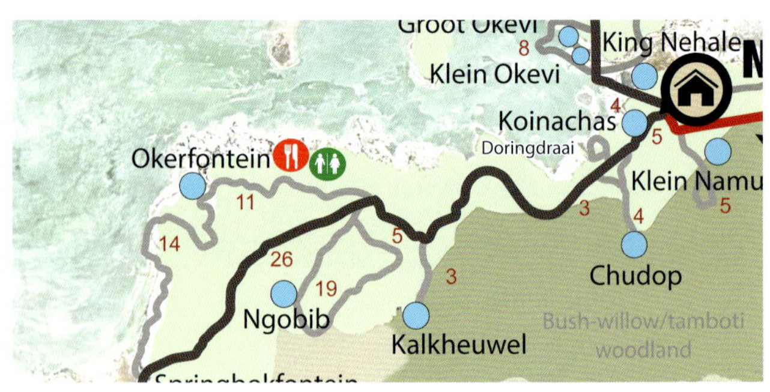

Moving towards **Chudop**, calcrete-surfaced **short grass flats** with **small shrubs** stretch on either side of the road, with a glimpse of the pan on your right. **Springbok** often graze on these plains early in the morning; watch for **cheetah** or **leopard,** which can conceal themselves well, even among the short shrubs. **African wild cats** are also sometimes seen along this stretch.

Chudop is usually productive in the morning for **spotted hyenas.** In the hot summer, they love to cool off in the waterhole before returning to their dens to escape the day's heat. **Lions** also favour the early morning hours; if you are lucky, they might have made a kill during the night, hanging about for a while. Various birdlife includes whydahs, doves, sandgrouse, lapwings, small raptors and some waterbirds. The vegetation zone around Chudop is described as **eastern karst woodlands**, specifically with purple-pod cluster-leaf and tamboti woodland.

Heading back towards the main road in the westerly direction, the pan stretches out to your right, with patches of dense shrub gradually giving way to thick patches of woodland on the left. White **termite mounds** are regular features on both sides of the road, with cheetah often seen near the termite mounds on the pan side. **Cheetahs** love these open areas adjacent to the pan, and you may see them as a coalition, as mothers and offspring, or on their own.

This stretch of road is also **scenic** to the turn-off to **Kalkheuwe**l. When navigating the three-kilometre access road to the waterhole, the calcrete surface tends to be rigid, uneven and badly corrugated. Look out for the diminutive **Damara dik-dik**, with its large, liquid eyes, and **leopard**. Kalkheuwel waterhole delivers the **best leopard sightings** in the vicinity.

Travelling towards **Okerfontein**, this picturesque 26 km detour (adding another two kilometres to return to the Okerfontein waterhole situated on the detour) should be teeming with wildlife from mid-morning onwards. The road meanders along the pan at places, affording visitors a wonderful glimpse of its vast expanse.

The vegetation is mainly sweet grass on lime and dwarf-shrub savanna in places. Splashes of colour from the white flowers of the **aambeibossie**, yellow flowers of the **forked geigeria**, **yellow-mouse whiskers**, **wing-stemmed daisy**, and striking blooms of the **dark-eyed hibiscus**, which grow next to the roadside, paint a pretty picture in the rainy season.

Massive herds of springbok, zebra and wildebeest are found here after the rains, crossing between the natural seepages on the pan side and extensive plains. Elephants, especially the old

Male lions and Angolan giraffe kill at Chudop waterhole

bulls, are regular visitors. They move between the seepages at the pan's edge and the Okerfontein waterhole, which is reminiscent of gigantic marble statues covered with the muddy white clay of the pan. **Red hartebeests** are always around, as are giraffe, warthog and ostrich. Predators, particularly lions, are often encountered with abundant prey animals around them. It is also one of the best areas to see **white rhino and cheetah with their offspring**.

High concentrations of **lilac-breasted rollers** and **European bee-eaters** hunting from their perches are found on this loop and frequently after the rainy season, providing brilliant splashes of colour. The **fork-tailed drongo** – master of flight and imitating other bird calls – is regularly seen, with the probably most common raptor in Etosha, the **pale chanting goshawk**, always close by. Other **birds of the plains**, like the Kori bustard, red-billed spurfowl, secretary bird and northern-black korhaan, can be found at regular intervals.

Look for the **common quail**. These terrestrial birds prefer to sit on the road and quickly run or fly for safety into the roadside shrubbery at the merest sight of a camera lens.

To the west of the Okerfontein waterhole, the low-spreading and many-stemmed **ink-bush** covers large parts of the salty soil. The halophytic ink-bush is particularly striking when its green leaves turn to vibrant shades of deep pinks and reds at certain times of the year.

Soon after the turn-off to the one-kilometre access road to the Okerfontein waterhole, there is a small **picnic site** with shaded seating in the form of a rustic concrete table and benches. It is conveniently situated before the road eventually connects with the main road. Many animals are drawn to the natural seepages on the pan side of the road, close to the exit of Okerfontein.

Although the water is not visible from the road, it is worth scanning the area with binoculars for predators. However, this scenic detour has a downside; the road warrants slow and careful navigation as numerous potholes and depressions fill up with water in the rainy season and can be tricky. It is not a road to be taken in haste but is one to be enjoyed if you take it slowly and appreciatively.

Exiting the Okerfontein loop, you can see **Batia** and **Springbokfontein** ahead of you, as they are not even a kilometre away. Depending on your schedule so far, it might be a good idea to add a few kilometres to your route and stopping there as well before travelling back to Namutoni, either via the **main road, which is 10 km shorter** or, if you prefer, back on the scenic Okerfontein detour. It's always worth the extra kilometres as it offers the most panoramic view.

You may consider taking this half-day excursion and turning it into a full-day adventure. If you choose the full-day excursion, ensure you have enough food and drinks. There are **two picnic sites** en route, six waterholes counting **Springbokfontein** and **Batia**, plenty of scope for fabulous wildlife encounters, and breathtaking scenery. Heading back in the glow of the late afternoon sun adds charm to the drive back to camp and the exciting possibility of good photographic opportunities in optimal light conditions.

Namutoni Camp to Ngobib

via Koinachas (p. 186), Doringdraai, Kalkheuwel (p. 181), to Ngobib waterhole (p. 187) and Ngobib loop

- 63 km (excluding Chudop loop)
- Hyena den next to the parking lot
- Sweet grassveld on lime; eastern karst woodland
- Leadwood tree; Tamboti tree
- Variety of raptors; laughing doves; red-headed finches; red-billed quelea
- Large predators; elephant; python; giraffe; kudu; black-faced impala

Ngobib is another scenic excursion, perfect for a **half-day outing** from Namutoni. Again, pack a few snacks, enough water and cool drinks and pop in at **Koinachas waterhole** before making your way to **Doringdraai** for a chance to spot early morning predators.

Doringdraai leads to a **smallish, wooded island**, circled by a short detour, about four kilometres **west of Namutoni**. It is an Afrikaans name, which translated into English, means 'thorn' and 'curve or detour', referring to the thickets of shrubs and bushes. Look for the **purple-pod cluster-leaf,** some of the larger trees around; the **stekelbossie**, a pretty, bushy perennial herb with pinkish-white flowers; the **forked Geigeria**, with conspicuous yellow flowers and **endemic to Namibia**; and the **lavender feverberry**, a woody shrub or tree with striking undersides of the leaves silverly when the wind blows and visible. Notice the **termite mounds** along the

White rhino female with calf

drive, often used by **cheetahs** to scent-mark in the form of faeces and urine.

Down the main road towards **Kalkheuwel**, keep an eye out for **cheetah,** mainly towards the pan side, especially in the vicinity of termite mounds. **Elephants** are often found on this stretch of road, too, foraging in the woodlands on the left-hand side. Kalkheuwel waterhole might deliver some exciting sightings, and it is usually a good idea to keep vigil here for a while despite the bumpy and rattling road to get there.

The **Ngobib waterhole** is situated on a 17 km circular drive, an open, picturesque stretch of wilderness that affords good game viewing. It is also a relatively quiet stretch of road without too much vehicle traffic. Thickets of **water thorn acacia** line the access road for one and a half kilometres. At the entrance of the loop, decide whether to take the left turn into the loop or carry on straight to the waterhole. The open grassland plains allow for good game viewing for most of the detour. Grasses like **nine-awned grass**, **foxtail buffalo grass** and **saw-tooth love grass**, interspersed with the **stekelbossie** are found in the first part of the loop, an incongruous sight of a few **Makalani** or fan palms are visible in the distance as the road makes a slow right turn.

Plan to be at **Ngobib** around mid-morning and settle for a coffee break at the waterhole. Spend at least an hour parked in the shade of the leadwood tree, soaking up the peaceful atmosphere of this utterly charming and scenic spot and waiting to see what turns up at the waterhole.

The area is also **excellent for birding**. The signatory **leadwood tree** towers over the waterhole and attracts various **raptors** that like to perch here. **Tawny eagle**, **black-chested snake-eagle** and **bateleur** are some of the larger raptors observed, with **lanner falcon**, **black-winged kite** and **Gabar goshawk** also prominently seen. **Laughing doves, red-headed finches, red-billed queleas** and various other smaller bird species like to hang about in the immediate vicinity of the waterhole, escaping to the safety of the purple-pod cluster-leaf close to the waterhole or surrounding vegetation when danger is near.

Towards the second half of the loop, white **termite mounds** dot the landscape, and both the **russet-bushwillow**, **red-bushwillow shrubs** and **three-leaved cotton** are more dominant, as is the **wether love grass**. You may spot black and white rhino, springbok, zebra, kudu and impala, elephant and lion. At some stage of the loop, the shortest distance to the Kalkheuwel waterhole is a mere 2.7 km as the crow flies, and the game moves quickly between the two waterholes.

Heading back, stop at Chudop waterhole, which should be bustling with wildlife towards midday.

Long detour roads for drives from Namutoni Eland Drive and Rhino Drive

Via Springbokfontein (p. 190); Batia (p. 175); picnic site

- 31 km Eland Drive; 29 km Rhino Drive
- Enchanting drive but bad road conditions in places
- Mopane/red bushwillow/purple cluster-leaf bushveld
- Wether love grass
- Pale-chanting goshawk
- Giraffe; kudu; black-faced impala; Burchell's zebra; elephant; rhino and predators

Eland Drive derived its name from a nearby seasonal pan three kilometres south of Noniams with the **Hai//om** name **!Khaneb**, which was frequented by large numbers of **eland**. None are found there now.

Eland Drive and Rhino Drive are **long detour roads that run east to west** through the Halali area, south of the rest camp. They run parallel to the southern edge of the Etosha Pan, with Eland Drive closer to the east and Namutoni.

From the Namutoni side of the main road, passing Springbokfontein and taking the left turn towards the picnic site, you will continue for three kilometres to Eland Drive, taking another left turn. The total **distance from camp should be approximately 40 km** until the turn-off to Eland Drive.

The vegetation zone is **mopane, red bushwillow and purple-pod cluster-leaf bushveld.**

The first part of the drive paints a beautiful picture in pastel with the peachy pink colours of **wether love grass** on either side of the road, interlaced with white calcrete rocks and stones. Lush green **mopane shrub** dots the landscape, the silver grey-green **trumpet thorn's** beautiful showy white flowers and ***Gossypium triphyllum*** with their mauve/lilac blooms, add a dash of colour intermittently, as do the shrubs of the russet bushwillow's russet-red fruit when ripe. **Mopane trees** and **water thorn acacias** line the road and a few shallow borrow pits are near the roadside. They fill up with water during the rainy season and make good mud wallows for elephants, warthogs and rhinos.

About halfway along the drive, you will find taller mopane trees and purple-pod cluster-leaf trees. **Giraffes** are fond of the flowers and young shoots of the purple-pod cluster-leaf, while elephants feed on the young branches, bark and leaves.

Dark grey **termite mounds** provide perches for the **African grey hornbills** and **lilac-breasted rollers** as they swoop down in their hunt for insects. This drive is appealing in autumn when the foliage of the tall mopane trees turns all shades of dappled gold and russet, a magical sight when a herd of elephants move silently and majestically under their canopies.

Unfortunately, the road condition is not always good. It is best described as adventurous in places – particularly the second half – and you must skilfully navigate around deep ditches and crags, which are deceptive and even dangerous in the rainy season. In times of prolific rainfall, the whole drive is closed because it gets waterlogged and muddy. However, it is an enchanting drive and delightful in dry conditions if carefully navigated.

You may encounter stately **kudu bulls**, which favour the area, as well as **black-faced impala**, **zebra**, **elephant**, **rhino** and their **predators.**

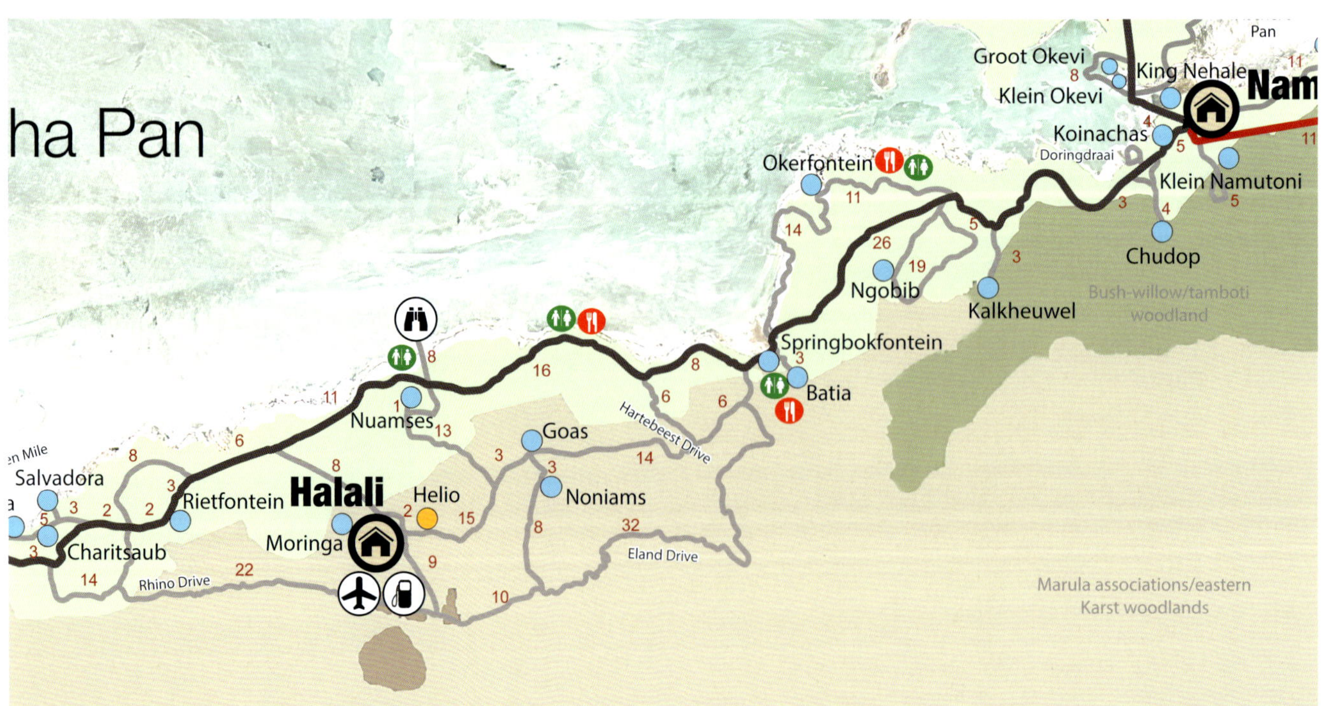

Spotted hyena playing with elephant dung

After 31 km, you reach a turn-off to the right, leading to **Noniams** for eight kilometres. Carrying on straight instead of turning towards Noniams takes you straight onto **Rhino Drive**. The vegetation resembles Eland Drive, alternating between dense shrubs and grasses lining the roadsides and extensive open plains dotted with tall mopane trees, purple-pod cluster-leaf, acacias and red bushwillow. **Spear grass**, a tall, variable perennial grass, grows prominently along the roadside.

Although the dirt road has a few corrugated areas and hard calcrete stone in places, there are no deep ditches and crags on Eland Drive. **Black rhinos** are often sighted on Rhino Drive, as are the usual browsers and grazers. There is an excellent chance to see **lions** walking along the road and a good chance of spotting **a leopard** as you head towards the end of Rhino Drive in the vicinity of Rietfontein. Although some people maintain they have yet to see much on both drives, don't miss it if time allows. There is always something special to find: either a pale-chanting goshawk with a lizard kill, a leopard tortoise, a yellow mongoose playing near a den, a flap-neck chameleon slowly rocking across the road or a spotted hyena on the move to the nearest waterhole. If a surprise awaits you, you may have it primarily to yourself.

There are a few options for routes leading back to Namutoni, depending on your choice of morning drive or full-day drive, time on your hands and sightings.

King Nehale LyaMpingana Gate to Tsumcor

Option A – Afternoon drive

Via Andoni (p. 174), Stinkwater (p. 192) and Tsumcor (p. 193)

- 61.4 km
- Termite mounds used as perches; deep depressions; picnic site
- Andoniveld; northeastern sandveld
- *Albuca pulchra*; purple-pod cluster-leaf
- blue crane; owls; raptors
- Lion; warthog; giraffe; Burchell's zebra; blue wildebeest; elephant; kudu; giraffe; common duiker

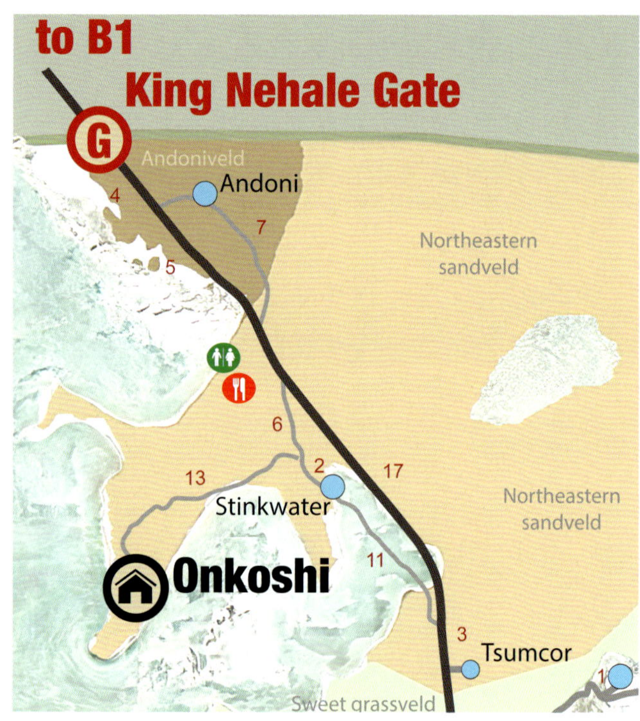

This route would suit an **early to mid-afternoon excursion** through King Nehale Gate. **Andoni waterhole** is situated only 3.8 km from the gate entrance, a particularly scenic and atmospheric welcome to the park's northern section.

The vast expanses of **Andoniveld**, primarily yellow, undulating grasslands, paint a beautiful picture when the sun has lost its harshness, rendering the landscape in a softer, more golden hue. You have a perfect chance of seeing the small, critically endangered **blue crane population** at the waterhole or surrounding area, even the presence of the entire small population, estimated at only 17 individuals, during the non-breeding season.

Blue cranes and springbok, Andoni plains

Blue wildebeest and Burchell's zebra, Andoni plains

The **short detour** along the main road is a more intimate and attractive alternative to the main road and just two kilometres longer. It produces exciting and unexpected sightings. Look out for the *Albuca pulchra*, a conspicuous, tall summer-growing geophyte with a conical white inflorescence.

Rollers, raptors and other birds use **termite mounds** along the roadsides as perches. The dense shrub thickets to the left of the road offer good concealment opportunities for predators. **Lions** are frequently reported on this stretch.

A series of **deep**, **round depressions** on the right side towards the end of the detour is fascinating and productive during the rainy season, drawing various birds and wildlife. **Warthogs** love to use these seasonal small waterholes as mud wallows. Multiple browsers and grazers, especially **giraffe**, **Burchell's zebra, blue wildebeest** and **elephant** are drawn to the plains and adjacent woodland.

When you join the main road, a small, scenic **picnic site** is situated conveniently to the right, shortly before you access the **Stinkwater Loop** road. This panoramic detour is a scenic alternative to the main road, a mere kilometre longer.

On the first stretch, you will see exceptionally tall and impressive specimens of **purple-pod cluster-leaf** and other woodland trees. Look out for **elephant**, **kudu** and **giraffe** here. If you scan these trees closely, you can sometimes observe **Verraux's** and **spotted eagle owls**.

The road navigates towards the pan after the turn-off to **Onkoshi Camp** on the right. It is a lovely stretch of road in the afternoon, with the expansive vista of the pan stretching out immediately to your right.

The **Stinkwater seasonal spring** is also situated to your right, nestled among predominantly **prickly brack grass** and consists of a few circular depressions that retain water during the rainy season. Several wildlife species occur in this area and it is fascinating if you have sightings of the **large cats** drinking from the springs.

Depending on your observations and schedule, a sundowner stop at **Tsumcor** is an excellent idea. There is always a possibility of a decent lion sighting towards late afternoon.

If time allows, you can take the scenic Pan Road or remain on the main road towards camp.

The one-kilometre-shorter main road can sometimes be corrugated as it carries substantially more traffic than the pan road. Still, travelling is worthwhile if alone, for the beautiful, diverse vegetation lining the roadsides. Elephants often make their way along the main road, and it is one of the **best areas to see the shy**, **common duiker**, which tends to be more elusive in the park.

King Nehale LyaMpingana Gate to Namutoni

Option B – Day drive

Via Andoni (p. 174), Stinkwater (p. 192) Tsumcor (p. 193), Groot Okevi (p. 180), Klein Okevi (p. 180), Namutoni, Koinachas (p. 186)

105 km

Panoramic views; Fort Namutoni; museum

Andoniveld

Purple-pod cluster-leaf; Kalahari apple-leaf; camelthorn; white bauhinia; common Commiphora; tall common corkwood; the rare sand acacia

Wetland birds; white-backed vulture; lilac-breasted roller; Verreaux's eagle owl

Herds of herbivores; predators; banded mongoose; common duiker; bullfrog

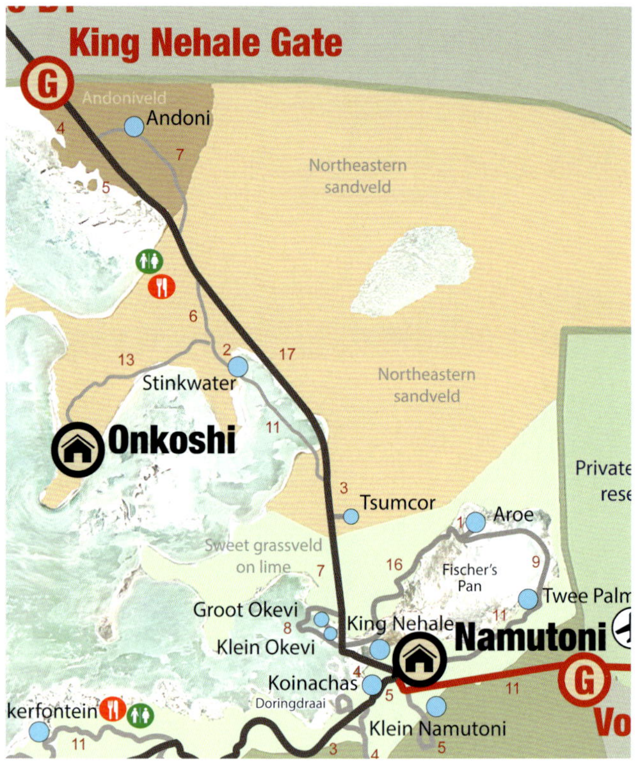

If you plan a **day trip** into the park and enter through King Nehale Gate, extending the route suggested for the afternoon drive and adding a few more options is a great recommendation for a full-day excursion.

Travel towards Namutoni on the main route from the Tsumcor waterhole. **Klein Okevi** is the next waterhole en route. In the morning, most wildlife heads to the waterholes.

Both the waterholes of **Groot-** and **Klein Okevi** will be active during this time and should produce good game viewing. Small numbers of **kudu**, **black-faced impala** and a few **elephants** are likely to be drawn to Groot Okevi, which is not as spacious and open as Klein Okevi, thus not drawing more significant numbers of wildlife. You may find small breeding herds of **elephant** and larger herds of Burchell's zebra, springbok, blue wildebeest and giraffe frequently encountered towards midday.

Namutoni, situated four kilometres from the Okevi waterholes is an ideal lunch option. The restaurant offers a small à la carte menu and an outside courtyard under big, shady

Lilac-breasted roller

White rhino female and calf

trees. A small curio shop and kiosk sells ice cream, souvenirs, snacks and cold drinks. The campground sports lush green vegetation with a variety of stately tall trees, most of them with identification tags for interested horticulturists and botanists.

A resident gang of **banded mongooses** are often near the green lawns on the fringes of the restaurant. They scuttle under tables, hoping to score tasty morsels from the plates of lunch-time guests.

Birdlife in the camp is varied and exciting, and a sparkling blue pool beckons when the summer heat can be simply overwhelming. The **King Nehale waterhole** close to the restaurant is also worth a visit for the avid birder, as the waterhole hosts a great diversity of birdlife, especially **wetland birds**. Those interested in history can look closer at **Fort Namutoni** or visit the small **museum**, which should have opened its doors again after a short renovation.

The **Koinachas waterhole** is close to camp and warrants a short visit.

On your way back, choose the **panoramic eight-kilometre edge of the pan detour**, which meanders along the pan. It runs parallel to the main road and should be productive early to mid-afternoon, with most grazers or browsers milling about on the grasslands and immediate vicinity of the mixed shrubland, either feeding or making their way to and from the **Okevi** waterholes situated between the main road and Pan Loop, well concealed by the vegetation. Stopping again at **Tsumcor** is advised; you can travel back via the scenic Stinkwater detour road meandering along the pan or the shorter stretch (by a kilometre) of the main road.

The light will have lost most of its harshness and the drive back to King Nehale Gate should be an enjoyable and enriching experience.

Onkoshi Camp to Andoni and Andoni Loop

Option A

Stinkwater (p. 192) Tsumcor (p. 193), Groot Okevi (p. 180), Klein Okevi (p. 180), Namutoni, Koinachas (p. 186)

- 50.6 km
- Scenic and varied access road
- Eastern sandveld; Andoniveld
- Lavender feverberry; purple-pod cluster-leaf; Kalahari apple-leaf; camelthorn; white bauhinia; common Commiphora; tall common corkwood; the rare sand acacia
- Blue crane; plains birds
- Bat-eared fox; elephant; kudu; lion

An essential point to remember is that **Onkoshi is closed to day visitors**, catering only to booked overnight guests. The access road to Onkoshi Camp leading from the Stinkwater road is 13.3 km long, which limits your choices for afternoon outings from camp. The access road alone, though, is scenic and varied. The shrubs and trees of the woodland vegetation are dense and impenetrable in places, limiting visibility up to a few metres from the road and again opening intermittently, with widely spaced shrubs, smaller trees and bushes dominating the understorey, dwarfed by taller, more single-spaced trees.

Aerial view of Stinkwater mudhole seep and road

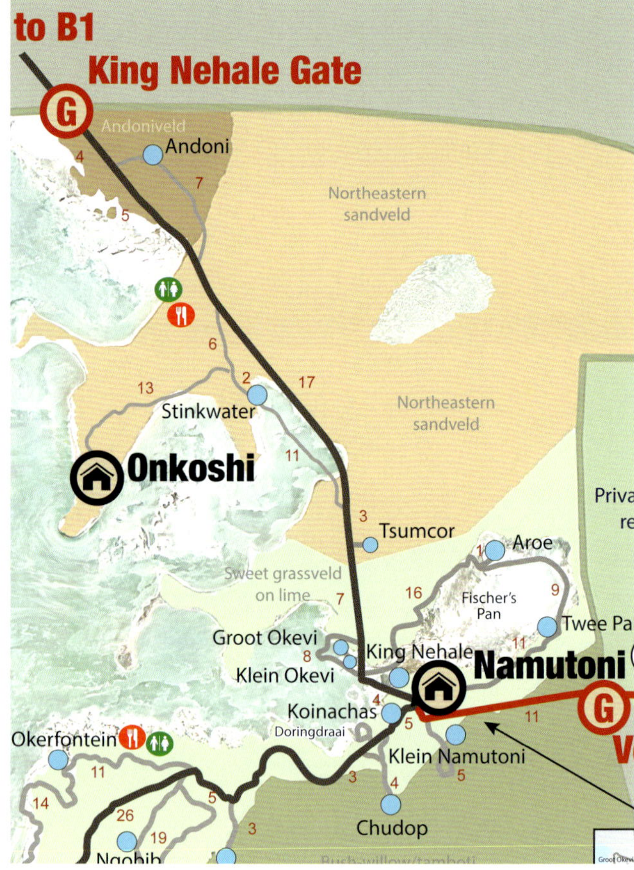

Look out for tall specimens of **lavender feverberry** in the vicinity. It is particularly noticeable that they, like the purple-pod cluster-leaf, occur more as smaller trees than smaller shrubs, a clear example of different effects of soil types on vegetation.

The road can get waterlogged and a few countermeasures were put in place in the form of culverts under the road and slightly sloping roadside edges, allowing water to run off more efficiently. A few medium-sized, **shallow depressions** occur next to the roadsides; when filled with water, these attract wildlife, especially **elephants**, as they favour the woodland habitat. **Bat-eared foxes, kudu** and **giraffes** are also frequently seen on this stretch of road. Sightings of **leopard** have been reported occasionally, with **lion** more regularly reported.

Turning left onto the main road towards Andoni, look for **elephant** along denser patches of vegetation along the roadside, as the road is narrower than the main road. It is better to be aware of them well before being manoeuvred into a tight spot when they suddenly appear right next to your car. Elephants in Etosha tend to be relaxed; however, breeding herds and solitary bulls in musth (a condition in bull elephants occurring when reproductive hormones spike, causing a rise in testosterone levels and can result in aggressive behaviour) should always be approached with caution and respect.

The **Andoni waterhole** and **short detour** are idyllic in the late afternoon sun as the golden grass bathed in good light is favourable for photographing wildlife. This is an atmospheric drive, guaranteed to leave you feeling content and appreciating nature's beauty.

Aerial view of Angolan giraffe, Andoni plains

Onkoshi Camp to Tsumcor
Option B

Via Stinkwater (p. 192)

- 57.4 km
- Pan views; scenic
- Eastern sandveld
- Prickly brack grass; trumpet thorn; wild sage; lavender croton; hook-thorn acacia; Kalahari apple-leaf
- Raptors
- Variety of wildlife; common duiker; bat-eared fox

Travelling right on the road in the direction of **Stinkwater**, this road equals the route to Andoni in respect of beauty and panorama. It's a good choice for an **afternoon drive** when the soft afternoon glow bathes the vast pan, interspersed with grass cover in pale yellow hues. The Stinkwater seasonal seeps, when holding water, draw a **variety of wildlife**. They nestle in predominantly **prickly brack grass** and are scenically positioned along the pan's edge.

The vegetation is varied and dense in places, with **trumpet thorn**, **wild sage**, **lavender croton** and **hook-thorn acacia** giving way to stately, widely spaced trees as you approach the main road. The three-kilometre stretch towards **Tsumcor**

Bat-eared fox

waterhole is equally appealing, with some of the tallest purple-pod cluster-leaf trees in the park supported on deep, **sandy soil**. Look out for the **Kalahari apple-leaf** tree, commonly found in the area. The reasonably large, greyish-green, once compound, oval to oblong leaflets are characteristic. Masses of small, violet, pea-shaped flowers are borne in large sprays around September, attracting various insects. The grass layer in the eastern sandveld area is poorly developed, with the annual **bushman grass** being the most prominent species. It is a tufted pioneer grass that is valuable as fodder in dry conditions. Look out for **elephant**, **kudu** and **giraffe**, often observed under the canopies of the taller trees by the roadside. The **common duiker**, not frequently seen in the park, is sometimes seen in the area.

The **Tsumcor waterhole** is usually busy, attracting a wide variety of game. **Lions** are often sighted here in the late afternoon. The scenic **Stinkwater** route along the pan exudes a particular charm in the last light and is bound to infuse you with a feeling of tranquillity and contentment. Be sure to look out for the **bat-eared foxes** on the access road leading to Onkoshi, where you can round off your day with an ice-cold beverage on the sundowner deck overlooking the pan.

Aardwolf

Onkoshi Camp to Fischer's Pan and Loop

Via Tsumcor (193), Aroe (175), Twee Palms (194) and Namutoni

- 119.5 km
- Loop particularly scenic
- Sweet grassveld on lime; eastern sandveld
- Lavender croton; purple-pod cluster-leaf; Kalahari apple-leaf; camelthorn; white bauhinia; common Commiphora; tall common corkwood; the rare sand acacia
- Large variety of waterbirds
- Bat-eared fox; aardwolf; cheetah; caracal; African wild cat; lion; rhino; eland

A half-day excursion via Stinkwater Road to explore the area around Fischer's Pan would be a good suggestion.

Head out of camp at first light via the Stinkwater Road that meanders along the pan. Early morning always heralds good fortune for **predator sightings**, especially in summer, when temperatures soar and big cats, particularly lions, seek shade and shelter early in the day. **Rhinos** are often seen at first light at the Stinkwater seasonal spring when it holds water, and you might even catch a glimpse of the more nocturnal creatures like **bat-eared foxes** or even **aardwolfs**.

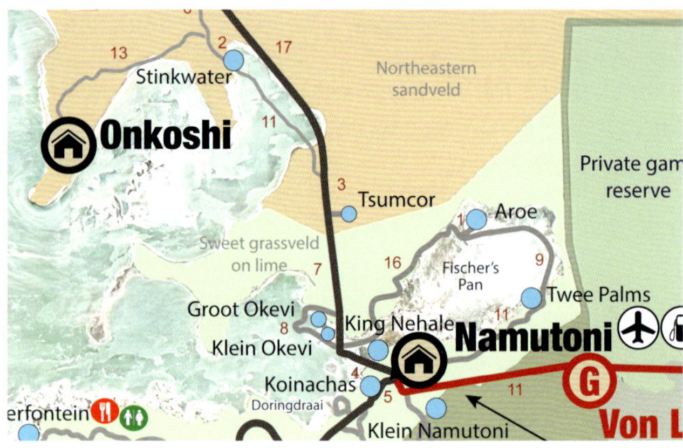

Drive slowly, wind down your windows and pay attention to the sounds of the bush. Look for **fresh spoor** on Stinkwater Road, which is easily detectable on the sand. Imagine seeing a fresh leopard or lion spoor on the road; it will add an exhilarating dimension to the morning drive when you eagerly follow the trail. Even if you don't find the animal, your senses will be heightened. The knowledge that it was there is bound to leave a sense of lingering excitement at the unpredictability of nature, where everything is possible.

Check in at Tsumcor to see the large carnivores or a solitary elephant bull before making your way towards Namutoni.

Opt for the access road leading to the **Edge of Pan Detour** instead of visiting the two Okevi waterholes. This detour is the more panoramic road and is very productive in the morning, with possible sightings of **cheetah**, **caracal**, **wild cats**, **lion**

African elephant and warthogs at Tsumcor waterhole

Aerial view of Fischers's Pan and loop

and **rhino**. These are fascinating possibilities in a scenic environment and scope for fantastic photographic opportunities before harsh light sets in. As the detour intersects with the main road, the **Fischer's Pan Loop's** start is directly opposite.

The loop is one of the **park's most scenic locations.** It is excellent when the area holds water and draws numerous migratory wetland bird species, including flamingos and pelicans. As the water dissipates, the scenery changes and holds a different allure when large parts of the pan are covered with yellow, undulating grass fields, hosting an abundance of herbivores.

Large numbers of browsers and grazers are a drawcard for predators, and many exciting **cheetah/springbok chases** are documented around the Fischer's Pan Loop area. **Lions** follow the large herds of zebra and blue wildebeest and are often observed in the area. You might see the shy **eland** around Fischer's Pan Loop if you are lucky.

The waterholes of **Aroe** and **Twee Palms** are situated on the loop. Twee Palms hosts a variety of waterbirds throughout the year.

Namutoni Camp is situated conveniently on your route back, ideal for a short stop to rest, refresh yourself and stretch your legs. **Heading back via the main road**, you can choose to **stop at the waterholes of Klein- and Groot Okevi** and **Tsumcor** before making your way back to Onkoshi.

WATERHOLES

Angolan giraffe at Okaukuejo waterhole

Waterholes

Water is life, and life in Etosha revolves around the many waterholes spread throughout the park, each with its specific flair and character. Initially, this so-called arid Eden of calcareous soil, calcrete rocks and a complete lack of vegetation surrounding many waterholes may greet the first-time visitor. However, this first impression of seemingly desolate places changes with the season.

Etosha's climate is considered semi-arid, with the average rainfall varying from 550 mm in the eastern part to only approximately 300 mm in the western region.

High animal pressure is usually experienced during dry months around perennial waterholes, with high concentration areas at the waterholes of **Ozonjuitju m'Bari**, **Okondeka**, **Okaukuejo**, **Gemsbokvlakte**, **Salvadora**, **Rietfontein** and **Halali seepage**.

With the onset of the rainy season – predominantly between January and April – the landscape changes dramatically and Etosha dons its coat of green. A prominent feature is the bright yellow carpets of arid devil's thorn *(Tribulus zeyheri)*, particularly noticeable at many waterholes. This prostrate, perennial herb, named after the German naturalist Carl Zeyher, has juicy green leaves and flowers consumed by many herbivores; ostriches are particularly fond of the flowers. When the lush yellow and green carpets turn into dry and desiccated fields, countless sharp thorns become a menace to wildlife.

As most animals in Etosha are migratory, they spread out, following the rains. This relieves pressure at the waterholes, allowing grasses to recover and transform the landscape completely. The cycle repeats itself when, after a few months, the grazing pressure and tracks of thousands of hooves have taken their toll on the vegetation and, once again, transform the lush landscape into seemingly bleak wastelands until the next rainy season. The waterholes, or sources of water, can be grouped into five different categories.

- **Shallow depressions:** Natural depressions in the form of pans or artificial depressions like roadside borrow pits. They are seasonal and usually dry out by June. Both are numerous and spread throughout the park and can be considered good-quality seasonal waterholes.
- **Contact springs**: This is underground water flowing from the Otavi mountains to the edge of the Etosha Pan at a gradient, where it meets with the clay-rich sediments of the salt pan and surfaces at several places in the form of contact springs. They depend greatly on rainfall and tend to dry up when rains are poor. Examples are **Kapupuhedi, Wolfsnes** and **Ondongab**, situated at the edge of the pan, which dry up following the persistent drought between 1980 and 1983. **Okondeka**, another contact spring at the pan's edge, has never dried up in living memory. **Sueda** and **Salvadora** are also good examples of contact springs.
- **Karst springs or water table springs**: These occur where depressions or holes in the calcrete are deep enough to contact groundwater. As groundwater levels can vary depending on the annual rainfall, these springs' levels can also differ. They are found quite far from the pan, with examples at **Aus** and **Olifantsbad**. They have often been hollowed out more by animal hooves and people, as is the case of **Ombika**, for instance, where the name refers to

hand picks used in earlier times by settlers and farmers to remove rocks to make the waterhole more accessible.

- **Artesian springs:** These spring are widespread in Etosha and occur away from the pan. Natural artesian water originates from underground aquifers where pressure within the underlying rock forces water under an impervious surface. Manually drilling into the surface can release the pressure or, in the case of Klein Namutoni, the water pressure is relieved naturally when the water seeks a natural escape through a weak point in the semi-permeable limestone bed. The waterholes of **Groot and Klein Okevi, Andoni, Goas** and **Rietfontein** are examples of artesian springs.
- **Artificial waterholes:** Boreholes sunk and created by park management. Borehole locations appear according to favourable hydrological conditions and are positioned to help distribute the game to underutilised areas. The **boreholes** drilled along the 19th latitude in western Etosha – for instance, **Olifantsrus, Rateldraf** and **Teëspoed** – are examples of artificial waterholes.

The chemical quality of water at waterholes varies significantly throughout the park. The waterholes in the western and southern regions are fit for human consumption and livestock. Waterholes in the central and eastern half region of the park, however, hold water that contains high levels of alkalinity, salinity and sulphates, rendering it unfit for human consumption and, in some cases, even for livestock. Most of Etosha's natural springs are fed by the relatively fresh Etosha limestone aquifer in the south and east of the pan, except for **Sueda**, where the salinity of the water is high. Hypersaline water also occurs in the northern parts of the pan.

The most conspicuous feature of the park, especially on the periphery of most waterholes, is the large expanses of white soil, rubble and boulders that cover the landscape.

The **Etosha Calcrete Formation** dominates the surface geology, covering the southern region of the pan and vast tracts to the east and west. **Calcrete** is a type of rock comprising grains of sand and small boulders cemented by microcrystalline calcite, the most essential lime mineral. The formation of calcrete is an interesting and complex process that depends mainly on rainfall.

Groundwater calcrete and **pedogenic calcrete** are distinguished. When calcite dissolves in groundwater, groundwater calcrete is formed by sediments as the water evaporates under a permeable or semi-permeable surface under semi-arid climatic conditions. The Etosha Calcrete Formation consists of the thickest deposits of this type of calcrete, which build up and create a ring around the carbonate rocks of the Otavi Mountain Land. The Etosha Calcrete Formation began 65 million years ago and continuously evolves.

Calcretes also undergo weathering processes. As they belong to the carbonate rocks group, one weathering process is **karstification**, a chemical weathering in which lime and dolomite dissolve by carbonated water containing calcium hydrogen carbonate.

Another form of weathering is **wind deflation**. In addition, biogenic activity, such as termites or humic acid, contributes to rock disintegration. Boulder calcrete, which covers large areas of Etosha – for instance, the waterholes of **Kalkheuwel** and **Olifantsbad** – is evidence of a former intact layer of this kind of material.

Thick calcrete layers are evident at the edge of the pan, shortly before the **Sueda contact spring**.

African elephants, oryx, springbok, ostrich and black rhino at Nebrownii waterhole

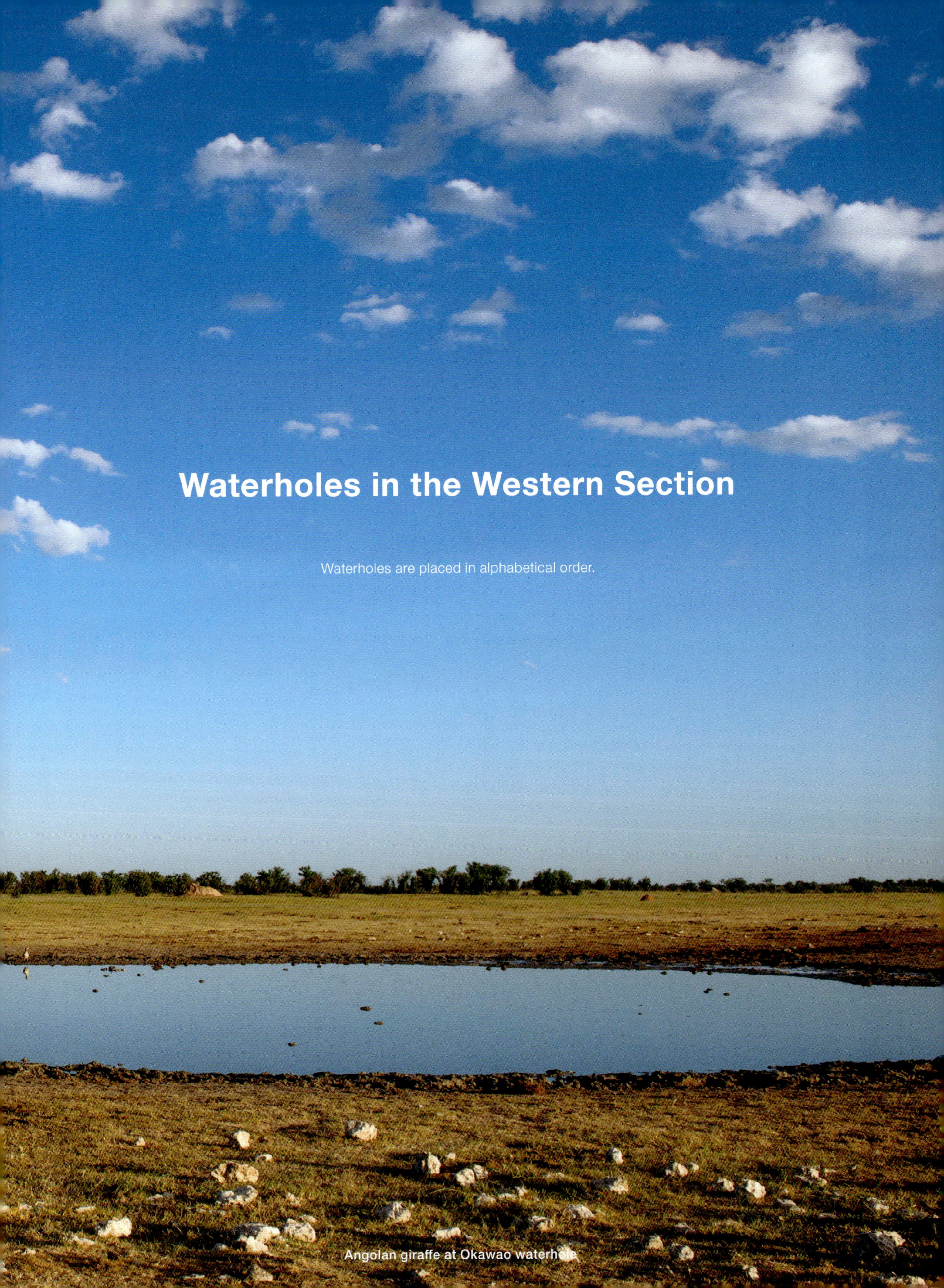

Waterholes in the Western Section

Waterholes are placed in alphabetical order.

Angolan giraffe at Okawao waterhole

African elephants and springbok at Dolomite point waterhole

Dolomietpunt/Dolomite Point ★★★

Borehole; solar power

Open plains; dolomite hill; smelly shepherd's tree

The main waterhole seen from the Dolomite Camp is on the sparsely vegetated, sprawling plains surrounding the dolomite hill and below the rocky outcrops on which the camp is situated. The artificial waterhole, run on solar energy, attracts a large variety and abundance of wildlife, from giant pachyderms to the tiniest bird species. Look out for the **Chacma baboons,** found only on the western side of the park; and **klipspringer** and **rock hyrax,** which you may see around the rocky ridges and outcrops of the dolomite hills. **Lions** are regulars, as are **black** and **white rhino**, and the usual herbivores like **mountain** and **Burchell's zebra**, **kudu**, **giraffe**, **blue wildebeest** and **springbok**.

Duineveld ★★★★

Borehole; solar power

Red soil; craggy dolomite hills

This artificial waterhole is in a typical **sandy cluster-leaf/ thorn tree shrubland, meaning 'dune veld'.** The first part of the access road to the waterhole – which is in good shape with white calcareous soil covering red sand – is fringed with tall mopane shrubs and isolated mopane trees. The road opens to vast plains on either side of the road. The red soil and craggy dolomite hills dominate the landscape, and undulating yellow grass fields paint a beautiful picture.

Vultures frequent the open waterhole, predominantly populated by **lappet-faced**, **white-backed** and **Cape vultures**. **Lions** usually follow the large herds of zebra that congregate here. **Wildebeest** and **red hartebeest** are regular visitors, and the ever-present **black-backed jackal** hovers on the perimeter.

The waterholes situated along the graded main road for almost 100 km eastwards from **Duineveld to Ozonjuitji m'Bari waterhole are referred to as the 19th latitude boreholes, as this road runs a few kilometres north of and parallel to 19° along the 19th latitude.** Duineveld, Nomab, Olifantsrus, Tobieroen, Teëspoed, Bitterwater, Sonderkop and Ozonjuitji m'Bari are all 19th-latitude boreholes.

Both **Hartmann's mountain zebra** and **Burchell's zebra** congregate here, and you can spend endless entertaining hours just watching the interaction between the zebras. They always seem to be noisily kicking, biting and chasing each other, with stallions rearing up to assert dominance. All this initiates spectacular stampedes, propelling the whole herd into action in the process, which is ideal for moody action photography when the red soil surrounding the waterhole swirls up and creates spectacular billowing clouds of dust.

The short access road leads to a corrugated iron basin into which the solar motor pumps fresh water. Once, a young **elephant** bull dipped its trunk into the basin's fresh water, keeping a few antelope standing at bay in the shade of the mopane shrub.

As the waterhole lies south of the main road, the light for photography is great throughout the day but particularly favourable in the afternoon. There is ample space to park, whether at the slight incline of the road leading to the basin or in the circular loop closer to the waterhole. When the grass is plentiful for grazers, herds of zebra and wildebeest like to graze on the open plains opposite the waterhole, with browsers nibbling on the mopane shrub nearby.

Lappet-faced and white-backed vultures

Jakkalswater ★★★

- Borehole; solar power
- Hartmann's mountain zebra

The two-kilometre access road to Jakkalswater tends to be slightly corrugated, with **trumpet thorn** and **mopane shrubs** lining the road in places. Look out for **ostrich, red hartebeest, springbok and black-backed jackals**, which make their way to or from the waterhole.

Jakkalswater is an artificial borehole run on solar power. As with most of the waterholes in the western section, they were given names deemed relevant by the early nature conservators. In this case, the Afrikaans name means 'water of the jackal' and was named after the carcass of a black-backed jackal was found, having probably drowned in the waterhole.

This waterhole and surrounding area are scenic, rendered in colourful hues of red sand, pale yellow grass, blue sky and the green fringes of mopane shrubland in the distance. They are best suited for photography in the late afternoon, as you shoot directly into the sun in the harsh morning light. The parking area is spacious enough to accommodate several vehicles, which enables you to perfectly position your vehicle for photography from any chosen angle. It is also situated close to the waterhole.

Set in a spacious and expansive area, Jakkalswater is visited by large herds of **Hartmann's mountain zebra**, **Burchell's zebra**, **red hartebeest**, **elephant**, **eland** and **springbok**, with most action from mid-morning onwards.

Particularly entertaining and rewarding subjects to photograph are the large colonies of **ground squirrels** with their extensive burrows on the parking lot's fringes and in the immediate vicinity of the solar pump, as they are gregarious and active creatures. Many bird species frequent the waterhole and surround it throughout the day. You may see **rollers**, **vultures**, **spurfowl**, **sandgrouse**, **waterfowl**, **korhaan**, **larks, birds of prey,** and even **South African shelducks**. **Marsh terrapins** have been seen on land, either making their way to or from the waterhole along the edges of the parking lot.

Southern ground-squirrels

Klippan ★★★★

Borehole; solar power

Scenically diverse landscape

What confronts you when you travel the six-kilometre access road leading to Klippan on your right is one of the most scenically beautiful and diverse landscapes of western Etosha. A **dolomite mountain ridge** is visible as you travel down the road, with open plains stretching out on either side of the road. The deep red soil is a perfect foil for the green vegetation.

Some isolated **camelthorn trees** dot the landscape, with two huge and beautiful specimens lining the roadside. The iconic camelthorn tree is a protected species in Namibia and one of the most widespread trees. They can reach heights of 15 m, with a deep tap root system that enables them to reach deep groundwater and thus survive under arid conditions. The leaves, flowers and pods are highly nutritious, and elephant, giraffe, rhino and most antelope species consume the pods. In contrast, the shoots and leaves are favoured by black-faced impala and the bright yellow flowers by ostrich. The situation of the waterhole is in a sprawling, shallow depression surrounded by calcrete rubble, hence the Afrikaans word 'klip' (stone) and 'pan'.

Burchell's zebra favours this area and you can see it nearby. **Vultures**, **martial** and **tawny eagles** are some of the large bird species observed in the area, perching in the widespread canopies of these trees. Look out for the striking and not commonly seen **Ludwig's bustard** patrolling the plains. It occurs in semi-arid areas with less than 500 mm of rainfall, including open lowland and upland plains with grass, light thornbush and sandy, open shrubveld.

Some plant species growing abundantly and conspicuously in the area are the **skew-leaved elephant root**, **wild sage** and **Osonanga lily**. The Osonanga lily – also known as slangkop – thrives in dry conditions. It has elongated, strap-shaped leaves and tubular white to cream flowers in December. It is toxic to game and livestock.

Look for the **red umbrella-thorn**, **mopane** and **purple-pod cluster-leaf** near Klippan. The vegetation zone around Klippan is ***Kowares sand mopane veld***, bordering on red umbrella-thorn, mopane and purple-pod cluster-leaf.

The smelly shepherd's tree features prominently. It is an evergreen shrub or small tree with stiff, small olive-green leaves on a short leaf stalk, densely arranged around branches. Dik-dik eats the leaves and young shoots, and various bird species and giraffe eat the fruit.

The whole area is incedibly scenic and productive for interactive wildlife sightings. **Lions** like to follow their favourite prey, zebra, drawing plenty of scavengers like **black-backed jackals** and **brown hyenas** in return. The area is exceptionally productive for brown hyena sightings.

Brown hyena and black-backed jackal interaction

African elephant, Kori bustards and Abdim's storks at Nomab waterhole

Nomab ★★★

Borehole; solar power

Skew-leaved elephant root plant; Abdim's stork

The name of this artificial waterhole comes from the Nama word for the **skew-leaved elephant root plant**, and the correct spelling is **!Nomab**, meaning '**root of a plant**'. The underground rhizome or tuber of the plant is much sought after by elephants. Before the gravelling of the main road or 19th latitude road, elephants often created significant obstacles for vehicles by digging holes up to one metre in depth to reach these tubers. Only a few of these plants are noticeable near the waterhole but they are plentiful in the area.

The round, concrete waterhole is situated on sprawling open plains in a beautiful setting. The waterhole runs on solar power, with the pump and corrugated iron basin a distance away. The round concrete basin is surrounded by a layer of calcrete rocks, with the **red sand** predominant in the west, as far as the eye can see. No tree was in sight in the spacious open area surrounding the waterhole, except for a single **stunted mopane** tree next to a **white termite mound**. After the rains, new green grass shoots cover these plains, growing into high, undulating grass so enjoyed by the grazers. **Mopane and acacia shrub savanna** fringe the plains in the distance, and white and red termite mounds peek out in between. Elephant dung scattered over the plains is a testament these pachyderms frequent the waterhole, usually single bulls. The ubiquitous Kori bustard is never far away, and you may see vultures and Abdim's storks, insectivorous summer migrants.

Okawao ★★★

Seasonal water source supported by solar-powered borehole

Thunderbolt flower; trumpet thorn; Bushman's poison

The **thunderbolt flower**, also known as wild sesame, is an annual, erect herb with lovely mauve to pink flowers. It is frequently encountered, providing splashes of colour next to roadsides and near these waterholes. **Trumpet thorn** thickets are particularly noticeable around Okawao waterhole and an approximately seven kilometres radius driving towards Olifantsrus. They are also known as rattle trees; the halves of the large, pendulous seed capsules – after splitting and releasing their seeds – remain on the plant and rattle against each other in a strong breeze. Okawao derives from the Herero word 'Okavao', referring to the 'place of the shield' (oruvao).

The area's grasses include **nine-awned grass**, a hardy grass that is beneficial in areas with low rainfall as it can quickly colonise and protect disturbed veld, and the palatable and drought-resistant **sand quick grass**, a valuable grazing grass that prefers the sandy loam and gravelly soil of the area.

Typical **mopane shrubveld** occurs in places. Look out for the small, elegant **steenbok** in the area, usually singly or in pairs. They are mixed feeders, browsing on grass, seedpods and fruit and digging for roots and bulbs with their front hooves. Medium- and large-sized raptors to look out for are the **Gabar goshawk, pale-chanting goshawk, black-chested and brown snake eagle, and bateleur.**

Cheetah and **lion** are regularly seen around Okawao, as well as **spotted hyena**.

Okawao Pan ★★★

Seasonal pan

Red termite hills

This seasonal pan is situated approximately four kilometres west of Okawao in a picturesque and tranquil setting. Beautiful, tall **purple-pod cluster-leaf** and **mopane** trees surround a vast vlei of white, calcareous soil capable of holding a large body of water in the rainy season.

Red termite hills dot the landscape. One of the conspicuous shrubs on the parking area's eastern side is the ***Gossypium triphyllum*** (no common name), a large woody shrub with beautiful blue or purple flowers. **Thunderbolt flower** (or wild sesame), an erect, sparsely branched annual herb with its funnel-shaped mauve flower, provides cheerful specks of colour in the vicinity.

Giraffes favour the flowers and young shoots of the purple-pod cluster-leaf and thus frequent the area, while **elephants** feed on the leaves, young branches and bark and use the opportunity to douse themselves with the white, muddy water of the vlei. **Zebra**, **springbok**, **red hartebeest** and **wildebeest** usually mill about, and the avid birder will most certainly be able to see **Namaqua doves**, **Kori bustards** and **sandgrouse**. Almost every waterhole boasts a resident pair of **Egyptian geese**.

Shaft-tailed whydahs flit about, and the purple rollers and **lilac-breasted** rollers hunt from their perches on shrubs at the fringes of the parking area.

The afternoons yield the best light and, when undisturbed, the water in the pan is ideal for capturing reflections.

Spotted hyena pair at Okawao waterhole

Olifantsrus hide

Olifantsrus ★★★★

- Borehole; solar power
- State-of-the-art viewing hide

An absolute highlight is the state-of-the-art hide overlooking the artificial waterhole. A wooden, elevated walkway connects the campsite to the waterhole, which is well lit at night. A double-storey construction, the upper viewing deck offers wooden benches arranged in a semicircle next to an open hatch, with spectacular views over the waterhole and surrounding area.

A wooden tablet fixture in front of the open hatch has enough storage space for your binoculars, camera, reading material or cold drink. Steps lead down to ground level, immersing you in an impressive eye-level experience with the waterhole and the wildlife. A glass front affords complete frontal visibility and allows dramatic photo opportunities, provided the glass is clean. Cleaning these windows, however, is highly challenging when a herd of elephant takes over, splattering the spectacular glass front with splashes of water and mud – an experience not to be missed, inducing an adrenaline rush.

An infrared light illuminates the waterhole at night, which attracts **black rhino**, **elephant, lion, leopard** and the usual **plains game**.

Male kudu bull

Burchell's zebra Olifantsrus waterhole

Ozonjuitji m'Bari ★★★★★

Borehole; solar power

Masses of game

Also known as **m'Bari**, this waterhole's name is Herero, which means '**two honey-bees**'. This also refers to the initials of two conservation-minded officials whose surname started with a B, Messrs. HA Böttger and LW Bermann, who donated funds for the windmill.

Powered by a solar pump, this entirely **artificial borehole** is the only source of water west of Okaukuejo and Okondeka that supplies water in the dry season, drawing large herds of game. Thus, it is a particularly busy waterhole frequented by various wildlife, guaranteeing action-packed game viewing. The area surrounding the waterhole is open and barren, offering clear and unobstructed viewing from all sides, especially in the dry season.

The vegetation zone is **sweet grassveld on lime,** bordering on **mopane shrubveld**. In a perfect rainy season, tall grass can surround the waterhole, hampering visibility. **Ostriches** are always around, and the highlight must be the **pride of lions**, often in residence, either lying concealed in the shade of the water tanks or causing havoc at the waterhole by engaging in hunting pursuits.

Particularly impressive are the approaching **herds of elephant**, usually at lunchtime. People see herds of **eland** drinking here, **as well as black rhino** and large herds of practically all herbivores that occur in Etosha. It is quite a spectacle to view the flocks of **Namaqua-** and **double-banded sandgrouse**, as well as masses of **red-billed queleas** swooping down in the morning, causing upheaval as the opportunistic **black-backed jackal** never misses the opportunity to dart in from the sideline to score a quick meal, with **Burchell's zebra** and **wildebeest** prompted into panic mode by all the noise and action. **Water thorn acacia** grows prolifically in the area further away from the waterhole and along the roadside.

Female ostrich

Blue wildebeest, Angolan giraffe, eland, ostrich and springbok at m'Bari waterhole

Rateldraf ★★★★

Borehole; solar power

Termite mounds; red soil; wild sage, wild sesame

Dolomite inselbergs are an iconic feature near the Rateldraf waterhole, and the vegetation zone is predominantly **red umbrella-thorn, mopane and purple cluster-leaf thorn scrub**. Named after the fearless and feisty honey badger, which apparently lived nearby in an abandoned ant bear hole and was often seen jogging to the water in typical purposeful badger-style fashion, this artificial waterhole runs on solar power. It comprises a circular concrete basin with a mud wallow to the left.

This expansive waterhole affords the best chance to **view herds of skittish eland, mountain zebra, leopard** and **lion**. **Black-faced impala** and **springbok** are regular features, as are kudu, **giraffe** and **oryx**. Birdlife is varied, with a good chance of spotting **Monteiro's hornbill, bateleur, martial eagle, helmeted guineafowl,** at least two sandgrouse species**, a few lark species and the usual smaller seed-eaters.** In the dry season, with most grass gone and the shrub dry and thinned out, the waterhole looks bleak and barren, and you wonder how the wildlife survives. All this changes with the onset of the rainy season, when the eternal cycle of nature starts afresh.

Termite mounds and **red soil** are regular features, especially along the two-kilometre access road leading to Rateldraf. **Wild sage** also grows abundantly.

Wild sesame

Burchell's and Hartmann's mountain zebra at Rateldraf waterhole

Springbok and Abdim's storks at Renostervlei waterhole

Renostervlei ★★★

Borehole; solar power

Herero sesame-bush

Renostervlei is the first waterhole accessible to the public on the left after entering Galton Gate. The short access road takes you to a large parking area facing west, suited to photography purposes from early to mid-morning. The scenery is quite picturesque, with calcrete rocks and rubble scattered near the waterhole and termite hills dotting the landscape. The parking area is exceptionally spacious and faces westwards.

An artificial borehole, it features a customary round concrete basin, with the overflow of water collecting in a large, muddy, shallow depression, thus aptly named 'rhino wallow or bog'. **Black rhino** favour this waterhole and wallow in the mud or dusty terrain, and **Hartmann's mountain and Burchell's zebra** congregate here in large numbers, equally fond of the mud wallows.

Isolated **smelly shepherd's trees**, **russet bushwillow** and taller **mopane** trees break the monotony of the relatively flat, stunted mopane shrubveld, with a few low, rolling dolomite hills and ridges in the background. The **Herero sesame bush** – a several-stemmed tree or shrub with thick white trunks and stiff thorny branches – is conspicuous in the area.

Elephants like to drink here, as do **oryx**, **springbok**, **wildebeest**, **black-faced impala**, **ostrich**, **giraffe** and **black-backed jackal**. **Lion** and **cheetah** are frequent visitors.

Martial eagle on Damara dik-dik kill

Sonderkop ★★★★

Borehole; former windmill; now solar power

Open and sparsely vegetated

An Afrikaans name, **Sonderkop**, translates to '**without a head**'. In earlier days, a windmill serviced the borehole. Strong whirlwinds wrenched off the head wheel three times within two months, after which the exasperated nature conservation official reported to park's headquarters that this windmill is '**alweer sonder kop**' (headless again). Nowadays, the borehole runs on solar power.

This waterhole has a unique flair, with many **termite hills** varying in size dotting the landscape. The area is spacious and open, sparsely vegetated, especially in the dry season

African elephant, Angolan giraffe, male lion and oryx at Sonderkop waterhole

and set in typical mopane shrubland. Various game species congregate here, and the **resident lion pride** is always close to the waterhole. They often prefer to lie at the base of the concrete basin, moving only when the day's heat gets too much, to the extreme frustration of the other wildlife desperate for a drink, or near the water tanks to the left of the parking lot.

Nearly all plains game congregate in large numbers, as do **giraffe**, **ostrich**, **black-backed jackal** and **elephant**. **Tawny eagles** – probably the most common in the park – **bateleurs** and **lanner falcons** are some of the larger raptors hunting around the perimeters of the waterhole, which are frequented by doves, sandgrouse and helmeted guineafowl.

The **Kori bustard** struts his stuff on the plains among the termite mounds.

Teëspoed ★★

Borehole; solar power

Skew-leaved elephant root

Teëspoed is the Afrikaans word for '**adversity**'. It refers to the hardships, misfortune and setbacks of drilling this borehole, making it a place of adversity.

Situated south of the main road, the light is best suited for afternoon photography. The waterhole is again composed of a round concrete basin, overflowing to an adjacent but smaller mud wallow than Tobieroen's.

The prolific **trumpet thorn** thickets, mopane shrub and termite hills mark the landscape open and with good visibility.

A few species of **skew-leaved elephant root**, a multi-stemmed shrub, and the common **gemsbok bean**, a creeper-like plant, are found near the parking lot. For some reason, **solitary bull elephants** and the usual **herbivores** and **rhinos** prefer to drink from this waterhole. **Blacksmith lapwings** patrol the water's edge, a resident pair of **Egyptian geese** are present, and **Cape-** and **lark-like bunting**, **great sparrows** and other small seed eaters are present.

Tobieroen ★★★

Borehole; solar pump

Elephant

Derived from the Afrikaans word, originally spelt '**Tobieroem**'. The name Tobias is Afrikaans, abbreviated to '**Tobie**' and '**roem**', which means '**fame**'. This borehole was named in honour of a fearless Hai//om tracker called Tobias. The story is told that a nature conservation official left his vehicle without his rifle to inspect the area and neglected to check the vicinity for possible danger. Upon completion of the inspection, to his dismay, a pride of lions was lying between him and the safety

Burchell's zebra near Tobieroen waterhole

of his vehicle. In desperation, he called Tobias, sitting at the back of the truck, to bring his rifle. The courageous Tobias promptly got off, circled the lions and handed over the gun to a somewhat embarrassed conservator. They both reached the vehicle safely.

Set in a large open area fringed by typical **mopane shrubland**, the waterhole consists of a typical round concrete basin overflowing into a sprawling, large mud wallow in the rainy season. **Termite hills** dot the landscape and the thickets of **trumpet thorn** are conspicuous. Situated south of the main road, the light for photography is excellent in the morning and afternoon, depending on how you park, and the spacious parking area enables you to jostle for the best possible angle. It is popular with **elephant**; single bulls or small breeding herds favour the waterhole from mid-morning onwards, while the usual herbivores like **zebra** and **wildebeest** quench their thirst throughout the day.

Closed or Inaccessible Waterholes

Arendsnes (inactive and not accessible)

Bitterwater (inactive but accessible)

An artificial borehole, the Afrikaans name means 'bitter water' and refers to the bitter-tasting water owing to the high magnesium content. It is situated in a depression, overlooked by a short, circular drive fringed by mopane shrubland, which can still be accessed. It has been dry for a few years but water collects in a small mud wallow in the rainy season.

Duiwelsvuur (inactive)

Another Afrikaans name meaning 'devil's fire', this artificial borehole obtained its name when a hellish fire ravaged the area in the late 1960s. The campfire of a nature conservator accidentally spread to the surrounding veld, setting fire to the tall grass and predominant mopane shrub. Aromatic oils found in mopane leaves accelerated the blaze, and nature conservators, trackers and farmers fought for six days and nights to extinguish the inferno. The fire had laid waste almost the entire area between **Charl Marais Dam** in the east and **Otjovasandu** in the west, and it was spreading to farms on Etosha's southern border.

Luiperdskop, Aasvoëlbad and Miernes

The three waterholes Luiperdskop, Aasvoëlbad and Miernes – which lie near each other – have been closed as they lie too close to the western boundary fence, and national park authorities considered them too much of a temptation for poachers. Duikerdrink, near Okawao waterhole, has been closed for the same reason: the 11 km long access road tends to become saturated in the wet season.

African elephant breeding herd at Goas waterhole

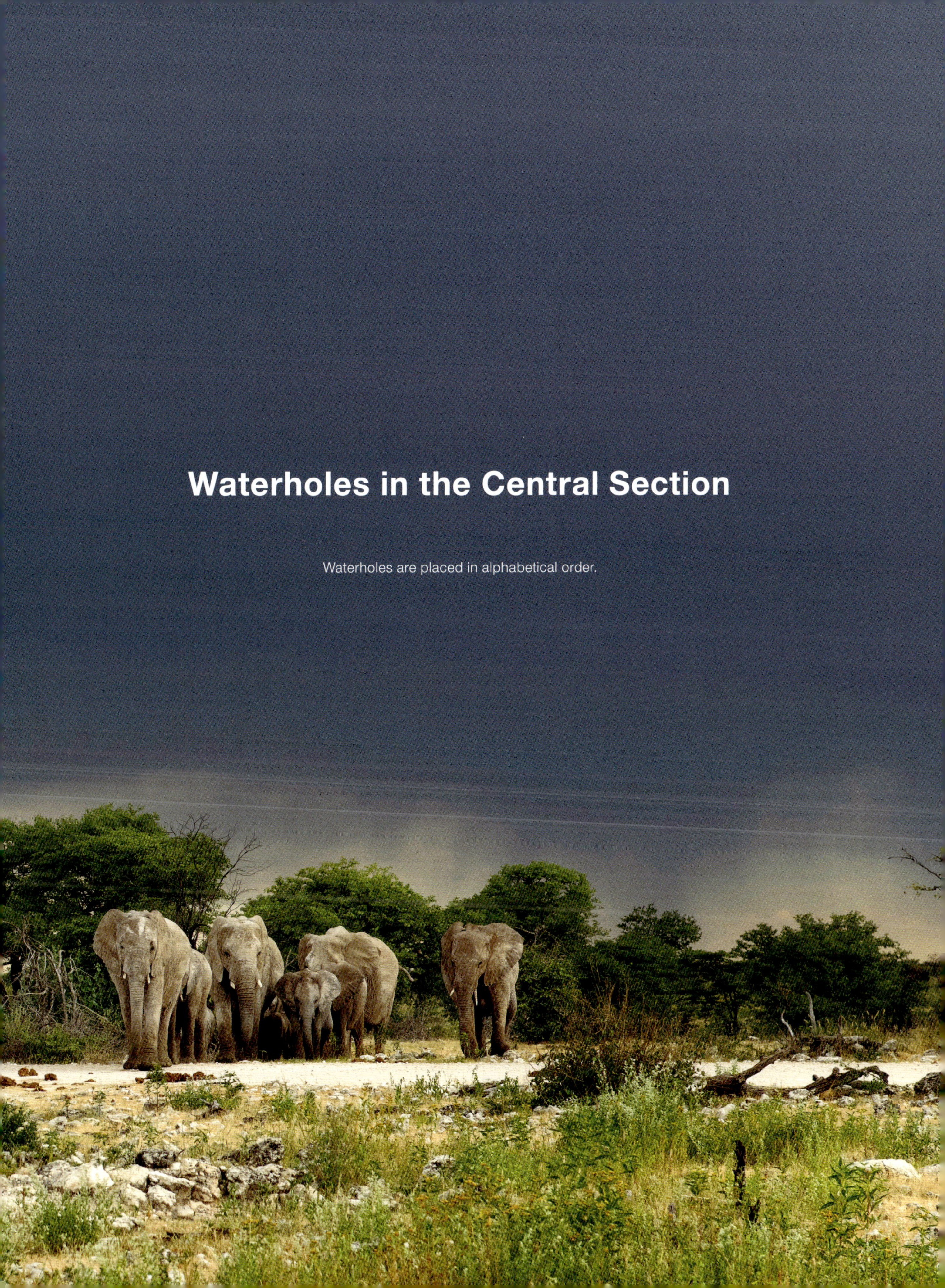

Waterholes in the Central Section

Waterholes are placed in alphabetical order.

Adamax ★★★ (inactive but accessible)

💧 Closed borehole; rainwater

⚑ Plains game

The name of this **borehole** was derived from the combination of the Christian names of a Swiss couple, **Ada and Max Kessler**, whose generosity contributed to the construction of the borehole. Management permanently discontinued the water supply to the waterholes of Adamax, Leeubron, Natco and Gaseb to prevent further habitat degradation as a result of overgrazing of plains game. You can also observe signs of degradation and erosion damage in these areas. Although the Adamax waterhole is inactive, it is on a **scenic route** and well worth visiting in the **rainy season**. Some waterholes still hold water and are situated in a much sought-after area by plains-game species for grazing and birthing during the rainy season.

Lioness with cubs

Aus ★★★

💧 Karst spring in a natural depression, supplemented by a solar pump

⚑ Open and spacious

The Aus waterhole is a **water-table spring** in a sprawling, **natural depression**, surrounded by mopane, red bushwillow and purple-pod cluster-leaf bushveld. Aus is a German name meaning '**out or finished**' and refers to its remote location when it was the furthest point tourists could travel to. It is also the Hai//om word, which has two meanings; '**spring**' and other Hai//om refer to the spring as '**/Os**', meaning '**salty water**'.

An additional solar pump supplements the spring water; the pumped spring water flows into a round, concrete waterhole with excess water overflowing into the natural depression below. During the rainy season, the **lake-like conditions** draw huge flocks of red-billed queleas, which descend on the waterhole. Opportunistic raptors like lanner falcon and tawny eagle swoop down in pursuit of a quick meal, fork-tailed drongo sing a merry tune, perched on solitary branches of mopane shrub and lilac-breasted rollers swoop and dive in their search for a tasty morsel, while uttering harsh and discordant cries.

Aus is a sprawling, **open, and spacious waterhole** where you can watch the approaching game from far away and, simultaneously, have the binoculars close at hand to carefully scan the dense mopane shrub near the water tanks for predators like leopards. It is also a firm favourite with elephant, large herds of black-faced impala, zebra and kudu.

Lion cub

Charitsaub ★★★★

- Artesian and perennial spring
- Kalahari acacia

An **artesian spring** surrounded by thick strands of desert sedge grass got its name from the San language as '**Geikoitsaub**', a large waterhole. Another Hai//om word for this spring is '**Kaikhoetsaub**', which means '**the spring of the old man**'.

This perennial spring is known to become dormant during Etosha's exceptionally harsh and climatic phase. The elevated parking area affords a superb view over the waterhole, and the rolling **Charitsaub plains** surrounding it, all the way to the pan, are visible as a long white sliver in the distance. A perennial herb with white, woolly flowers, with the common Afrikaans name '**aambeibossie**', adds colour to the edge of the elevated parking lot.

A solitary **Kalahari acacia** is an iconic landmark, with small raptors like greater kestrels, black-winged kites and red-necked falcons favouring its canopy. Lions have often been observed under the tree, seeking shade under the bushy mustard tree, which grows at the base of the tree trunk. They also love to lie in ambush in the dense sedges surrounding the waterhole.

Cheetahs pass by, as do black- and white rhino. Large herds of zebra and springbok favour this waterhole, and a pair of blue cranes can be observed during the breeding season, as well as the odd flamingo or two. The vast expanse of the plains surrounding Charitsaub on the route to Salvadora draws enormous herds of zebra, wildebeest and springbok after good rains. The plains are also an excellent place to view secretarybirds, red-capped larks, the omnipresent Kori bustard and northern-black korhaan (white-quilled bustard).

Aerial view of Charitsaub waterhole

Charl Marais Dam ★★★ (seasonal)

Seasonal

Elephants playing in water; waterbirds

This **dam** was named after a former secretary of the former SWA Administration because he secured funds for the dam's construction. The intention was to **supply drinking water to plains game.** The constructors built the dam wall across the narrowest point of a drainage system, covering about 100 km^2 of pans in the southwest. The road leading past m'Bari to Otjovasandu was built over the wall to allow tourists to view the game from there. However, following a study by Dr Hymie Ebedes in 1976, veterinarians established this site was a **possible source of anthrax**. Consequently, to prevent the accumulation of stagnating water, which might facilitate the proliferation of anthrax, several **aqueducts** were laid at the base of the wall for drainage purposes.

The dam can still hold a **large body of water** in the rainy season, attracting a wide variety of wildlife, especially elephants. Elephants love frolicking and playing in the water, sometimes wholly submerging themselves with only the trunk showing, especially the youngsters. A mud bath equals a spa treatment, providing protection and coolness against the burning sun and getting rid of parasites.

Look out for wetland birds like flamingos, grey herons, white egrets and marabou storks, among others. An elevated small parking area affords a beautiful vantage point over the whole region. Lions are frequently encountered in the area, moving between the m'Bari waterhole and the dam.

Gaseb (inactive)

The waterhole was closed owing to overgrazing, causing habitat degradation.

A true story

A gruesome, dramatic story played out at Okondeka in 1950. Four migrant workers on contract with farmers south of Etosha abandoned their work and travelled to Ovamboland via Okaukuejo on foot. While quenching their thirst at Okondeka, the lions attacked and killed one man, while the other three escaped into the nearest tree, which was standing where the parking area for tourists is today. After eating the unfortunate victim in full view of his terrified comrades, a lioness pulled two more men from the tree and killed them. The fourth man hoisted himself through the thorns right to the tree's crown, where he lay spread-eagled for three agonising days and nights, with the man-eaters lying in wait beneath the tree. A South African Police patrol from Okaukuejo passed by and rescued him from certain death. The unfortunate survivor, however, was mentally deranged from a combination of thirst, fear and horror of witnessing his companions' death. Nobody recorded whether he ever fully recovered from this horrendous ordeal.

African elephants at Charl Marais Dam

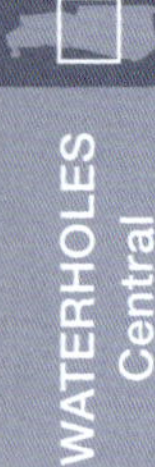

Gemsbokvlakte ★★★★★

- Solar-powered borehole
- Excellent game viewing and lion sightings; brown hyena

Translated as 'plain of the oryx', this borehole was the first waterhole in Etosha to be converted from wind power – with the stand-by of a diesel pump – to solar energy. Surrounded by sprawling, open plains, it offers tourists excellent game-viewing opportunities. It is particularly active in the dry season and visited by large herds of herbivores like Burchell's zebra, spring-bok, oryx, giraffe and wildebeest from mid-morning onwards.

Elephants are particularly fond of the waterhole thanks to the ample space of its surroundings. It is also one of the best waterholes for **good lion sightings**, Etosha's apex predator, usually early morning and towards late afternoon. The reward to early risers may be a sighting of the predominantly **nocturnal and shy brown hyena**. You may also see amusing interactions between black crows and black-backed jackals on the perimeters of the waterhole and parking area. Thickets of trumpet thorn grow prolifically in the area, attracting black rhino, which eat the branches; zebra and springbok, which prefer the foliage; and kudu, which favour the flowers. Typical components of **dwarf shrub savanna**, like saltbush, cork-bush and petal-bush, are near-endemic shrubs in Namibia that occur on the plains surrounding Gemsbokvlakte.

Breeding herd of African elephants approaching Gemsbokvlakte

Goas ★★★★★

- Artesian spring
- Scenic and productive; elephant breeding herds; lion and leopard

Probably the **most productive** and **scenically pleasing** waterhole near **Halali Camp**, Goas is characterised by its sprawling surroundings and **two pools** of water. One theory is that each waterhole has its underground water supply, but they are more likely linked. The artesian-confined water surfaces through two weak points in the semi-permeable surface, forming two distinct pools of water. The upper pool maintains a constant water level throughout the year, while the lower one empties in the dry season. After copious rainfall, the upper spring can sometimes overflow into the lower pool.

The Hai//om referred to the waterhole as **!Gō-ās**, meaning !gō (**to knock**) and ās (**to drink**), referring to the stomping of the hooves on the calcrete rocks and rubble on the ground when the game approached the water.

The setting is picturesque, with the waterhole **fringed by** typical **dense mopane woodland**. Mopane, red bushwillow and purple-pod cluster-leaf trees of six metres and higher are common and offer excellent shade, shelter for wildlife and ideal places of concealment for predators.

The added attraction for visitors is the **access road**, which winds around the two separate water sources. The road enables different angles for photography in a spacious setting and good light conditions throughout the day.

Goas is well known for **good sightings of elephants** – especially breeding herds – and black-faced impala. Zebra, giraffe, wildebeest, red hartebeest and kudu are regular visitors, setting the stage for predators that follow the ample prey. Look out for **lion, leopard and spotted hyena**.

Raptors such as the tawny eagle, lanner falcon and African harrier hawk follow proceedings from the tree line while the cleaning crew, in the form of marabou storks and vultures, hovers in the background. The vast flocks of red-billed queleas descend in the thousands to quench their thirst here, which is also significant.

Breeding herd of African elephants at Goas waterhole

Three-leaved cotton *(Gossypium triphyllum)*

Moringa tree at the 'enchanted forest'

Grünewald ★★★ (inactive, but accessible)

- Former borehole; closed
- Mopane woodland; Gossypium triphyllum; Grootvlakte; Moringa trees

This **former borehole**, situated on the eastern edge of **Grootvlakte**, was permanently closed off to prevent further degradation of the habitat from overgrazing by plains game. It was also to stop the elephants utilising the area and causing further destruction to the moringa trees of Sprokieswoud. The rather unimaginative German name 'Grünewald' literally means '**green forest**' and refers to the extensive mopane woodland, boasting some of the largest specimens of mopane trees in Etosha, as well as short grasses that sprout here after the rainy season.

Trumpet thorn thickets line the road in places where wild sage and ***Gossypium triphyllum*** also occur. *Gossypium triphyllum* is a near-endemic, perennial woody shrub sporting beautiful flowers ranging from purple and lilac to pink. It is a lovely, lush setting during the rainy season when shallow depressions in the area hold water. Large herds of grazers are drawn to the whole region, attracting predators like lion, spotted hyena and cheetah. However, winter and the dry season paint a completely different picture, one of dryness and bleakness with little wildlife found.

Halali Plains Seep ★★★

(not waterholes but a series of contact springs seepages at the edge of the pan)

- Contact spring seepage
- Large herds of plains game, especially springbok; black rhino

The Halali plains are the extensive open plains you pass along the main road between Namutoni and Okaukuejo. The western plain is the section west of the turn-off to Halali, and the eastern plain is two kilometres east of the turn-off after passing through a **water-acacia thicket**.

The **Halali plains seep** is located on the eastern Halali plain just north of the westernmost road culvert. About 600 m north of this vantage point, an area of dark green vegetation – consisting of ***Juncus* sedges** – is visible around the edges of the seep, with the wide vista of the pan as a backdrop. From mid-morning, you can encounter large herds of plains game arriving from various directions on their way to the seepage.

Herds of **springbok** are prolific in the area, and it is quite a spectacle when they approach over the plains, often **pronking**, before crossing the road to the pan side. Pronking is characteristic of springbok, bouncing and bounding into the air in a series of high leaps as they run. This spectacle infuses joy and admiration when witnessing these acrobatic feats. Some say this behaviour demonstrates strength, agility and stamina; others argue it serves to outrun predators. The actual reason, when observing this behaviour, seems to be a display of pure fun and enjoyment by these agile gazelles.

Many **small contact-spring seeps** are in the area, not visible nor accessible by car but the Halali plains seep is visible. Keep an eye out for rhino, which frequent the area, usually early or mid-morning. The large carnivores also favour the seeps and springs as the dense sedges traditionally found in the vicinity offer ideal concealment opportunities for ambushing prey.

Helio (inactive but accessible, adjacent to Helio Hills)

- Closed borehole
- Helio twin hills

This **borehole** got its name from the heliograph station on top of one of the adjacent twin Helio hills. After 1992, the waterhole was closed, with the intention that wildlife would use the Moringa waterhole, two kilometres away at Halali Camp.

Helio hills

Aerial view of Homob waterhole

Homob ★★★★

Karst and artesian springs

Bulrushes with wetland birds; tawny eagle; lion pride

A **karst** and an **artesian spring**, emerging from two distinct sources in a calcareous depression, afford great game viewing from the elevated parking area. Homob is named after a Hai//om word, meaning '**place without swarms of locust**'. The larger waterhole has a small island filled with bulrushes, an ideal habitat for wetland birds.

A pair of binoculars would come in handy for leisurely observing birdlife, such as little grebes, black crakes, Egyptian geese, red-billed ducks, Eurasian moorhens and red-knobbed coots going about their business in the recesses of the bulrushes, from the comfort of your car. Look for tawny eagles on nearby trees and helmeted guineafowl that mill about in great numbers.

Well-worn animal highways traverse the calcrete landscape, utilised by large herds of wildebeest, zebra, springbok and impala on their daily pilgrimages to the waterhole. Homob is **known for its considerable lion pride**, often found in residence. You can expect sightings of leopard and black rhino. The morning light is best for photography.

The white, sprawling, predominantly calcrete landscape around the waterhole is fringed by **mopane treeveld**, with some beautiful, tall, old mopane trees and purple-pod cluster-leaves. A pair of spotted thick-knee birds may be breeding at the entrance of the access road leading to Homob, or leopard tortoises could be encountered on the same route.

The condition of the four-kilometre access road varies, with some corrugation and a few shallow potholes, mainly owing to the different sizes of calcrete rocks and rubble, especially near the end of the access road leading to the waterhole.

Kapupuhedi ★★★

Contact spring

Scenic; mopane aloe; Haas islands; ostrich

Kapupuhedi is set in an atmospheric and incredibly **scenic setting** at the edge of the pan, with the parking area at an elevated angle overlooking this **contact spring** offering an exceptional view over the vast, white expanse of the pan. It holds water during and after the rainy season but can run dry after a prolonged drought. The Hai//om referred to it as '**Tsam**', meaning soft mud or soil. It may also be interpreted as '**small earthworm mounds**', called '**e/hedi-hedi**', meaning earthworm in Oshindonga.

Ostrich and oryx often make their way across the shimmering expanse of the pan, and black rhino enjoy browsing here in the early morning. **Spotted hyena** are frequently observed loping over the nearby plains, pot-bellied and heads hung low, muzzles and parts of the neck caked with dried blood, all indicators of a recent, substantial banquet. Hyenas are successful hunters, with enough speed and stamina for the

Lion pride at Kapupuhedi waterhole

pack to bring down a fully grown oryx.

The vegetation is typically **dwarf-shrub savanna** on **sweet grassveld on lime**, favoured by springbok. The main components consist of saltbush, petalbush and woolbush. Look for the **mopane aloe** from the elevated parking area to the left on the plains. The grass is palatable and attracts large herds of zebra when the grazing at Nebrownii and Gemsbokvlakte has been exhausted.

The **Haas islands** (loosely translated as 'hare islands') refer to the **scrub hare**. These islands are found four kilometres north of Kapupuhedi, and you can see them situated at a distance in the pan.

Lions often occur in the vicinity. Another unforgettable experience early one morning was watching a pride of 10 scattered lazily among the prickly brack grass and ink bushes on the pan. They would play and interact with each other before meandering to the spring for a drink and settling down in the shade of the calcrete ridge for the remainder of the day. The view from this waterhole is scenic and it's a tranquil spot for early morning and late afternoon photography in the golden light.

Leeubron ★★★ (inactive but accessible)

💧 Borehole permanently closed

⚑ A variety of tree species

Leeubron, literally translated into '**lion fountain**' from Afrikaans, was first established by the German Schutztruppe during their time of occupation as a **water source for their horses**. A **borehole** later replaced the well, and there is an intriguing story about how Leeubron acquired its name. Prof. Schoeman, chief game warden in the 1950s, came across an emaciated lioness and her offspring in the area and thought it prudent to feed them, as lions were relatively scarce during that time. As more lions joined the small family, shooting two Burchell's zebra was deemed necessary to feed the lions every week. Nature conservation officials were privy to the spectacle. After tourists complained this was discriminatory and wanted to witness the feeding, a maximum of 10 visitors' cars were allowed to partake in the spectacle. The so-called '**lion party**' took place every Wednesday and Saturday under the supervision of the wardens. However, this was later entirely disbanded for safety's sake when things got completely out of control, for instance, with people getting out of cars to film the spectacle.

The borehole was **permanently closed** after research indicated habitat degradation as a result of overgrazing.

Buffalo thorn, confetti spike-thorn, tall common corkwood and the smelly shepherd's bush occur here. A few acacia species, like the red umbrella-thorn, dense thickets of hook-thorn, three-hook acacia (rare) and candle-pod acacia, are also found here. In the rainy season, the natural depression where the remnant of the old waterhole used to be still holds water and attracts a variety of wildlife.

Moringa waterhole

Moringa ★★★★★ (Halali Camp)

💧 Artificial floodlit waterhole; solar power

⚑ Moringa trees; excellent game viewing, silhouette photography

The Moringa waterhole is an **artificial**, **floodlit waterhole** established in 1992 on the boundary of the Halali Camp to enable tourists to enjoy wildlife sightings. Many people rate this as the **most scenic and beautiful waterhole** of the main camps, where a semi-natural rock wall separates wildlife and visitors. The seating area is partially covered and situated at an elevated angle, with adequate seating on wooden benches and greyish carbonite rocks. The rocks were deposited as carbonate reefs during Damaran times (a geological term difficult to describe) about 750 million years ago – certainly a historical and unique seating. A small wooden walkway also enables people to stand on or walk to the furthest point of the viewing area. The vista over the waterhole stretches over the mopane thickets to the distant horizon. The waterhole is

Black rhino silhouette

set between natural rocks, its surface reminiscent of a pane of glass, without a ripple to disturb its surface. This lends itself beautifully for silhouette shots at dusk. The many **moringa or ghost trees** gracing the site also provide a particularly charming and unique character to the setting.

Getting there well before the sun sets is advisable to secure a good place and set up your photographic equipment or enjoy a sundowner with your favourite drink and a pair of binoculars. The first black rhino usually appears when the sky turns a dusky orange, accompanied by a flock of chattering **double-banded sandgrouse**. As more rhino emerge from the fringes of the mopane shrub – often up to six individuals – the cacophony of sounds consisting of snorting, huffing and screaming can be heard well into camp. **Elephant** usually join the fray, and **spotted hyena** hang around the perimeter, waiting for their turn to nip to the water's edge for a hasty drink. **Lion** and **leopard** appear regularly, and there is never a dull moment.

Birdlife is constantly entertaining. The distinct calls of the **pearl-spotted owlet** and at least two nightjar species and the eerie bloodcurdling screech of several **barn owls** penetrate the night. They fly over the waterhole or settle on the ground. Be prepared for an absolute spectacle during and after the rainy season, when thousands of **red-billed queleas** descend on the waterhole, especially at dusk. Individuals always get pushed into the water by the supercolony of birds. Struggling, they will try to reach the waterhole's edge, only to be gobbled up by an opportunistic **spotted hyena**.

The floodlights attract myriad **insects**. They swarm and provide a banquet for the fork-tailed drongo, rufous-cheeked nightjar or familiar chat, which make short work of what is on offer. Feisty **honey badgers** used to scuttle among the visitors' legs, looking for food scraps, not shy to deliver a quick nip to a sandalled foot, which would have several visitors jumping onto the benches out of reach of sharp teeth. This problem, however, resolved itself during the Covid-19 pandemic when visitor numbers declined, with only a few scraps in the dustbins throughout camp. It forced most honey badgers to seek greener pastures and return to their natural foraging locations.

Natco ★★★ (inactive but accessible)

- Closed borehole owing to habitat degradation
- Game viewing during the rainy season

Drilling the **Natco borehole** between Leeubron and Adamax aimed to attract wildlife for tourist viewing. The National Trading Company of SWA bore this cost, hence the name Natco. The abundance of artificial water in this fragile area of sweet grassveld on lime proved a mistake and was closed when research indicated **habitat degradation owing to overgrazing**. Water collects in several depressions in the rainy season, and wildlife frequents the area, drawn by the excellent grazing. The area looks barren and bleak during the long, hot summer months.

African elephant bull at Nebrownii waterhole

Nebrownii ★★★★★

- Artesian borehole, later boosted by solar power
- Masses of game in the dry season, lion, ghost elephant, water thorn acacia

The Nebrownii waterhole is picturesque and approximately seven kilometres east of Okaukuejo. The park administration opened the artesian borehole in 1992 to relieve pressure on the vegetation around the Okaukuejo waterhole from the many animals, especially elephants, coming to drink. This initiative seemed successful in drawing other game species, like Burchell's zebra, away from Gemsbokvlakte, which had also been impacted by overgrazing. In 1997, management installed a solar pump to boost the flow.

Nebrownii derives its name from the **water thorn acacias** (*Vachelia nebrownii*), which are found in the area and often form dense thickets that line parts of the roadside west of Nebrownii to Okaukuejo. With the onset of spring, masses of bright yellow, fluffy flowers explode, covering these usually rather colourless shrubs. The sweet scent attracts plenty of insects. Springbok, giraffe and kudu consider the flowers a delicacy, while elephant and rhino prefer the twigs and leaves.

Nebrownii offers **exceptional game viewing** as the waterhole lies at an elevated angle, offering great views of the vast, open plains surrounding it. Various game species visit the waterhole and large herds of herbivores like zebra, springbok and wildebeest mill about from mid-morning. Oryx, ostrich and giraffe also come to drink. The **great whites** or **ghost elephants** are **iconic** as they approach the waterhole with their flapping ears and trunks held high. They coat themselves with the white clay, hence their white countenance. The ever-opportunistic black-backed jackal hovers on the perimeter, always looking for a quick meal. Expect a black rhino or two to arrive at dusk.

Best **predator sightings** are early morning and towards evening, as lion and spotted hyena are regular visitors to the waterhole. Lions often retreat to the culverts under the main road to escape the day's heat. Some people fail to observe the proper park etiquette of keeping a respectful distance, even driving off the road to glimpse the lions inside the culverts. Park management eventually had to erect short poles on either side of the road to prevent this.

The light is best for photography early in the morning and especially favourable in the afternoon. The proximity to Okaukuejo main camp makes it an ideal sundowner spot and a quick foray from camp.

Spotted hyena pup

Springok at Nebrownii waterhole

Kudu bull at Nuamses waterhole

Noniams ★★ (inactive but accessible)

Seasonal karst spring

Black-faced impala

Noniams derives its name from the Hai//om word **/Honi-ams**, used for the **smelly shepherd's bush** that grows near the spring. A **seasonal spring**, it becomes dormant in the long dry period of Etosha and is active only in the rainy season. Wildlife utilises the nearby Goas waterhole, a mere two kilometres away. Still, you can always find large herds of black-faced impala, Burchell's zebra, steenbok and black rhino.

Find the waterhole about two kilometres along the 10 km access road that joins Rhino Drive and Eland Drive. Beautiful old, gnarled, single-stemmed mopane trees create a peaceful atmosphere and afford good visibility, interspersed with red bushwillow trees and purple-pod cluster-leaf. Wether love grass and stunted mopane shrubs grow along the roadside, as do thickets of sicklebush.

A few uneven, deeper depressions in the road fill up with water in the rainy season but can be navigated relatively easily by sedan cars.

Mating pair of leopards at Nuamses waterhole

Nuamses ★★★★

Karst spring

Leopard; black-faced impala, elephant

Nuamses is a **karst spring** producing dark, murky water, at least in appearance. The water is clear and palatable, and the dark colour results from the depth of the circular sinkhole, which has a dark base within calcrete rock. The Hai//om refer to this spring as **#Nu-amses**, which means black water. Numerous **rock crevices** are preferred by shyer species, lending the waterhole a secretive and secluded appearance. **Leopards** are particularly fond of **mopane/red bushwillow/ purple-pod cluster-leaf bushveld** south of Nuamses.

It is one of the favourite waterholes, and I have spent many hours here, patiently waiting for the elusive leopard to appear. The long hours of patient vigilance eventually paid off when a mating pair of leopards appeared one morning, briefly drinking at the waterhole before melting back into the bush. Another visitor was privileged to see a female leopard hunting terrapins perched on the rocks near the waterhole.

Elephants love swimming and drinking here, especially small breeding herds with calves, coating themselves with the glistening dark mud at the waterhole's edge. Tall mopane trees and mopane shrubs are the dominant vegetation, a favourite with black-faced impala, which also quench their thirst here.

The golden glow of the late afternoon sun creates a scenic atmosphere at this waterhole, and the light is ideal for photography. As with many Etosha roads, the calcrete access road leading to the waterhole is rough, uneven and corrugated.

Aerial view of Nuamses waterhole

Abidm's storks, Burchell's zebra, oryx and springbok at Okaukuejo waterhole

Okaukuejo ★★★★★

- Former karst spring; water supplied by solar power
- Nearly all game species; black rhino; brown hyena

Probably the **flagship waterhole of Etosha**, situated at the edge of one of the main rest camps, Okaukuejo and pronounced **O-ka-kwi-you**. Hai//om referred to it as ***Thekwi***, meaning '**place of the small bush**', and one Hai//om called it specifically **Hui-e**, meaning '**place of the saltbush**', referring to the saltbushes, the significant component of the dwarf shrub savanna around Okaukuejo. This **floodlit** waterhole, situated at the edge of the rest camp, is an important tourist attraction with a low stone wall combined with a game-proof fence, separating wildlife from people. Comfortable wooden benches, some shaded, and a **thatched lapa** with elevated stone benches enable guests to have superb game viewing virtually 24 hours a day.

Various **game** species frequent the waterhole, and the dry season ensures a continuous procession of animals. Towers of giraffe come to drink, as do herds of zebra, wildebeest, springbok, oryx and impala. Sunrise and sunset are optimal for photography as the benches all face west, with beautiful lighting for photographers. The setting sun, especially, is ideal for silhouette shots and reflections in the water. The Okaukuejo waterhole is one of the best waterholes to observe the endangered **black rhino**, which usually starts appearing

at dusk, with as many as eight rhino recorded at the waterhole simultaneously, if not more.

The stage is set for some action-packed moments when elephants appear. The fight for dominance, a strict pecking order, and simple socialising all play out, accompanied by loud trumpeting, snorting and mock charges among billowing dust clouds. **Lion** pass through regularly, and many kills take place at the waterhole. **Spotted hyena,** the elusive and nocturnal **brown hyena** and **leopard** usually drink here in the early hours of the morning.

Birdlife is prolific, with Verreaux's eagle owls roosting in the waterhole's signature huge leadwood tree and various raptor species like lanner falcon and Gabar goshawk hunting near the waterhole. Flocks of Burchell's and Namaqua sandgrouse fly in at sunrise; the males absorb water in their chest and belly feathers and then fly home for the chicks to drink. Double-banded sandgrouse frequent the waterhole after sunset. Red teal and Egyptian geese are permanent fixtures and blacksmith lapwing are the most vocal birds, especially when they attempt to deter many hooves from trampling their nests.

Various bird species feed off the fruit of the **buffalo thorn**, as do black rhino, giraffe, springbok and kudu. However, owing to the high pressure of animals, there is evidence of soil erosion damage and the destruction of vegetation around the Okaukuejo waterhole.

Aerial view of Okondeka waterhole

Okondeka ★★★★★

- Contact spring
- Different grass species; scenic with masses of game; pan panorama

Okondeka, a **contact spring** that has never dried up in living memory, is one of the **most scenic locations** right at the edge of the pan, offering uninterrupted viewing over the vast white vista. The Okondeka duneveld stretches along the western side of the pan and constitutes one of the **tall grassveld** communities in the park. The sands often overlie calcrete and free lime is also present. Woody plants are not prominent in these grasslands, but the **trumpet thorn**, **sickle bush** and **wool bush** are locally common.

The light is best in the afternoon as most of the day, the view from the parking area across the shimmering expanse of the pan is direct, harsh light, which creates a heat haze and transforms wildlife into silhouettes. With its favourable afternoon light, Okondeka is one of Etosha's top landscape photography locations. Animals appear from kilometres away to drink, and you have a great diversity, spread far and wide. Okondeka is the place to photograph the masses of wildlife in the distance, with lions drinking in the foreground. Look for **brown hyena** and **Cape fox** dens on the plains, west of Okondeka.

Okondeka, an Oshindonga name, has at least four names, each with a completely different interpretation. One means '**place of sedges**', referring to the desert sedge grass growing in the vicinity, and another means '**place of the small (or wild) dog**'. In earlier literature, the word '**Ondeka**' was used, which means '**creeping plant**', possibly referring to the halophytic grass growing along the edges of the pan, prickly brack grass or desert sedge. Another spelling **Onkondeka**, means to **encircle** or set up an ambush, referring to the resident lion pride ambushing their prey, with the surrounding grassy dune hummocks offering ideal concealment. When in residence, the pride is also often found under the sprawling, extensive candle-pod acacia scrub on the other side of the main road, parallel to the spring.

Olifantsbad ★★★★

- Originally karst spring, now solar power
- Ostrich; vultures; raptors, stately kudu bulls

This **artificial waterhole** is on the southwestern side of Etosha Pan. Seasonally, a **natural seepage** in the form of a **karst spring** occurred in a depression, which was later supplemented and enlarged by drilling a **borehole** run on a **solar pump** and an additional concrete basin. Like many of Etosha's waterholes, Olifantsbad is in a **predominantly calcrete landscape**.

The Hai//om referred to this waterhole as **#Gaseb** or **#Aseb**, meaning '**to scoop water from a deep hole**'.

Olifantsbad, translated from Afrikaans, means '**elephant's bath**' and, indeed, large herds of elephants frequent this waterhole. Owing to its size and the openness of the surrounding area, Olifantsbad is a haven for a great variety and abundance of game; in fact, you may see all species here. **Mopane/red bushwillow/purple-pod cluster-leaf bushveld** is the predominant vegetation, favoured by elephants, black-faced impala and kudu. Red hartebeest and large herds of zebra come to visit, and predators like lion, leopard and spotted hyena, in turn, follow the browsers and grazers.

Ostriches are often seen at Olifantsbad, as are **vultures**, especially lappet-faced- and white-backed vultures. Look for **raptors** perching nearby. Expect to see a tawny eagle, lanner falcon or pale-chanting goshawk. They wait for opportunities to pounce on the helmeted guineafowl, doves, sandgrouse and other small birds that quench their thirst at the waterhole's edge.

Light is best at mid-morning but an unused, former underground hide in the form of an unsightly concrete structure at the water's edge is not ideal for a panorama or landscape shot of the whole scenery.

African elephant bull and red-billed quelea swarm at Olifantsbad waterhole

Ombika ★★★★

- Artesian spring and new borehole supplemented by solar power
- Good lion and black rhino sightings

Ombika is near the **Andersson Gate** en route to Okaukuejo. It is the first waterhole on your left as you enter the park. It was also known by the Otjiherero name '**Ompica**' but originally spelt '**Ombike**'. The names refer to hand picks used to remove rocks from this original spring to make the water more accessible to early travellers.

A natural **artesian spring**, it dried up for the first time in living memory in 1994, after 14 years of prolonged drought in Etosha. Park management installed a borehole 300m away, driven by a solar pump, to ensure a water supply to Ombika. Initially, the waterhole was quite a distance away in a deep calcrete depression, in which animals sometimes completely disappeared when the water level was low, especially in dry conditions. Visibility from the parking area was a challenge, and park management has recently constructed a new waterhole closer to the parking area, which provides much better accessibility for wildlife and visibility for visitors.

Ombika is **renowned for good lion sightings**, attracting many browsers and grazers like zebra, oryx, wildebeest and springbok. Visitors recently saw Burchell's and Hartmann's mountain zebra together at the waterhole, which is unusual as Hartmann's mountain zebra occurs only in western Etosha. You may even see a black rhino here. In springtime, the blooms of the trumpet thorn or ghabbabos and water thorn acacia attract giraffe.

The tawny-eagle is a regular feature; African harrier-hawks, Marabou storks, hornbills, fork-tailed drongos, helmeted-guineafowl and at least two species of sandgrouse are just a few of the bird species that frequent the waterhole. In times of exceedingly good rainfall, the calcrete basin of the old waterhole tends to fill up and overflow, often flooding the surrounding area and leaving pools of water everywhere.

Ondongab ★★

- Seasonal contact spring
- Scenic

Ondongab is a **seasonal contact spring** at the bottom of a rocky ledge at the edge of the pan, near a water thorn acacia thicket. It is a **scenic location** with a lovely view over the expanse of the pan.

Water thorn acacia thickets and desert sedges line the access road to Odongab in places. Look for the **confetti spike thorn**, a large woody shrub or tree, and **halophytic grass** near the spring. The name is probably derived from the Oshindonga-speaking people of Ovambo, as alternative spellings are **Ondonga** or **Ndonga**. The Hai//om referred to it as **IHaodommi**, with IHao meaning '**coming together**' and '**dommi**' – '**depression**', thus translated into '**the place where two depressions meet**'.

Good game viewing is best in the rainy season as the spring empties in dry phases. It is an excellent spot to occasionally see lion, black rhino, elephant and even scrub hares.

Black-backed jackal

Female leopard marking her territory

Rietfontein ★★★★★

Strong artesian spring

Extremely popular and active waterhole; good leopard sightings; raptors and predators

This waterhole is one of the biggest in the park and a powerful **artesian spring** carrying sweet water with a fascinating history. Rietfontein received its name from the *Dorsland trekkers in 1876, which means '**reed fountain**', named after the prolific common reeds which grew there. The Dorsland trekkers used the spring as a resting place for themselves and their oxen on their long journey to Angola. Later, they settled in the spring to farm but found the lush reed beds and fresh-water belied a harsh environment. Malaria, lung sickness which plagued the cattle, and raids from the Ovambo, Herero and Hai//om prompted them to abandon Rietfontein and seek greener pastures elsewhere. To this day, the grave site of a trekker woman, Johanna Alberts (1841–1876), lies under a mopane tree and can be viewed at Rietfontein.

The Hai//om referred to it as **llNasuneb**, meaning '**to let oneself fall**', relaxing after a long journey and refreshing oneself with good water. Elephant, whose numbers increased significantly after being given protected status, demolished the former lush reed beds.

Still visible to the left upon entering the parking area of the waterhole are the remains of a **bone meal factory,** built in 1952 on the initiative of former game warden and noted hunter Prof. P Schoeman, who believed there was an excess of Burchell's zebra and wildebeest, thus over utilising the grazing. The official record states that 293 zebra and 122 wildebeest were culled and processed, but many reports state the numbers were far higher and that they shot thousands of animals of several species. Nature lovers and environmental organisations greatly opposed this, and their protests eventually resulted in the plant's permanent closure in the same year.

Rietfontein is still an **extremely popular and active** waterhole today. The spacious plains surrounding the waterhole can attract hundreds of plains game, especially zebra, which can all quench their thirst there because of the abundance of water. It can be gratifying to photograph zebra at Rietfontein, as such large herds offer ideal photographic opportunities for fascinating and action-packed interludes.

There are two parts of the waterhole; the eastern end on the left has an islet covered with bulrushes and green vegetation but holds dark, muddy water, a favourite with elephants. The other end of the waterhole is shallower and holds cleaner water, which other animals prefer to drink. Good sightings of **black rhino** can be guaranteed, especially in the late afternoon, while **lion** are regulars in the morning. I once witnessed a spectacular leopard ambush, resulting in a springbok kill at noon.

Female leopard in stalking mode at Rietfontein waterhole

Birdlife is prolific and varied, with the most unusual being good sightings of **African fish eagle**, especially in the rainy season. Tawny eagle, black-chested snake eagle, African harrier-hawk and lanner falcons are raptors that often circle the waterhole from above or swoop down from lofty heights in search of prey. Marabou storks, white-backed- and lappet-faced vultures, hyenas and black-backed jackals are the cleaning crew when there is carrion. Egyptian geese, blacksmith lapwings and sandgrouse hover around the water's edge, and a few opportunistic pied crows usually harass visitors, hoping for some tasty morsels tossed their way.

The mid to late afternoon light is best for photography, as the sun is directly behind the parking lot.

Rietfontein waterhole, as well as the Rietfontein detour, is well known for **good leopard sightings**. I have followed three generations of territorial females in the area for almost 10 years, each sharing and later leaving the territory to their female offspring. My first encounter with the first of these particular females occurred in December 2014, when my daughter and I had the privilege to spend a whole day in the company of the first females on the detour, with no other vehicle in sight, which is a rare phenomenon. In May 2015, my husband and I re-encountered her when she was stalking springbok at the Rietfontein waterhole, and after a few suspenseful hours, the leopard secured a meal of springbok for herself. Her offspring joined her, and this was my last sighting of her. The female offspring took over the territory and became well known in the area, fondly referred to as the 'Rietfontein female' by many. She became habituated around cars and relaxed in their presence. I was privileged to follow her progress over the next few years, sometimes utterly alone with her. In June 2018, I photographed her and one of her cubs, a little female, on the main road directly opposite the waterhole. The other little cub, a male and an adult now, also roams the territory around the Rietfontein waterhole but is more aloof and less approachable. My last sighting of the Rietfontein female was October 2021. The leopard joined us on the main road, much further north of Rietfontein, again leaving the immediate vicinity of Rietfontein for her offspring. It was fanciful, but almost as if she were saying goodbye, and we never saw her again. On our most recent trip to Etosha in March 2023, researching material for this book, we came across an adult female leopard with a cub, again at almost the exact spot where we had first encountered the Rietfontein female with her female cub in 2018. Looking at the spot pattern in the photos, we could identify the same tiny female cub, now an adult, with her offspring. May the legacy continue…

***Dorsland trekkers** – Boer settlers from South Africa explored various destinations to eventually settle in a place with better living conditions and political independence.

Female cheetah and offspring overlooking the pan

Salvadora ★★★★★

- Contact spring
- Picturesque; active; Kalahari acacia; mustard bush; blue cranes

Salvadora is a **more extensive contact spring** than in previous years. The Hai//om referred to it as **#Kharitsaub** or **#Aritsaub**, meaning small spring. The water is sweet, and 90% of wildlife prefers to drink here rather than the very salty water of Sueda, a few kilometres along the edge.

Salvadora is rated as the **most picturesque waterhole** in the park and named after the once prominent evergreen **mustard bush**, which has considerably diminished in size over the years. It is situated on the calcrete ridge at the edge of the parking area. Located at an elevated angle with glorious, uninterrupted views over the Salvadora waterhole and the dramatic backdrop of the pan, the scenic beauty of the landscape lends itself superbly for **landscape photography**, especially in the golden glow of the morning light.

Another iconic landmark is the single **Kalahari acacia**, situated on the Salvadora plains near the waterhole and probably the most photographed tree in Etosha. A few visitors have had tremendous luck lately when they could photograph a leopard around or in the tree and mating leopards in the immediate vicinity.

From mid-morning, the approach of large herds of zebra and springbok moving over the adjacent grassland plains towards the waterhole is a spectacle to behold, and the surrounding reeds and grasses along the water's edge are ideal places of concealment for lion lying in ambush. The rare **blue crane** is occasionally seen in the area during the breeding season. Red-billed queleas usually descend on the mustard bush. Black- and pied crows frequently sit on the concrete marker at the edge of the parking lot, begging for handouts. Egyptian geese, black-smith- and crowned lapwings frequent the fringes of the waterhole, with smaller raptors like falcons and kestrels silently hunting from above.

Cheetah on plains of Salvadora

Aerial view of Salvadora plains and waterhole

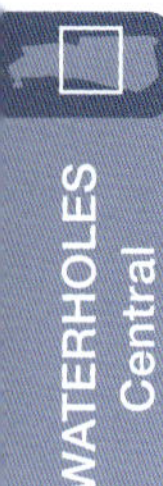

Sueda ★★★★

Contact spring

Lion; cheetah; black rhino; surreal landscape

Another **contact spring** on the southern edge of the pan, Sueda, was named after the **ink bush**, a fleshy-leafed halophyte growing on brackish, low-lying areas fringing the pan. Halophytic grasses like **prickly brack grass** and **salty dropseed** grow along the edge. Sueda offers a glorious, sweeping panoramic view of the vast, white expanse, overlooking the spring, lined by thick stands of desert sedge and situated in a **depression west to the parking area**.

Only a few animals frequent this waterhole because the water has a **high salt content.** Interspersed on the dramatic landscape are ridges and projections of snow-white limestone rocks and protrusions, an almost surreal and unique setting. Limestone is a sedimentary rock, consisting largely of calcium carbonate. If you have the good fortune to spot a lion or

Black rhino

cheetah, which likes to frequent the area, you can capture some unusual images in the morning or late afternoon.

I have had good sightings of a **black rhino** drinking from the spring and a **pride of lions** with cubs resting in the shade of a sizeable calcareous mound. The males came to drink in the late afternoon, and the cubs chased each other up and down an elevated calcrete mound. Females like to hide their cubs in the nearby calcrete rock crevices at the edge of the pan while going off to hunt. It is also a good area for **cheetah** sightings.

Immature black-winged kite

Wolfsnes ★★

- Contact spring
- Scenic; Kalahari acacia; hyena den; colonies of small mammals

Another Afrikaans name meaning '**wolf**' and referring to hyena, combined with '**nes**' meaning nest/haunt/den, relates to the **dens of the spotted hyena** in the vicinity. Situated on the southwestern edge of the main pan, this natural **contact spring** – particularly active and flowing into the pan in the wet phases – was also one of the first to dry out and become dormant in Etosha's dry period starting 1980. Nevertheless, it is scenic, with a single prominent **Kalahari acacia** at the edge of the parking lot, views of the pan and rolling grassland on either side of the road leading up to Wolfsnes.

Springbok favour the area, colonies of **ground squirrels** have their burrows near the road, and you may see **secretary-birds** strutting their stuff and looking for rodents, snakes and other tasty morsels. Be on the lookout for **Cape foxes**, which also have dens close to the main road before and after the access road to Wolfsnes.

Lion pride at Springbokfontein waterhole

Waterholes in the Eastern Section

Waterholes are placed in alphabetical order.

Andoni ★★★★

Borehole; two artesian aquifers

Surrounded by extensive plains

The origin of the name Andoni is obscure but people suggest the word is derived from Oshindonga and refers to the **extensive flat plain** characteristic of the area. Another interpretation is that it stems from Anton, a colonial family in Angola whose name was difficult to pronounce for the Ovambo-speaking people, hence naming the family Andoni.

In 1923, a geologist drilled a borehole looking for minerals but it needed to be more viable. However, later, they located **two aquifers**: the upper was fresh water and the lower was filled with salty water. Management attempted to close the waterhole when Andoni became an anthrax-endemic area. Owing to the corrosive content of the water and its pressure, the plug in the borehole casing ruptured, and this is how Andoni unintentionally continued to supply water to a large **saline depression**.

It is an incredibly **scenic place**, characterised by wide open spaces of vast grasslands of **Andoniveld**, reminiscent of the plains of the Serengeti. These plains attract a variety of **plains game**, as well as enormous herds of Burchell's zebra and wildebeest. These extensive plains are grazed chiefly in the late dry season, though, when forage is scarce elsewhere.

Andoni is also one of the best places in the park to see **warthog**. Various **wetland bird species** come to the area, and it is the best place to see endangered **blue cranes**, the national bird of South Africa, of which Etosha hosts a small breeding population.

Aerial view of King Nehale gate and Andoni plains

Blue cranes in flight over Andoni plains

African elephant bull

Aroe ★★

💧 Artesian spring; supplemented by solar power

⚑ Seasonal watercourse; productive after rains

Also known as **Aru**, the name refers to the **worm-cure albizias** that occur in the vicinity, especially near the start and left side of the access road. Looking at the vegetation zone map, Aroe borders the vegetation zone called **Andoniveld** and the extensive **northeastern sandveld.** Trumpet thorn thickets are widespread, as are cork bush and wild sage. The short, relatively narrow, two-kilometre access road to the waterhole has one or two deep depressions requiring slow and attentive driving. Careful navigation is advised in the rainy season when the depressions hold water but are completely manageable by sedan cars. A natural artesian spring is supplemented by a **borehole** driven by a **solar pump**. It erupts next to the **Omuramba Omuthiya**, a seasonal watercourse named after the camelthorn trees growing along the banks. The spring became dormant but the solar pump still supplies water. Aroe is a productive waterhole in the rainy season. It is situated on a long, large, dry watercourse, forming a natural depression lined by prickly brack grass and trumpet thorn, which carries water during prolific rain. Kudu frequents the area, and elephants favour this spring, especially in the rainy season when water is scarce in the sandy area further north, as well as lion and black rhino. It is worthwhile to spend an hour here early or mid-morning and again towards late afternoon, with good chances of surprise sightings.

Batia ★★★

💧 Artesian spring

⚑ Desert sedge; elephant; predators

A small **artesian spring** seeping south of Springbokfontein ran dry at the end of Etosha's long, dry period starting in 1981. The area still holds a lot of water during periods of good rainfall. It derives its name from **Bernabè de la Bat**, a former biologist and later warden of Etosha who became the first director of Nature Conservation in SWA. Limestone and large stands of desert sedge grass dominate the area to the west**. Eastern karst woodlands** border Batia to the east.

Predators like lion and leopard use thickets to lie in wait for passing prey, especially springbok, which are plentiful in the area. The vast, extensive open plains are ideal for sighting cheetah chases as this is also the preferred habitat of springbok, their favourite prey.

Red hartebeest frequent the area and are found along the Okerfontein loop. However, most game prefer to drink at the nearby Springbokfontein waterhole.

Small seepages occur on the left side of the access road leading back to the main road from Batia. Elephants, mostly the solitary old bulls, love to drink the water from these seepages and then dust themselves with the white, powdery clay of the area. Secretarybirds strut their stuff, and lappet-faced vultures sometimes nest in the canopies of the larger trees further away at the edges of the plains. Blacksmith lapwings, three-banded plovers and red-billed teals are often seen at the roadside, when rainwater runs off the sides of the road, forming veritable small lakes stretching alongside the road.

Etosha agama

Female cheetah in pursuit of black-backed jackal

Chudop ★★★★★

Artesian spring

Scenic; calcrete rubble/rocks; reed island

One of Etosha's most scenic and active waterholes is surrounded by open plains littered with calcrete rubble and rocks, making it ideal for game viewing. Chudop is an **artesian spring** sunken in a calcrete basin with a thick overlay of black mud and a clump of dense, common reed in the middle. It is a San name meaning '**black mud**'. When the water level drops, the muddy substratum may trap animals, which drown or suffocate, unable to free themselves.

You will see a constant stream of animals throughout the day, including spotted hyena, elephant, giraffe, zebra, kudu, warthog, black-faced impala, cheetah, black-backed jackal, the shy and elusive eland and black rhino. Chudop is so close to Namutoni that it is advisable to head out first thing in the morning and spend a few hours here, as it's usually a **hive of activity from early on**, with good light as a bonus.

Spotted hyena tend to stop by for a drink early in the morning and often use the waterhole as their private bathtub. A few years ago, visitors saw a couple of hyenas swimming to the middle of the waterhole, diving down bottoms up, retrieving chunks of meat, and swimming back to the edge. The hyenas probably cached the carcass there themselves.

On another occasion, a black-backed jackal kept teasing a cheetah at first light by approaching and backtracking repeatedly. The cheetah subsequently chased the jackal around the waterhole a few times. Watching the expressions on their faces, you could have believed that both were having fun.

Lions often lie around the waterhole early in the morning, chewing on the carcass of an unfortunate zebra or giraffe they caught during the night, later retiring to the shade of some trees east and west of the waterhole. Many **helmeted guineafowl** mills are near the waterhole, and it is a comical sight when they approach a single file at top speed, chattering non-stop. **Kori-bustards**, **blacksmith lapwings**, **crowned lapwings**, and **Namaqua doves** favour this waterhole. **Shaft-tailed** and **long-tailed paradise whydahs** flitting over the dense bed of reeds are a regular sighting.

Chudop is one of the best places to see the **endemic Etosha agama**, usually perched on small calcrete rocks lining the parking area's fringes.

The light is optimal for photography in the late afternoon, and it pays to head to Chudop in time if you plan to secure the best spot. Again, the proximity to camp is ideal, utilising the golden glow of the setting sun to maximum effect. **Elephant** often come to drink in the afternoon, and usually, black rhino approach the waterhole just before sunset. Good sightings of **African wild cat** and gregarious, chattering packs of **banded mongoose** are regularly seen in the area as they scuttle across the road or use the elevated mounds of the termite hills to scout the area.

Helmeted-guinea fowl and Angolan giraffe at Chudop waterhole

Kori bustard at Chudop waterhole

Fischer's Pan ★★★★★

Omuramba Ovambo River, Omuramba Omuthyia, seasonal

Masses of wetland birds

Fischer's Pan is the extensive delta of the **Omuramba Ovambo**, a river that originates about five kilometres from Tsintsabis and flows only when there is heavy rainfall. Named after Lieutenant Adolf Fischer, this **finger-like eastward protrusion** of Etosha Pan covers an area of about 56 km^2.

Fischer's Pan receives water almost yearly but the amount received and the duration of wetland conditions varies. The pan is connected to the main Etosha Pan, and water may flow in either direction via a small channel that links them. After prolific rainfall, various wetlands and other migratory species descend on the pan. **Great white pelicans** sometimes visit, and **storks**, **egrets** and **herons**, **pied avocets** and **black-winged stilts** stalk the shimmering expanse of water. **Cape-** and **red-billed teals**, **knob-billed ducks**, **Cape shovelers** and **Egyptian geese** often glide across it. Travelling the main road from Namutoni to Tsumcor, the causeway next to Fischer's Pan is one of the best places to see both **lesser-** and **greater flamingos** at close range.

The early morning light is excellent for sunrise and silhouette photography, and the late afternoon glow is spectacular for photographing birds, especially flamingos, from the causeway. Hues of pastel colours ranging from pinks to blues create a magical, dreamlike atmosphere; here, you can take some spectacular and wonderfully moody images.

Once again, early morning and late afternoon is the best time to explore the approximately 33 km Fischer's Pan loop. Encompassing the pan and accessible from two sides, the loop is a scenically diverse and picturesque drive that often yields excellent surprises.

Aerial view of Fischer's Pan carrying water

Fischer's Pan with flamingo at dusk

Klein Okevi and Groot Okevi ★★★★

A pair of artesian springs in calcrete depressions

Red bushwillow; mustard tree in parking lot

Situated west of Namutoni, the Okevis are a **pair of artesian springs** set approximately 1.5 km apart in calcrete depressions. Okevi derives from Oshindonga and means '**from under the ground or rocks**', referring to the perennial springs. 'Klein' means small, and 'groot' means large.

Sandveld dominates the area, and the typical vegetation includes **purple-pod cluster-leaf**, **lavender croton** – a pretty shrub with silver-green leaves – and the false umbrella thorn. **Foxtail buffalo** and **African lovegrass** grow on the plains near the two waterholes.

Klein Okevi is near the road, and lion, hyena, elephant, black rhino, impala and giraffe visit regularly.

Elephants tend to approach the waterhole by meandering across the parking lot, extremely close to the cars, so be prepared for some heart-stopping moments if you focus on the waterhole in front of you and are unaware of their silent approach from behind.

If you closely watch the water's surface, you can often see water **terrapins** hunting **Cape turtledoves** and other small birds by catching them unaware and pulling them under the water when they drink. There is also a realistic chance that you will see **caracal** and **African wildcat** hunting birds at the water's edge.

Exiting Klein Okevi and travelling towards Tsumcor, the turn-off to Groot Okevi is a mere kilometre away to the left of the main road. The greyish silver trumpet thorn shrubs line the 1.5 km access road to the waterhole. The flowers are striking white, sometimes fringed with pink, and they flower soon after the rain until the end of summer. Visibility is limited in places, and slow driving is advised, as elephants can be nearby.

The parking lot overlooks the Groot Okevi waterhole, which is **in a depression** in a woodland setting. Long lines of well-worn animal paths lead towards the waterhole. Large **red bushwillows** are attractive, and a **mustard tree**, an evergreen shrub, can be seen in the middle of the parking lot.

In the rainy season, the setting is green and lush, with carpets of the **aambeibossie**, an herbaceous plant with white flowers, covering large areas.

It is worth spending at least an hour or two at this scenic and isolated spot, as there is a good chance of a **surprise sighting** of a lion or elephant approaching from any direction. It is also an ideal leopard habitat.

Kudu usually approaches carefully, constantly wary of hidden dangers.

The helmeted-guineafowl and red-billed spurfowl frequent this waterhole; their alarm calls often herald an approaching predator and it is an excellent place to observe red-headed finches, fork-tailed drongos and green-winged pytilia, lilac-breasted- and purple rollers. Swallow-tailed and European bee-eaters are also visitors in the wet season. The area around the waterhole is covered with dense vegetation, interspersed with calcrete rock, offering ideal hiding places for predators.

Lioness and black-faced impala at Groot Okevi waterhole

Leopard, African elephants and Angolan giraffe at Kalkheuwel waterhole

Kalkheuwel ★★★★

Artesian spring; borehole; solar power

White calcrete landscape; excellent leopard sightings

Directly translated from Afrikaans, the name means '**limestone hill**', an apt description for this **artesian spring** aided by a **borehole** driven by **solar power**. It is set in a predominantly **white calcrete landscape**, characteristic of Etosha. Large, irregular, carbonate boulders, which are weathered remnants of calcrete, dominate the landscape.

The vegetation zone with mopane, tamboti, leadwood and purple-pod cluster-leaf trees is classified as **purple-pod cluster-leaf/tamboti bushveld**. Black-faced impala, elephant, zebra, giraffe and kudu are regular visitors. The animals drink from a square concrete basin, and in times of good rainfall, the area around the basin floods, often as far as the right side of the parking lot, creating a large surface of water.

The dense woodland surrounding Kalkheuwel and large carbonate rocks offer ideal predator concealment opportunities. Kalkheuwel can guarantee **excellent leopard sightings**, with lion often found as well. Plenty of helmeted guineafowl roam the waterhole. Bateleurs favour this area, as do **Meyer's parrots**, red-billed spurfowl, black-chested snake eagles and yellow-billed hornbills.

Unfortunately, the four-kilometre access road to Kalkheuwel is not in good shape most of the time owing to complex, irregularly sized calcrete boulders and fine calcareous soil, which makes it difficult to maintain. Careful and slow navigation is required, with **potholes and hard corrugation** encountered at intervals, but this should not be a deterrent; it is well worth a visit.

Attempted hunt of lioness and Burchell's zebra

The one that got away

Often, genuinely spectacular wildlife interactions happen at waterholes within split seconds, and this is what my husband and I experienced pretty recently.

Arriving at Kalkheuwel first thing in the morning, we were the only car in the parking area. We saw the carcass of a zebra foal lying almost at the edge of the parking lot, with no visible injuries.

Speculating we had disturbed a leopard without noticing any drag marks, we decided to wait for further developments. Not even five minutes later, we heard thundering hooves from the left, and a couple of zebra burst from the mopane bushes to the left of our parked car. I heard my husband shout: "Lion!" Thrown off-guard, all I could see initially were zebra and clouds of dust right in front of our car. Then, finally, a lioness, which was almost on top of a zebra, slowly sliding sideways, unable to hold on before disappearing under the belly of the zebra, one outstretched foreleg clawing on before making contact with the hard limestone surface, the zebra almost on top of her. The lioness was up in a flash but lost the game. The action happened in split seconds, the shutter of my husband's camera clicking merrily, perfectly capturing the entire scene. All I had to show was dust and one blurred image of parts of the lioness – a wildlife photographer's nightmare!

Nevertheless, an unexpected and surreal experience like this creates an adrenaline rush and remains etched in your memory forever.

We sat there for a while, still completely shell-shocked and reliving the experience, when I looked up straight at another lioness sitting in the grass in front of the concrete basin.

She crouched down immediately as a wildebeest appeared from the right. I was camera-ready this time, when the lioness charged the wildebeest, which made an abrupt right turn and headed back in the direction from which it came.

Again, the lioness clawed the rump off the fleeing wildebeest before losing her grip and tumbling down into the grass with the wildebeest gone.

Almost like magic, 10 lions popped up everywhere. They had been so well camouflaged in the grass and vegetation at the fringes of the waterhole, we had never noticed them. The pride and exhausted lioness from two attempted hunts flopped down by the waterhole, as did we in our seats – exhausted and completely overwhelmed by all the action from the morning.

The moral is be vigilant and prepared for the unexpected.

King Nehale Fountain ★★★

(Namutoni camp waterhole)

- Artesian fountain
- Thatched open-air viewing area

This **perennial and copious floodlit waterhole** was named **King Nehale Fountain** during a festive ceremony on 28 January 1996, commemorating the 92nd anniversary of the last battle at Namutoni. The name celebrates the chief of 500 Ndonga warriors who attacked the German fort that day.

The waterhole is situated on the **western side of the camp**, overlooked by a **thatched, open-air viewing area**. Several rows of banked seating are available but visibility is limited because the viewing area's elevation is shallow. A **dense reed bed** to the left also obscures the view, especially of smaller subjects. Owing to the proximity of other waterholes around Namutoni, there is **no great variety or abundance of wildlife** at the waterhole. However, a thrilling sight is that of elephants that rustle around the reed bed, pulling up the roots of the reed and eating them. Springbok, wildebeest, giraffe and zebra usually frequent the waterhole, spotted hyenas often pass by, and warthogs regularly wallow in the mud at the waterhole's edge.

The waterhole holds a great **attraction for bird lovers** as many bird species are found here throughout the year and are not found elsewhere in the dry periods, for instance, the red-knobbed coot and common moorhen. Others include sandpipers, three-banded plovers, Caspian plovers and greater painted-snipes. The reeds attract the red bishops, which nest here, and the African jacana and great snipes that feel safe in the protection of the reeds. Western cattle egrets, southern masked-weavers, red-billed queleas, red-eyed bulbuls, African reed warblers and lesser swamp warblers also occur here.

It is a peaceful and tranquil spot, perfect for photography in the afternoon light and relaxing with your favourite sundowner beverage in hand.

Burchell's zebra approaching King Nehale waterhole

Aerial view of Klein Namutoni waterhole

Klein Namutoni ★★★★

- Perennial, copious, artesian fountain
- Close to Namutoni camp

This perennial and copious artesian fountain is located just 2.2 km from Namutoni Camp and is ideal for game viewing. It attracts a variety of wildlife, including birds.

The name derives from the Hei//om language '**=Khari-!Namob**', with '**=Khari**' meaning small and '**!Namob**' describes an attractive or **pleasant place**. Approaching the waterhole, the sight greets you of giraffe elegantly walking towards it, their tall silhouettes beautifully offset against the spectacular colour of the sky at dusk or dawn.

Elephant usually come to drink in the evening, while **spotted hyena** use the large body of water as their giant bathtub. Marabou storks and vultures favour this waterhole, and lions often use the area as their hunting ground. Visitors have unhampered views of the open area surrounding the waterhole, with the extensive **purple-pod cluster-leaf/ tamboti woodland** and **bushveld** fringing the backdrop. The greatest asset is the proximity to camp, making it ideal for sunrise and sunset photography and maximising the time to utilise the excellent light before returning to camp in under five minutes.

As you exit the parking lot and take a left turn towards **Dik-Dik Drive**, look for the **spotted hyena den** in proximity on the right side of the road. The den is quite active and the jet-black, droll hyena pups are frequently frolicking outside the den under the close supervision of at least one or two adults.

The white, dusty calcrete road is usually bustling with a continuous stream of thirsty wildlife trekking to the waterhole. Drive slowly and keep an eye under the shrubs lining the roadside for the diminutive **dik-dik** and **leopard**. Smelly shepherd's bush, mopane, red bushwillow, purple-pod cluster-leaf and leadwood are some of the dominant trees and shrubs next to the roadside, featuring prominently throughout the Dik-Dik Drive.

Koinachas ★★★

Artesian spring

Unexpected sightings; plains game

Situated about one kilometre from Namutoni Camp in a westerly direction lies the slightly elevated **Koinachas waterhole**, a picturesque artesian spring set in a calcrete basin. You can see this is an artesian spring as the **water level is higher than the surrounding plains**. The middle of the waterhole is dominated by a dense thicket of **bulrushes**, obscuring most visibility to the back of the waterhole. The mustard bush occurs here, and in times of the Hai//om, beautiful old leadwood trees used to encircle the waterhole but have since been destroyed by elephant. You can expect good sightings of leopard, cheetah, lion, zebra, springbok, black-faced impala and spotted hyena. Again, the proximity to camp and easy access from the main road makes it ideal for checking in often, any time of the day. Two surprise leopard sightings occurred recently; one just before lunchtime with a leopard crossing the road from the waterhole in front of our vehicle and the second was one day around mid-noon when a female leisurely strolled down the short access road from the waterhole, again crossing the road in front of the vehicle. Another memorable experience was a cheetah kill right next to the road, opposite the access road to the waterhole. A single female cheetah took the opportunity to secure herself a meal from the significant number of springbok that usually graze near the waterhole.

Black-faced impala

Spotted hyena with black-backed jackal carcass

Ngobib ★★★★

🌢 Perennial artesian spring

⚑ Leadwood tree

The Ngobib waterhole is on a **17km circular drive**, which is exceptionally picturesque and affords good game viewing. The waterhole was named **!Nabob** by the Hai//om, meaning '**the water is less**', which is a very apt description as it is a **perennial artesian spring** that **dries up** in the hotter months of the year.

The small parking area is near the waterhole, with a magnificent single specimen of **leadwood tree** standing guard next to the waterhole and parking lot. The Herero's call it **omumborombonga**. Herero and Ovambo consider this an **ancestral tree** from which the first humans, cattle, sheep and wild animals originated. The bark is characteristic, deeply fissured lengthwise, splitting into rectangular pieces. The wood is hefty and hardy and produces excellent charcoal. Elephant, giraffe, kudu and other antelope feed on the leaves, while rhino feed on the branches.

The waterhole is in a **substantial depression**, entirely enclosed by a round basin of calcrete rock, and the water level is not visible from the outside. Therefore, it is a perfect ambush spot for predators, especially leopards. The game needs to be wary on its approach to the waterhole and prefer drinking at Kalkheuwel. However, you are still privy to good sightings of elephant, zebra and black-faced impala drinking at the waterhole, as well as abundant birdlife.

Giraffe and kudu are found on the surrounding plains, as are cheetah. The Hai//om also referred to this waterhole as the 'waterhole of snake', as **pythons** in particular preferred this spot, which is perfect for hiding in the water and ambushing prey like birds and small game in this manner. A **spotted hyena den** is situated near the road on the edge of the small parking area under the leadwood trees, providing great entertainment when it is active and pups are around. The road is in reasonably good condition, slightly corrugated in places, with a few minor potholes along the detour. In rainy conditions, these will fill with water and become muddy, and you should navigate with extra care in wet conditions.

Okerfontein ★★★★

- Contact spring
- Scenic; dense sedges

The Hai//om referred to this waterhole as **!Ammûb**, which means 'the green eye', as lush green **desert sedge** and **prickly brack grass** surround it. The strong **contact spring** is on a blunt peninsula at the edge of the main pan.

The word 'Okerfontein' can be directly translated from Afrikaans, meaning '**ochre fountain**', which refers to the sometimes yellowish-brown colour of the water. A possible cause for the colouration might be micro organisms or dissolved solids flourishing under saline conditions.

Elephants love this waterhole – usually old, solitary bulls or small bachelor herds – but I have observed breeding herds,

African elephants approaching Okerfontein waterhole

too. Lions pass through regularly, as do cheetah, which favour the plains surrounding Okerfontein. The dense sedges provide ideal concealment opportunities for leopards ambushing prey. **Forked geigeria** is a Namibian endemic that adds a dash of colour with its bright yellow flowers. Interspersed with the white flowers of the **ambeibossie** and the striking **dark-eyed hibiscus** in springtime are the pinkish flowers of the ***Cyathula lanceolata*** (no common name).

Dense **bitter karee** shrubs occur in the vicinity and rhino particularly favour the branches of this bush.

If you gaze at the horizon of the main pan, you can see shimmering pink mounds of flamingos in the distance, breeding in their thousands on the pan, especially when the rain has been prolific and it holds water. It is a spectacle to behold.

Springbokfontein ★★★★

Contact spring

White/olive-green sediments

A strong freshwater spring **drainage line** extends along the edge of the pan and runs through Etosha on the **other side of the main road**.

This Afrikaans name can be directly translated into '**springbok fountain**' owing to the many springbok that come here to drink.

This contact spring has sources on either side of the main road, i.e. north and south, the signpost pointing to the southern spring. The Hai//om word **/Arixas** or **!Arighas** can be interpreted widely, with some referring to it as a song, which is sung during a traditional gathering in the spring for young girls approaching puberty. In contrast, others insist it describes the dry, cracked, wrinkled appearance of the clay of the pan. Others again refer to the dry skin of their hands and feet cracking during the approaching cold winter months at this low-lying spring. A Hai/om clan resided in the wooden area south of the spring.

Desert sedge grows abundantly on both sides of the road and the access road leading to Batia, offering predators good concealment opportunities.

Elephant and **rhino** frequently visit the spring and love to cover themselves with the white, muddy clay, lending them the distinct white countenance so characteristic of Etosha. There is also a patch of olive-green clay sediment next to the spring, and one memorable sighting was that of a huge elephant bull flinging the green clay all over himself.

Expect predators like lion, leopard and spotted hyena.

After the rainy season, when adjacent plains and parts of the pan are covered in palatable grasses, large herds of wildebeest, zebra and springbok congregate, a proverbial feast for the eyes.

Lilac-breasted roller

Aerial view of lion pride at Springbokfontein waterhole

Helmeted guinea fowl vocalising the presence of a female leopard

Angolan giraffe

Stinkwater ★★★

- Seasonal mudhole seeps
- Great viewing /photographic opportunities

Stinkwater is a seasonal water source situated along the eastern edge of the pan, along a picturesque detour, affording some beautiful views of the pan for long stretches of road. The Afrikaans name can be translated into English as '**stinking water**' because of its obnoxious smell and **high sulphur content**. This spring is active only during the rainy season and is a **series of mudhole seeps**. Its beautiful location along the pan offers excellent game viewing and photographic opportunities.

Elephant and warthog often take mud baths. **Oryx** usually lie out on the pan and enjoy grazing on the surrounding grassland. **Kori bustards and black-backed jackals** favour the area. Journeys of **giraffe** are an impressive sight when they gracefully walk along the edge of the pan. The dense **shrub thickets** lining parts of the road away from the pan are often impenetrable and limit your sight, but the glorious, open views over the vast expanse more than make up for it.

Tsumcor ★★★★

💧 Borehole; solar power

⚑ Sightings of the shy eland; white bauhinia

The name is a compilation of the Tsumeb Corporation in honour of the mining company's donation of a windmill for the **borehole**. The sand instantly absorbs rainwater in this extensive sandveld area. Therefore, a borehole was drilled and, as a result, no surface water remains for the animals to drink. Tsumcor is **situated on top of an age-old Kalahari dune**, surrounded by mixed tree and shrub savanna, which the elephants have considerably thinned out and opened while foraging. The borehole failed in 1994, probably because of the relentless drought and was temporarily closed, but a new one, driven by a solar pump, is now in use.

There is a shallow concrete basin from which wildlife drinks. Tsumcor is among the best places to see the extremely shy and skittish **eland** in the park. The eland produces loud knee-clicks, presumably through vibrations of tendons, and demonstrates remarkable intelligence. The clicking is a sign of social signalling between males, designed to intimidate rivals and avoid physical conflict unless necessary – an excellent strategy to prevent fighting and killing each other.

Oryx, kudu and **warthog** also frequent this waterhole. Look for a **leopard** but **lion** regularly patrol their territory. The light is tricky as it is harsh and best in the afternoon. The waterhole could be more scenic, especially for photography, but wildlife is abundant, varied and action-packed.

You may see lilac-breasted rollers, yellow- and red-billed hornbills, emerald-spotted wood doves, crested francolins, and blacksmith- and crowned lapwings.

White bauhinias are rare in Etosha but occur near Tsumcor, with **purple-pod cluster-leaf** especially conspicuous; some beautiful old specimens reach a height of up to eight metres. Find the **silver cluster-leaf** and the two **croton species**, the lavender croton and the balsam bush.

Aerial view of Tsumcor waterhole with eland

Twee Palms ★★★★

Contact spring

Scenic

Twee Palms is the Afrikaans name for '**Two Palms**', a contact spring situated on the southeastern fringe of Fischer's Pan, with the iconic landmark of two fan palms (makalani) standing at the waterhole's edge. Sadly, we may have to think of a new name for this waterhole. The first palm toppled over on 14 May 2019, with the second palm following suit as recently as 12 June 2022. The speculative reason that elephants were responsible for the demise of the palms seems the most likely, especially given the following anecdote:

One of the authors of the booklet *Etosha National Park Centenary Edition – Guidebook to the Waterholes and Animals* described witnessing a large elephant bull lean its head against the trunk of one of the palms and rocking back and forth. The giant pachyderm fortunately tired of the game and left, leaving the waterhole's name intact, until recently.

Before the demise of the palms, this was a picturesque

Great white pelican, marabou stork and grey heron at Twee Palms waterhole

waterhole and surrounding scenery, especially in the rainy season when the adjacent Fischer's Pan also held water. The presence of the two palm trees was a significant factor that added to its charm and unique character. The landscape certainly looks bereft without them. A cluster of 13 fan or makalani palms still stands guard in the vicinity of the waterhole, while dense thickets of the sickle-bush, with their conspicuous and striking pink/yellow flowers, occur in the area.

It is one of the best areas in the park to observe **cheetah**, often with their offspring, perched on one of the many termite hills dotting the landscape or stalking springbok. It is also a haven for **bird lovers**, as many species of wetland birds can be observed here, especially in the rainy season. You may see the rare blue crane here and have the good fortune to spot a pair with chicks.

The light is suitable for landscape photography or silhouette shots in the morning or late afternoon. Underexposing is a good idea if there is an opportunity for rim-lit shots.

ADDITIONAL INFORMATION

Male leopard on patrol with blue wildebeest and Burchell's zebra

A brief historical overview of the Etosha National Park

Etosha has a chequered and turbulent history, shaped by many ethnic groups and events.

The **Ovambo-speaking people** first gave Etosha its name, referring to it as '**Etotha**', which means bare place, or '**great white place**'.

The earliest humans to settle in Etosha were the **Hai//om Bushmen**, a nomadic tribe that settled around waterholes and followed the game, true to their **hunter-gatherer lifestyle**. They left their mark on Etosha as a place of rich cultural history. They referred to Etosha as '**Khubus**' because of the blisters that appear on the surface of the pan as it dries up, or '**Khushu**', meaning a bare, white place with lots of dust.

The **Ovambo people** were also active in Etosha, living off the land as **farmers**, **fishermen**, **hunters**, **artisans**, **salt-gatherers** and **traders** around the Namutoni area. The Hai//om recognised the authority of the **Ovambo king** at Ondonga, while the Herero tribe disputed his authority.

1851: The first Europeans to have recorded the existence of Etosha were the explorers **Sir Francis Galton** and **Charles Andersson** when they reached what is now known as Namutoni on 29 May 1851. Galton Gate, through which you can access the western part of Etosha, was named in honour of Galton; Andersson Gate, the gateway to Okaukuejo, was named after Andersson. Other explorers, hunters and traders soon followed in the footsteps of Galton and Andersson, among them the missionary **Hugo Hahn** and the artist/hunter-trader ornithologist **Axel Eriksson**.

1879: The **Thirstland (Dorsland) trekkers**. Boer settlers from South Africa explored various destinations to eventually settle and also left their mark in Etosha. They settled around Namutoni and Rietfontein in 1879 and again in 1885, when a few returned from Angola.

1881: People drove the last elephant herd into a marsh near Namutoni in 1881 and wiped them out.

1885: In 1885, businessman **William Worthington Jordan** from the Cape **bought** an extensive tract of **land** from Ovambo Chief Kambonde, which included strategic fountains such as Okaukuejo, Okakahana, Ombika, Namutoni, and Fischer's Pan, an area of almost 2 500 km^2, to **help the trekkers farm**. Herero Chief Maharero tried to nullify the contract and lay claim to the land. This claim, as well as the onset of **malaria** and the outbreak of **rinderpest**, eventually forced the farmers to abandon the farms and move away.

1886: White rhino had **disappeared**.

1892: The implementation of **hunting regulations** in 1892 was the first official step in an attempt to protect the game in Etosha.

1896–1879: Meanwhile, the advent of modern-day **firearms** and **indiscriminate hunting** soon became a severe threat to the game in Etosha. The outbreak of the **rinderpest** in 1896–1897 was another severe blow to the game. The authorities established control posts at Namutoni, Okaukuejo and Rietfontein, and the German Reich gave orders to shoot all migrating game to curb the spread of rinderpest.

1900: People **exterminated lions** in the Namutoni area.

1901: German colonial forces built **two forts**: an unfired clay brick structure at Namutoni and another one of limestone in 1901.

1904: During an uprising against the German colonial forces by the Ovaherero in 1904, the Herero requested military support from Chief Kambonde and Chief Nehale lyaMpingana. The Ovambo attacked and destroyed Fort Namutoni. The Germans rebuilt it the following year, and it became a **police station**.

1906: Lt. Adolf Fischer became the **first game warden** of the not-yet-proclaimed Etosha in 1906. In 1881, he reported the demise of the last herd of elephants in a marsh near Namutoni. By 1886, the white rhino had disappeared, with the black rhino finding refuge only in the most inaccessible areas. Fischer also reported the extermination of lions in the Namutoni area.

1907: On **22 March 1907**, the Governor of German South West Africa, **Dr F von Lindequist**, unimaginatively proclaimed Etosha as Game Reserve No. 2. Hence, the entrance gate close to Namutoni is called Von Lindequist Gate. The total area – encompassing a vast expanse of approximately 93 240 km^2 from the Kunene and Hoarusib river mouths on the Skeleton Coast eastwards to Namutoni – made it the **largest wildlife reserve in the world**.

1912: People heard the first lion roar again.

1947: The Afrikaans author **AA Pienaar (Sangiro)** was appointed game warden to publish a book on the territory's wildlife. The book never came to fruition. However, he was instrumental in advocating the necessity of protecting Etosha and for **stricter application** of the **game laws**.

1953: Bernabé de la Bat was appointed chief game warden at Okaukuejo 1953. He served 10 years in Etosha before being transferred to Windhoek as the first Nature Conservation and Tourism Division director. He was instrumental in **creating a rich legacy of game parks, nature reserves and rest camps**, which have provided the basis for the phenomenal growth of Namibia's tourism industry, mainly thanks to his remarkable vision, courage and foresight.

1957: The reconstructed Fort Namutoni opened its gates to tourists.

1958: The officials shifted the park's boundaries, and its size shrank to about 55 000 km^2. Game Reserve No. 2 became the **Etosha Game Park**.

1961: Following an **outbreak of foot-and-mouth disease,** a veterinary cordon fence, also known as the **Red Line**, was erected along Etosha's eastern and southern borders.

King Nehale warriors memorial

1965: The Director of Nature Conservation and Tourism established a **permanent research section** in Etosha. H Ebedes was the first wildlife veterinarian, and KL Tinely and E Joubert were the ecologists. The same year, a **ranger station** replaced the existing veterinary control post at Otjovasandu, western Etosha and Kaross. The authorities bought three other adjoining privately owned farms in the west to form a **rare animal enclosure** adjacent to the park. Adding the government-owned farm Khoabendes as a quarantine camp completed this phase of Etosha's development.

1967: An Act of Parliament in South Africa awarded the park national park status and made it the **Etosha National Park.** Also, in 1967, the park commissioned the **Halali Rest Camp** and greatly enlarged **the Okaukuejo Rest Camp**, which opened in 1955.

1970: Following the recommendation of the Odendaal Commission, the park boundaries were changed once again. The **park area was drastically reduced**, with total disregard for ecological boundaries, to cater to the land needs of Namibia's indigenous population. The size decreased by 72% to its **present size of 22 270 km²**.

1971: The frustration and bitterness caused by this decision, despite well-documented scientific evidence in opposition to the plan by KL Tinley MSc, prompted the then director of Nature Conservation and Tourism, Bernabè de la Bat, to utter his famous remark: "After Odendaal, Etosha resembled a plucked fowl."

1973: The park officials **completely fenced** the entire park with 850 km of fencing, which proved inadequate for warthog, lion and elephant and, subsequently, the 'elephant-proof' cable strengthened 130 km of the fence, while electrified fencing strengthened other strategic sections. The fencing severely impacted the **natural migration routes of wildlife**, contributing to a drastic decline in numbers of the blue wildebeest by reportedly 90%, Burchell's zebra by 80%, as well as eland and oryx.

1974: The park established the **Etosha Ecological Institute** to conduct studies of game diseases like anthrax, the development of game-catching techniques, ecological surveys, grazing and the analysis of problem animals.

1980–1982: The **terrible drought** experienced in the park, especially in the western part, necessitated drastic measures, including the capture, sale and culling of 2 235 Hartmann's mountain zebra and the capture of 450 Burchell's zebra in western Etosha. The **culling of the elephants** at Olifantsrus is directly related to this event.

1982: A severe blow to conservation occurred when a **light aircraft crashed near Halali** during a game census, killing the pilot and five nature conservation officials. In their memory, the park officials built a small monument on the lawn outside Halali's tourist office and restaurant.

1988: The park established the **Anti-poaching Unit** (APU).

MODERN-DAY ETOSHA NATIONAL PARK

Today, despite being a fraction of its original size, Etosha is a vital ecosystem supporting various plant and animal species. It has some of the highest wildlife densities in the world for a semi-arid region. The highest concentration of game occurs in the eastern and southern fringes of the pan, with reported statistics of an average of more than 70 large mammals per square kilometre.

The west also holds large concentrations of game and wildlife can still migrate vast distances throughout the whole park, following seasonal migration routes. Today, active management strategies focus on infrastructure, such as fence lines, road and borehole maintenance, mitigating human-wildlife conflict, and reducing rhino poaching.

A 40 km buffer zone surrounds Etosha, comprising an area of 36 160 km² and is known as the **Greater Etosha Landscape** (GEL). The GEL buffer comprises communal land, communal conservancies, state-owned concessions, private freehold and resettlement farms, urban areas and private game reserves. Various tourist accommodations are part of the buffer.

Etosha National Park is one of Africa's most incredible national parks and Namibia's number one tourist destination. More than 300 000 visitors pass through the park gates annually.

Common occuring trees, shrubs, herbs and grasses

Makalani palm
(Hyphaene petersiana)

Strangler fig
(Ficus burkei)

Kaoko Ceraria
(Ceraria longipedunculata)

Smelly shepherd's tree
(Boscia foetida)

Camelthorn
(Vachellia erioloba)

Floodplain acacia
(Vachellia kirkii subsp. Kirkii)

Kalahari acacia
(Vachellia luederitzii var luederitzii)

Sickle-bush
(Dichrostachys cinerea)

Skew-leaved elephant root
(Entada rangei)

Mopane
(Colophospermum mopane)

Butterfly leaf
(Adenolobus garipensis)

Corkbush
(Mundulea sericea)

Kalahari apple-leaf
(Philenoptera nelsii)

Tall common corkwood
(Commiphora glandulosa)

Lavender feverberry
(Croton gratissimus var. gratissimus)

Tamboti
(Spirostachys Africana)

Marula
(Sclerorcarya birrea)

Buffalo-thorn
(Ziziphus mucronata)

Velvet raisin
(Grewia flava)

Small-leaved crossberry
(Grewia tenax)

Mallow raisin
(Grewia villosa)

Red bush-willow
(Combretum apiculatum subsp apiculatum)

Russet bushwillow
(Combretum hereroense)

Leadwood
(Combretum imberbe)

Purple-pod cluster-leaf
(Terminalia prunioides)

Bushman's poison/Kaoko impala-lily
(Adenium boehmianum)

Herero sesame bush
(Sesamothamnus guerichii)

Namibian Resin-tree
(Ozoroa crassinervia)

Cup-and-saucer plant
(Albuca pulchra)

Pan ganna
(Caroxylon etoshense)

Cerise stars
(Commicarpus pentandrus)

Cape saltbush
(Atriplex muelleri)

Barleria
(Barleria prionitis)

Ecbolium clarkei

Forked geigeria
(Geigeria odontoptera)

Three-leaved cotton
(Gossypium triphyllum)

Grey-leaf heliotrope
(Euploca ovalifolia)

Ink-bush
(Suaeda articulata)

Arid devil's thorn
(Tribulus zeyheri)

Pogonospermum cleomoides

Mountain thistle
(Blepharis obmitrata)

Osonanga lily
(Pseudogaltonia clavata)

Petal-bush
(Petalidium englerianum)

Saltbush
(Caroxylon etoshense)

Stekelbossie
(Cyathula lanceolata)

Stink-bush, wild sage
(Pechuel-loeschea leubnitziae)

Horse-bush
(Leucas pechuelii)

Wild sesame, thunderbolt flower
(Sesamum triphyllum)

Wool-bush
(Leucosphaera bainesii)

Yellow cleome, yellow mouse-whiskers
(Cleome augustifolia subsp. Diandra)

Poison apple
(Solanum campylacanthum)

Gazania group
(Roessleria gazaninoides)

Spider-wisp
(Cleome gynandra)

Cephalocroton mollis

Aptosium decumbens

Momordica humilis

Trumpet thorn
(Catophractes alexandri)

Vlei lily
(Nerina laticoma)

Porcupine root
(Talinum caffrum)

Hibiscus
(Hibiscus caesius)

Gemsbokboontjie
(Neorautanenia mitis)

Foxtail buffalo grass
(Cenchrus ciliaris)

Lüderitz grass
(Monelytrum luederitzianum)

Natal red top
(Melinis repens)

Salt drop-seed
(Sporobolus spicatus)

Saw-tooth love grass
(Eragrostis superba)

Silky Bushman grass
(Stipagrostis uniplumis)

Silver-wool grass
(Anthephora argentea)

Spear grass
(Heteropogon contortus)

Turf grass
(Ischaemum afrum)

Blue-stem, Vleivingergras
(Dichanthium annulatum var. papillosum)

Feather-top chloris
(Chloris virgata)

Invertebrata and herpetofauna

It is human nature to focus more on charismatic mammal species such as lion, leopard, rhino and elephant, which trigger strong emotional responses. These flagship species are successful conservation drivers, while reptiles and amphibians seem to garner less attention. They evoke feelings of distaste, fear or plain disinterest and receive virtually little or no attention. However, they are an integral part of our biological diversity and are crucial in any ecosystem, such as in a national park like Etosha.

Invertebrates

Easily overlooked and often inconspicuous, all national parks – not only Etosha – host a large population of invertebrates, including scorpions, butterflies, moths, numerous beetle and spider species, locusts and grasshoppers.

Boulton's Namib day gecko

Amphibians

Etosha hosts approximately 16 species of frogs, the most conspicuous of which is the **Giant African bullfrog** *(Pyxicephalus adspersus)*. It surfaces only during the rainy season, though, when it breeds. Outside the rainy season, these frogs bury themselves underground in dry mud, waiting for rain to fall. During their brief period above ground, they must consume enough food to sustain them through hibernation. They are cannibalistic, have a great appetite and swallow any animal that fits into their large mouth, including small birds, other invertebrates, small rodents and other amphibians.

Other frog species only found above ground during the rainy season are:

- The **bushveld rain frog** *(Breviceps adspersus)*
- Ornate **frog** *(Hildebrandtia ornata)*
- Spotted **rubber frog** *(Phrynomantis affinis)*

Western Etosha hosts one endemic, namely **Hoesch's pygmy toad** *(Poyntonophrynus hoeschi)* and a near-endemic, the **marbled rubber frog** *(Phrynomantis annectens)*.

Reptiles

Of Namibia's approximately 261 reptile species, 112 occur in Etosha alone. Of these, approximately 52 snake species occur in the park.

VENOMOUS SNAKES

Venomous snakes, such as the **black mamba** *(Dendroaspis polylepis)*, **Anchieta's cobra** *(Naja anchietae)*, **western-barred spitting corbra** *(Naja nigricincta)*, and **puff adder** *(Bitis arietans)*, are conspicuous owing to their size and mannerisms. They are often spotted near waterholes or crossing the road.

WHIP- AND SAND SNAKES

Usually, you see these snakes as thin, elongated flashes that race across the roads at top speed. Nine species occur in Namibia, all in the park, with the yellow-bellied sand snake probably the most conspicuous.

PYTHONS

The southern African python *(Python natalensis)* can reach a length of 5.5 m and prefers the vicinity of waterholes, often hiding in dense reeds and sometimes even in the water, lying

Horned adder

Namib rock agama

in wait for prey. The near-endemic, beautifully patterned Anchieta's dwarf python *(Python anchietae)* is found more on the western side of the park, preferring the granite habitat.

OTHER NEAR-ENDEMIC SNAKES

Two more near-endemics found in the granites are the **western keeled snake** *(Pythonodipsas carinata)* and the **viperine rock snake** *(Hemirhagerrhis viperina)*, which occurs in the dolomites and Otavi highlands extending to southeastern Etosha.

TORTOISES, TURTLES AND TERRAPINS

Two tortoise species can occur in the park, the most common being the **leopard tortoise** *(Geochelone pardalis)* and the **Kalahari tent tortoise** *(Psammobates oculiferus)*. The latter is relatively rare and occurs more in sandveld habitats like Kaross and Mushara, which favour the red sand with its scattered growth of perennial grasses and shrubs.

The African helmeted turtle, also known as the marsh terrapin (*Pelomedusa subrufa*), is often perched on rocks and is a common sight at various waterholes throughout the park. It is strictly carnivorous and lives on frogs, fish, worms, tadpoles, insects and birds, which it tries to ambush at waterholes by grabbing and pulling underwater when it drinks.

MONITORS OR LEGUAANS

The **rock monitor lizard** *(Varanus albigularis)* occurs abundantly in Etosha. It is particularly active in the rainy season and is only sometimes encountered otherwise. Depending on the habitat, it can attain a length of 140 cm, sometimes more. Its best method of defence is dishing out painful, swift whips with its muscular tail.

LIZARDS, SKINKS AND AGAMAS

A whopping 54 different lizard species are known or expected to occur in Etosha, the granite habitat of the western part hosting many endemics and near-endemics. The near-endemic **Namib rock agama** *(Agama planiceps)* is a colourful and striking example; the male sports a showy metallic purple-blue back and fiery orange-red head, neck, throat and tail and the female has a mottled grey and yellow head and orange flashes on its shoulders.

The common **ground agama** *(Agama aculeata)* is regularly encountered. It favours high perches on termite mounds, boulders or shrubs. In contrast, the endemic **Etosha agama** *(Agama etoshae)* favours rocky, sandy plains at the pan's edges. An excellent place to see this special agama is the Chudop waterhole, where it perches on stones lining the fringes of the parking lot.

Of the skink family, the stocky, smooth **Ovambo tree skink** *(Trachylepis binotata)* is of particular interest as it is the largest, reaching a length of over 20 cm. These lizards can occur in the mopane trees in the Halali Rest Camp. Another conspicuous species in the camps is the **black-lined plated lizard** *(Gerrhosaurus nigrolineaturs)*, which can grow to over half a metre in length.

GECKOS

Turner's thick-toed gecko *(Chondrodactylus turneri)* is the most encountered gecko species. The near-endemic **rough thick-toed gecko** *(Pachydactylus rugosus)* and endemic **large-scaled gecko** *(Pachydactylus scutatus)* are more secretive, mainly nocturnal and also favour the western part of Etosha. The common **barking gecko** *(Ptenopus garrulus)* prefers a habitat of gravel plains and harder sand with scattered grasses. You can hear the males' high-pitched, territorial, distinctive chirping towards dusk.

CHAMELEONS

The **flap-neck chameleon** *(Chamaeleo dilepis)* is commonly found in Etosha as it crosses the road, while the **Namaqua chameleon** *(Chamaeleo namaquensis)*, a near-endemic, only occurs marginally.

Rock monitor lizard

Birds

Etosha supports approximately 412 species of birds, of which a third are migratory. The richness and diversity of birdlife can be attributed to the varied habitat, which ranges from pans – with the main pan and Fischer's Pan changing into seasonal wetlands after prolific rain – to waterholes, grassveld savanna, woodlands, mopane shrub and treeveld, and sandveld.

Damara red-billed hornbill

Local specials

Near-endemic species found in the park are Hartlaub's spurfowl, Rüppell's korhaan, Rüppell's parrot, violet wood-hoopoe, Monteiro's hornbill, Carp's tit, bare-cheeked babbler, rockrunner, Herero chat and white-tailed shrike.

Breeding species of international concern include a small, isolated breeding population of blue cranes – which are listed as critically endangered in Namibia and occur only in Etosha – and the lesser flamingo. Over a million flamingos, including the greater flamingo, have been breeding on the pan during years of exceptional rainfall. The great white pelican and chestnut-banded plover also breed on the pan.

Bare-cheeked babbler

Violet wood hoopoe

Southern red-billed hornbill

Lanner falcon

Raptors

A total of 46 raptor species occur in the park. The martial eagle is the largest of the eagles, with the tawny eagle probably the most common eagle in the park. Of the snake eagles, the black-chested snake eagle is more common than the brown snake eagle. African hawk-eagles often nest in the Helio hills region near Halali. The striking and flamboyant bateleur is found more in the eastern section. It is classified as highly endangered in Namibia, with numbers seemingly dwindling in the park. Sightings of the African fish eagle have also been reported, for instance, around the Rietfontein waterhole, with sightings of the African harrier-hawk at the Rietfontein waterhole and the Namutoni area. The smallest raptor, the pygmy falcon, also occurs in the park.

The southern pale-chanting goshawk must surely be the most common raptor seen. The Gabar goshawk is the most common of the small bush hawks. The melanistic form is also found in the park, constituting about 10 % of the Gabar population.

Lanner falcons are abundant in Etosha, especially during the rainy season, and their hunting skills are awe-inspiring. The peregrine falcon is a summer migrant and less common than the lanner. The black-winged kite, greater kestrel and shikra are standard in Etosha. The migratory yellow-billed kites arrive in significant numbers in summer.

All vulture species found in Namibia occur in the park, including the Cape vulture and Egyptian vulture.

Kori bustard female with chicks

Plains birds

Some of the most frequently seen birds of the plains are the northern-black korhaan, helmeted guineafowl, red-billed-, as well as Swainson's spurfowl, Burchell's sandgrouse, Namaqua sandgrouse, double-banded-sandgrouse, Burchell's and Temminck's coursers. You can also see spotted-thick knees. Of the larger birds of the plains, common ostrich, secretary-birds and Kori bustards occur throughout, with the less common Ludwig's bustard seen more in the western region of Etosha. The density of Kori bustards in the park is estimated to be the highest worldwide. The migratory Abdim's stork occur in great numbers and are abundant around Okaukuejo waterhole and Gemsbokvlakte.

Grassland birds

Some of the grassland birds observed in the park are a variety of larks:

- Spike-heeled, red-capped, rufous-naped, fawn-coloured, Sabota and pink-billed larks
- Blue-, violet-eared, and black-faced waxbill
- Green-winged pytilia
- Red-headed finches and red-billed quelea
- Long-tailed paradise whydah, shaft-tailed whydah, pin-tailed whydah
- Several weaver species

Birds in trees

Some of the more colourful birds in and around trees, such as the crimson-breasted shrike, lilac-breasted and purple roller, swallow-tailed, and European bee-eaters, are found in association with trees and shrubs.

KEY SPECIES TO LOOK OUT FOR IN THE THREE MAIN CAMPS

Okaukuejo: African hoopoe, groundscraper thrush, crimson-breasted shrike, fork-tailed drongo, yellow-bellied- and burnt-necked eremomela, dusky-and Marico sunbird, pied crow, scaly-feathered finch, pearl-spotted owlet, Cardinal woodpecker, chestnut-vented warbler, acacia pied barbet and southern-pied babbler make camp life very interesting for birders. Look out for the colonies of sociable weavers, mainly near the campsite area and the charming little pygmy falcon usually close by.

Halali: The best place to tick off most owl species, with the western barn owl, African scops-owl, southern white-faced owl, spotted eagle-owl and pearl-spotted owlet found in camp. Marsh owls drinking at the waterhole at night are also sighted occasionally. Violet wood-hoopoe, common scimitarbill, white-crested helmetshrike, southern white-crowned shrike, bare-cheeked babbler and purple roller are some of the noticeable birds in the camp. The hornbills are also well represented, with African grey-, southern yellow-billed-, southern red-billed and Damara red-billed hornbill sighted here – the ultimate is to see and photograph the Monteiro's hornbill.

Crimson-breasted shrike with armoured ground cricket catch

African scops-owl

Namutoni: Hailed as the waterbird camp, Namutoni attracts several exciting species and a variety of wetland species. The reeds at the King Nehale Waterhole attract several species like the little grebe, Egyptian goose, South African shelduck, hamerkop, pied avocet, lesser swamp warbler, great reed warbler, western cattle egret, red-knobbed coot and black-headed heron. Red-billed buffalo weavers often nest in the tall trees around the restaurant, while African red-eyed bulbul, red-faced mousebird and Cape starling feast on the fruit of the fig trees when ripe. Namutoni and its surroundings are an excellent place to look out for black-faced babblers.

KEY SPECIES TO LOOK OUT FOR IN WESTERN ETOSHA

In the western areas of the park, look for Monteiro's hornbill, Hartlaub's francolin, white-tailed shrike, rockrunner, great sparrow, Rüppell's parrot, and bare-cheeked babbler.

KEY SPECIES TO LOOK OUT FOR AT FISCHER'S PAN DURING WETLAND CONDITIONS

Fischer's Pan is exceptional for sightings of greater and lesser flamingos, great white pelican, African spoonbill, saddle-billed stork, grey heron, black-headed heron, pied avocet, black-winged stilt, black-necked grebe, little grebe, red-knobbed coot, Cape teal, red-billed teal, greater-painted snipe, blacksmith lapwing, chestnut-banded plover, three-banded plover, Kittlitz's plover, blue crane, great egret, little egret, intermediate egret, western cattle egret, knob-billed duck, southern pochard and Ruff.

Lappet-faced vulture pair

GAIA Vulture Research Project in Etosha

One of the most recent research studies conducted in Etosha in May 2022 by the GAIA team (Guardian of the Wild using Artificial Intelligence Application) on the vulture population involved highly technical, innovative and increasingly sophisticated research methods applied to research on vultures. AI, camera footage, energy-efficient electronics and satellite-based communication technology enabled unprecedented insight into ecosystems and the gathering and evaluation of much more comprehensive information, such as flight patterns and movements in the park using such sophisticated technology.

The study's primary objective involved capturing and tagging vultures using 42 g solar-powered GPS tags to determine their role in detecting disease outbreaks and recapturing previously ringed vultures.

Vultures play a **crucial role in Etosha's ecosystem**, which is well known for the presence of anthrax *(Bacillus anthracis)* by finding and quickly disposing of animal carcasses, thus reducing the spread of the disease. Tracking the vultures enables scientists to promptly detect the locations of carcasses, collect samples from them and determine the cause of mortality. Recapturing ringed vultures also provides fascinating insight and information. In one instance, a vulture ringed in Etosha on 13 September 2001 (21 years old) and another ringed on 7 February 2009 was recaptured in May 2022. According to knowledge, these were the longest-recorded living white-backed vultures. Etosha hosts all six vulture species found in Namibia, even the rare Egyptian- and hooded vulture.

Blue cranes *(Anthropoides paradiseus)*

Etosha hosts a small and isolated breeding population of blue cranes. Consistent sightings of resident breeding birds have been reported only from 1918; at no stage are there more than 150 birds. There are tree possible scenarios regarding the origin of blue cranes in such an odd location. It could be a relict population, the last survivors of a formerly more comprehensive range, or natural dispersal in southern Africa since approximately 1800, leading to an establishment of a breeding population in Etosha; or these birds were deliberately introduced at some point in the past (this last option is most probably the least likely possibility).

However, one thing is sure: this is the only population in the whole country and they are listed as **critically endangered** in Namibia. Regular summer counts, ringing exercises and observations before the rainy season starts and during the breeding season by the Namibia Crane Working Group (NCWG) and MEFT staff, and observations by the public and tour operators have revealed the numbers of these birds are drastically declining. Poaching is, unfortunately, a threat. Other threatening factors are natural mortalities, habitat loss, fires, predators like jackals or raptors and, lately, climate change.

Records show researchers counted 138 blue cranes in 1976. By December 1994, only 60 of these rare birds had occurred; in 2017, the numbers had decreased to between 30 and 35.

Blue cranes usually **congregate at Andoni** and are mainly found around the southeastern edges of the Etosha Pan later in the season, where some breed in summer. Visitors had sightings of pairs and, on two occasions, pairs with chicks at the Salvadora and Charitsaub waterholes, Fischer's Pan and Twee Palm waterholes, as well as sightings of up to 18 individuals at Andoni a few years ago. Unfortunately, according to the latest statistics by Hanjo Böhme and Dirk Heinrich of the NCWG revealed in April 2023, a current estimated number of **just 17 blue cranes left in Etosha**.

We can only hope that the blue crane population stabilises, and should applaud the hard work and constant monitoring by the Namibia Crane Working Group and officials from MEFT (Ministry of Environment, Forestry and Tourism).

GENERAL INFORMATION ON THE BLUE CRANE

The blue crane is a tall ground-dwelling bird with a height of 1.20 m, a weight of 1.0 to 5.0 kg (males are heavier), and a wingspan of 2.0 m.

The long feathers are wingtip feathers that trail to the ground.

They stay near water, but feeding occurs on dry open grassland and dwarf scrubland, which fringes Etosha. Here, they find small bulbs, seeds, grasses, sedges and roots, although they also feed on numerous, sizeable insects, such as grasshoppers, crabs, snails, frogs and even small lizards and snakes. Such protein-rich food is often broken down and fed to the young.

Blue cranes are monogamous, and reproduction of offspring starts only after 3–5 years. Laying dates are between December and January after the first rains. There is a direct connection between rainfall and triggering breeding activity. They usually lay only two eggs at an interval of 2–3 days, so the chicks hatch asynchronously. The period of incubation is about 30 days. During this period, the male generally incubates the eggs at night, while the female takes over during the day.

When feeding, they fly far away from the feeding grounds to avoid giving away the nest location to their incubating counterparts. The female feeds the chicks, regurgitating food into the chick's beak/mouth.

Blue cranes silhouetted against Fischer's Pan

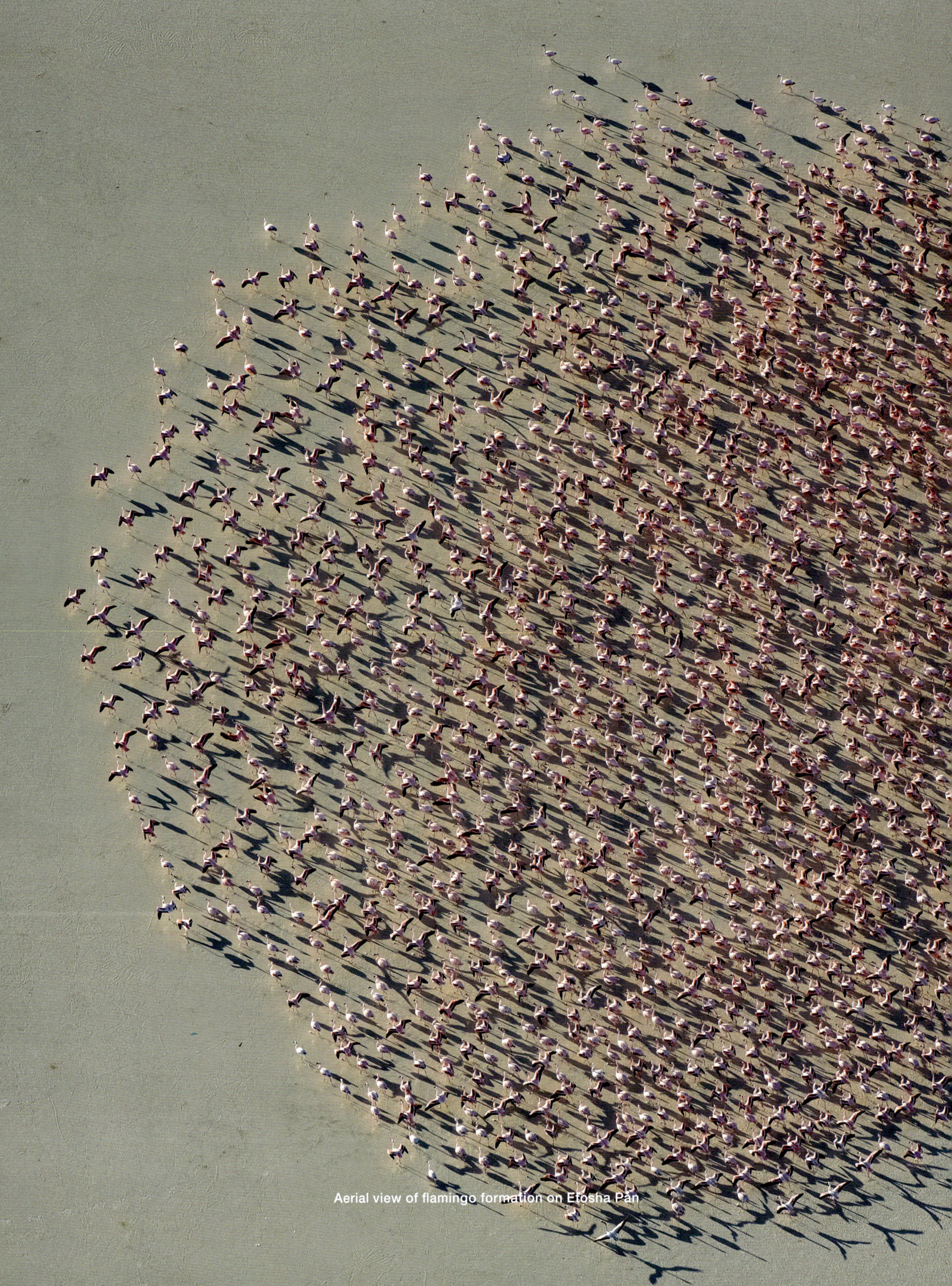

Aerial view of flamingo formation on Etosha Pan

General information on the flamingo

The floodwaters attract vast numbers of lesser and the greater flamingo to the pan. The combination of the levelled topography, clay sediments rich in salinity and alkalinity, and available seasonal water are highly favourable conditions. The presence of blue-green algae and micro-organisms form the main diet of the flamingo.

The earliest published record of both species of flamingo occurring on the pan and its surroundings is by Sauer and Sauer (1959 a, b; 1960) when they identified greater flamingo *(Phoenicopterus roseus)* and lesser flamingo *(Phoeniconaias minor)* during the rainy season of November 1957. In an above-average rainy season ending in April 1971, a total of 514 mm was recorded in Namutoni, with the additional three supplying rivers of the Ekuma, Oshigambo and Omuramba Ovambo running strongly, resulting in approximately 40% of the pan being covered in water. Scientists estimated that as many as a million flamingos were feeding off the rich supply of micro-organisms, which bloom in the pan's unique conditions.

In 1971, almost 60 000 nests, made by both species of flamingo, were built on Etosha Pan. Flamingos favour total isolation when they breed and, therefore, choose to nest far into the pan, out of sight, sound and scent of predators. Their main nesting sites and breeding areas occurred in a radius of 8–13 km northwest of Okerfontein.

On average, the pan floods sufficiently for flamingos to attempt breeding once every two years. However, the mean rainfall (400 mm) is below the threshold for successful breeding, usually above 440 mm. When the rain stops too early, water stops flowing, and the pan starts drying out, terrible tragedies occur when the chicks cannot yet fly, and parents have no choice but to move on and leave them to their fate. In some instances, the premature drying of the pan drastically impacted newly hatched flamingo chicks in June 1969, when 20 000 chicks were caught by hand and released at Fischer's Pan, which still held water. In another instance, in 1971, up to 30 000 hatchlings, guided by adult birds, which fed them on the way, walked 80 km from their nests until they reached deeper water, which is an incredible feat.

In 1989, hundreds of flamingo chicks were captured in a rescue operation and later airlifted to bird sanctuaries in South Africa. In April 1994, 144 greater flamingo chicks were taken from the pan and hand-reared at Okaukuejo, following the drying of the shallow water of the pan and the death of hundreds of chicks.

However, flamingo breeding frequency and success at Etosha Pan could be higher owing to receding pan water, which reduces food supplies and increases predation. Of 24 breeding attempts by greater and lesser flamingos at Etosha in 57 years, only eight produced thousands or tens of thousands of chicks.

Checklist for birds of Etosha

The list below is in accordance with the latest Roberts 2 Field Guide
Key: ***=Endangered; **= Vulnerable; *=Near threatened

INFO Birds

Ostriches
- ☐ Common ostrich *Struthio camelus*

Ducks and geese
- ☐ Knob-billed duck *Sarkidiornis melanotos*
- ☐ Egyptian goose *Alopochen aegyptiaca*
- ☐ South African shelduck *Tadorna cana*
- ☐ Blue-billed teal *Spatula hottentota*
- ☐ Cape shoveler *Spatula smithii*
- ☐ Cape teal *Anas capensis*
- ☐ Red-billed teal *Anas erythrorhyncha*

Guineafowl
- ☐ Helmeted guineafowl *Numida meleagris*

Francolins and spurfowls
- ☐ Crested francolin *Ortygornis sephaena*
- ☐ Hartlaub's spurfowl *Pternistis hartlaubi*
- ☐ Red-billed spurfowl *Pternistis adspersus*
- ☐ Swainson's spurfowl *Pternistis swainsonii*

Flamingos
- ☐ Greater flamingo *Phoenicopterus roseus*
- ☐ Lesser flamingo* *Phoenicoparrus minor*

Grebes
- ☐ Little grebe *Tachybaptus ruficollis*
- ☐ Great crested grebe *Podiceps cristatus*
- ☐ Black-necked grebe *Podiceps nigricollis*

Pigeons and doves
- ☐ Ring-necked dove *Streptopelia capicola*
- ☐ Laughing dove *Spilopelia senegalensis*
- ☐ Emerald-spotted wood-dove *Turtur chalcospilos*
- ☐ Namaqua dove *Oena capensis*

Sandgrouse
- ☐ Namaqua sandgrouse *Pterocles namaqua*
- ☐ Yellow-throated sandgrouse *Pterocles gutturalis*
- ☐ Double-banded sandgrouse *Pterocles bicinctus*
- ☐ Burchell's sandgrouse *Pterocles burchelli*

Bustards and korhaans
- ☐ Kori bustard* *Ardeotis kori*
- ☐ Ludwig's bustard*** *Neotis ludwigii*
- ☐ Red-crested korhaan *Lophotis ruficrista*
- ☐ Northern black korhaan *Afrotis afraoides*

Cuckoos
- ☐ Black cuckoo *Cuculus clamosus*
- ☐ African cuckoo *Cuculus gularis*
- ☐ Senegal coucal *Centropus senegalensis*
- ☐ Pied cuckoo *Clamator jacobinus*
- ☐ Levaillant's cuckoo *Clamator levaillantii*
- ☐ Diederik cuckoo *Chrysococcyx caprius*
- ☐ Klaas's cuckoo *Chrysococcyx klaas*
- ☐ Great spotted cuckoo *Clamator glandarius*
- ☐ Jacobin cuckoo *Clamator jacobinus*

Nightjars
- ☐ Rufous-cheeked nightjar *Caprimulgus rufigena*
- ☐ European nightjar *Caprimulgus europaeus*
- ☐ Fiery-necked nightjar *Caprimulgus pectoralis*
- ☐ Freckled nightjar *Caprimulgus tristigma*

Swifts
- ☐ Alpine swift *Tachymarptis melba*
- ☐ Common swift *Apus apus*
- ☐ Bradfield's swift *Apus bradfieldi*
- ☐ Little swift *Apus affinis*
- ☐ White-rumped swift *Apus caffer*
- ☐ African palm swift *Cypsiurus parvus*

Crakes, coots and moorhens
- ☐ African crake *Crex egregia*
- ☐ Spotted crake *Porzana porzana*
- ☐ Common moorhen *Gallinula chloropus*
- ☐ Red-knobbed coot *Fulica cristata*
- ☐ Black crake *Zapornia flavirostra*
- ☐ Baillon's crake *Zapornia pusilla*

Cranes
- ☐ Grey crowned crane*** *Balearica regulorum*
- ☐ Blue crane** *Anthropoides paradiseus*
- ☐ Wattled crane** *Bugeranus carunculatus*

Thick-knees
- ☐ Spotted thick-knee *Burhinus capensis*
- ☐ Water thick-knee *Burhinus vermiculatus*

Avocets and stilts
- ☐ Black-winged stilt *Himantopus himantopus*
- ☐ Pied avocet *Recurvirostra avosetta*

Plovers and lapwings
- ☐ Common ringed plover *Charadrius hiaticula*
- ☐ Three-banded plover *Charadrius tricollaris*
- ☐ Blacksmith lapwing *Vanellus armatus*
- ☐ Crowned lapwing *Vanellus coronatus*
- ☐ Caspian plover *Anarhynchus asiaticus*
- ☐ Kittlitz's plover *Anarhynchus pecuarius*
- ☐ Chestnut-banded plover* *Anarhynchus pallidus*

Painted-snipes
- ☐ Greater painted-snipe *Rostratula benghalensis*

Sandpipers and allies
- ☐ Marsh sandpiper *Tringa stagnatilis*
- ☐ Wood sandpiper *Tringa glareola*
- ☐ Common greenshank *Tringa nebularia*
- ☐ Ruff *Calidris pugnax*
- ☐ Little stint *Calidris minuta*

Pratincoles and coursers
- ☐ Bronze-winged courser *Rhinoptilus chalcopterus*
- ☐ Three-banded courser *Rhinoptilus cinctus*
- ☐ Double-banded courser *Smutsornis africanus*
- ☐ Burchell's courser *Cursorius rufus*
- ☐ Temminck's courser *Cursorius temminckii*
- ☐ Black-winged pratincole* *Glareola nordmanni*
- ☐ Collared pratincole *Glareola pratincola*

Terns
- ☐ Whiskered tern *Chlidonias hybrida*
- ☐ White-winged tern *Chlidonias leucopterus*

Storks
- ☐ African openbill *Anastomus lamelligerus*
- ☐ Black stork *Ciconia nigra*
- ☐ Abdim's stork *Ciconia abdimii*
- ☐ Saddle-billed stork *Ephippiorhynchus senegalensis*
- ☐ Marabou stork *Leptoptilos crumenifer*
- ☐ Yellow-billed stork *Mycteria ibis*

Cormorants
- ☐ Reed cormorant *Microcarbo africanus*
- ☐ White-breasted cormorant *Phalacrocorax carbo*

Herons, egrets and bitterns
- ☐ Dwarf bittern *Ixobrychus sturmii*
- ☐ Little bittern *Ixobrychus minutus*
- ☐ Western cattle egret *Bubulcus ibis*
- ☐ Grey heron *Ardea cinerea*
- ☐ Black-headed heron *Ardea melanocephala*

Secretarybird
- ☐ Secretarybird** *Sagittarius serpentarius*

Birds of prey

- ☐ Black-winged kite *Elanus caeruleus*
- ☐ African harrier-hawk *Polyboroides typus*
- ☐ Palm-nut vulture *Gypohierax angolensis*
- ☐ Egyptian vulture*** *Neophron percnopterus*
- ☐ White-headed vulture** *Trigonoceps occipitalis*
- ☐ Lappet-faced vulture** *Torgos tracheliotos*
- ☐ Hooded vulture*** *Necrosyrtes monachus*
- ☐ White-backed vulture*** *Gyps africanus*
- ☐ Cape vulture** *Gyps coprotheres*
- ☐ Bateleur* *Terathopius ecaudatus*
- ☐ Black-chested snake-eagle *Circaetus pectoralis*
- ☐ Brown snake-eagle *Circaetus cinereus*
- ☐ Martial eagle** *Polemaetus bellicosus*
- ☐ Wahlberg's eagle *Hieraaetus wahlbergi*
- ☐ Booted eagle *Hieraaetus pennatus*
- ☐ Tawny eagle *Aquila rapax*
- ☐ Verreauxs' eagle *Aquila verreauxii*
- ☐ African hawk-eagle *Aquila spilogaster*
- ☐ Lizard buzzard *Kaupifalco monogrammicus*
- ☐ Pale chanting-goshawk *Melierax canorus*
- ☐ Gabar goshawk *Micronisus gabar*
- ☐ Pallid harrier* *Circus macrourus*
- ☐ Montagu's harrier *Circus pygargus*
- ☐ Shikra *Accipiter badius*
- ☐ Little sparrowhawk *Accipiter minullus*
- ☐ Ovambo sparrowhawk *Accipiter ovampensis*
- ☐ Yellow-billed kite *Milvus aegyptius*
- ☐ Common buzzard *Buteo buteo*
- ☐ Augur buzzard *Buteo augur*

Falcons

- ☐ Pygmy falcon *Polihierax semitorquatus*
- ☐ Lesser kestrel *Falco naumanni*
- ☐ Rock kestrel *Falco rupicolus*
- ☐ Greater kestrel *Falco rupicoloides*
- ☐ Red-necked falcon *Falco chicquera*
- ☐ Red-footed falcon* *Falco vespertinus*
- ☐ Lanner falcon *Falco biarmicus*
- ☐ Peregrine falcon *Falco peregrinus*

Barn owl

- ☐ Western barn owl *Tyto alba*

Owls

- ☐ African scops-owl *Otus senegalensis*
- ☐ Southern white-faced owl *Ptilopsis granti*
- ☐ Spotted eagle-owl *Bubo africanus*
- ☐ Verreaux's eagle-owl *Bubo lactea*
- ☐ Pearl-spotted owlet *Glaucidium perlatum*
- ☐ Marsh owl *Asio capensis*

Mousebirds

- ☐ White-backed mousebird *Colius colius*
- ☐ Red-faced mousebird *Urocolius indicus*

Kittlitz's plover on eggs

Hoopoes

- ☐ African hoopoe *Upupa africana*

Woodhoopoes and scimitarbills

- ☐ Green woodhoopoe *Phoeniculus purpureus*
- ☐ Violet woodhoopoe *Phoeniculus damarensis*
- ☐ Common scimitarbill *Rhinopomastus cyanomelas*

Hornbills

- ☐ Bradfield's hornbill *Lophoceros bradfieldi*
- ☐ African grey hornbill *Lophoceros nasutus*
- ☐ Monteiro's hornbill *Tockus monteiri*
- ☐ Southern red-billed hornbill *Tockus rufirostris*
- ☐ Damara red-billed hornbill *Tockus damarensis*
- ☐ Southern yellow-billed hornbill *Tockus leucomelas*

Kingfishers

- ☐ Grey-headed kingfisher *Halcyon leucocephala*
- ☐ Brown-hooded kingfisher *Halcyon albiventris*
- ☐ Striped kingfisher *Halcyon chelicuti*
- ☐ Pied kingfisher *Ceryle rudis*

Bee-eaters

- ☐ Little bee-eater *Merops pusillus*
- ☐ Swallow-tailed bee-eater *Merops hirundineus*
- ☐ Blue-cheeked bee-eater *Merops persicus*
- ☐ European bee-eater *Merops apiaster*

Rollers

- ☐ European roller* *Coracias garrulus*
- ☐ Lilac-breasted roller *Coracias caudatus*
- ☐ Purple roller *Coracias naevius*

Barbets and tinkerbirds

- ☐ Yellow-fronted tinkerbird *Pogoniulus chrysoconus*
- ☐ African pied barbet *Tricholaema leucomelas*

Woodpeckers

- ☐ Cardinal woodpecker *Dendropicos fuscescens*
- ☐ Bearded woodpecker *Chloropicus namaquus*
- ☐ Bennett's woodpecker *Campethera bennettii*
- ☐ Golden-tailed woodpecker *Campethera abingoni*

Parrots and lovebirds

- ☐ Rosy-faced lovebird *Agapornis roseicollis*
- ☐ Meyer's parrot *Poicephalus meyeri*
- ☐ Rüppell's parrot *Poicephalus rueppellii*

Wattle-eyes and batises

- ☐ White-tailed shrike *Lanioturdus torquatus*
- ☐ Chinspot batis *Batis molitor*
- ☐ Pririt batis *Batis pririt*

Helmetshrikes

- ☐ White-crested helmetshrike *Prionops plumatus*

Bushshrikes

- ☐ Brubru *Nilaus afer*
- ☐ Black-backed puffback *Dryoscopus cubla*
- ☐ Black-crowned tchagra *Tchagra senegalus*
- ☐ Brown-crowned tchagra *Tchagra australis*
- ☐ Crimson-breasted shrike *Laniarius atrococcineus*

Shrikes
- ☐ Lesser grey shrike *Lanius minor*
- ☐ Magpie shrike *Lanius melanoleuca*
- ☐ Southern fiscal *Lanius collaris*
- ☐ Southern white-crowned shrike *Eurocephalus anguitimens*

Orioles
- ☐ African golden oriole *Oriolus auratus*
- ☐ Eurasian golden oriole *Oriolus oriolis*

Drongos
- ☐ Fork-tailed drongo *Dicrurus adsimilis*

Crows
- ☐ Cape crow *Corvus capensis*
- ☐ Pied crow *Corvus albus*

Larks
- ☐ Spike-heeled lark *Chersomanes albofasciata*
- ☐ Dusky lark *Pinarocorys nigricans*
- ☐ Chestnut-backed sparrow-lark *Eremopterix leucotis*
- ☐ Grey-backed sparrow-lark *Eremopterix verticalis*
- ☐ Sabota lark *Calendulauda sabota*
- ☐ Fawn-coloured lark *Calendulauda africanoides*
- ☐ Monotonous lark *Mirafra passerina*
- ☐ Rufous-naped lark *Mirafra africana*
- ☐ Eastern clapper lark *Mirafra fasciolata*
- ☐ Red-capped lark *Calandrella cinerea*
- ☐ Stark's lark *Spizocorys starki*
- ☐ Pink-billed lark *Spizocorys conirostris*

Swallows and martins
- ☐ Banded martin *Neophedina cincta*
- ☐ Bank swallow *Riparia riparia*
- ☐ Rock martin *Ptyonoprogne fuligula*
- ☐ Barn swallow *Hirundo rustica*
- ☐ Western house-martin *Delichon urbicum*
- ☐ Rufous-chested swallow *Cecropis semirufa*
- ☐ Mosque swallow *Cecropis senegalensis*
- ☐ South African cliff swallow *Petrochelidon spilodera*

Tits
- ☐ Carp's tit *Melaniparus carpi*
- ☐ Ashy tit *Melaniparus cinerascens*

Bulbuls
- ☐ African red-eyed bulbul *Pycnonotus nigricans*

Crombecs, rockrunners, warblers, erenomelas, aplises, prinias, cisticolas
- ☐ Long-billed crombec *Sylvietta rufescens*
- ☐ Rockrunner *Achaetops pycnopygius*
- ☐ Willow warbler *Phylloscopus trochilus*
- ☐ Icterine warbler *Hippolais icterina*
- ☐ Sedge warbler *Acrocephalus schoenobaenus*
- ☐ Common reed warbler *Acrocephalus scirpaceus*
- ☐ Yellow-bellied eremomela *Eremomela icteropygialis*
- ☐ Burnt-neck eremomela *Eremomela usticollis*
- ☐ Barred wren-warbler *Calamonastes fasciolatus*
- ☐ Grey-backed camaroptera *Camaroptera brachyura*
- ☐ Yellow-breasted apalis *Apalis flavida*
- ☐ Black-chested prinia *Prinia flavicans*
- ☐ Rufous-eared warbler *Malcorus pectoralis*
- ☐ Rattling cisticola *Cisticola chiniana*
- ☐ Zitting cisticola *Cisticola juncidis*
- ☐ Desert cisticola *Cisticola aridulus*
- ☐ Garden warbler *Sylvia borin*
- ☐ Chestnut-vented warbler *Sylvia subcaeruleum*

White-eyes
- ☐ Southern yellow white-eye *Zosterops pallidus*

Babblers
- ☐ Bare-cheeked babbler *Turdoides gymnogenys*
- ☐ Southern pied babbler *Turdoides bicolor*
- ☐ Black-faced babbler *Turdoides melanops*

Flycatchers
- ☐ Spotted flycatcher *Muscicapa striata*
- ☐ Marico flycatcher *Bradornis mariquensis*
- ☐ Chat flycatcher *Agricola infuscatus*

Scrub-robins
- ☐ Kalahari scrub-robin *Cercotrichas paena*
- ☐ White-browed scrub-robin *Cercotrichas Leucophrys*

Thrushes
- ☐ Short-toed rock-thrush *Monticola brevipes*
- ☐ Groundscraper thrush *Turdus litsitsirupa*

Chats and wheateaers
- ☐ Southern ant-eating chat *Myrmecocichla formicivora*
- ☐ Mountain wheatear *Myrmecocichla monticola*
- ☐ Capped wheatear *Oenanthe pileata*
- ☐ Familiar chat *Oenanthe familiaris*

Starlings
- ☐ Wattled starling *Creatophora cinerea*
- ☐ Violet-backed starling *Cinnyricinclus leucogaster*
- ☐ Pale-winged starling *Onychognathus nabouroup*
- ☐ Burchell's starling *Lamprotornis australis*
- ☐ Greater blue-eared starling *Lamprotornis chalybaeus*
- ☐ Cape starling *Lamprotornis nitens*

Sunbirds
- ☐ Marico sunbird *Cinnyris mariquensis*
- ☐ White-bellied sunbird *Cinnyris talatala*
- ☐ Dusky sunbird *Cinnyris fuscus*

Wagtails and pipits
- ☐ Cape wagtail *Motacilla capensis*
- ☐ Western yellow wagtail *Motacilla flava*
- ☐ African pipit *Anthus cinnamomeus*
- ☐ Buffy pipit *Anthus vaalensis*

Sparrows
- ☐ Great sparrow *Passer motitensis*
- ☐ Cape sparrow *Passer melanurus*
- ☐ Southern grey-headed sparrow *Passer diffusus*

Weavers and bishops
- ☐ Red-billed buffalo-weaver *Bubalornis niger*
- ☐ Scaly-feathered finch (weaver) *Sporopipes squamifrons*
- ☐ White-browed sparrow-weaver *Plocepasser mahali*
- ☐ Sociable weaver *Philetairus socius*
- ☐ Red-headed weaver *Anaplectes rubriceps*
- ☐ Lesser masked-weaver *Ploceus intermedius*
- ☐ Southern masked-weaver *Ploceus velatus*
- ☐ Chestnut weaver *Ploceus rubiginosus*
- ☐ Red-billed quelea *Quelea quelea*
- ☐ Southern red bishop *Euplectes orix*
- ☐ Yellow-crowned bishop *Euplectes afer*

Waxbills finches and pytilias
- ☐ Black-faced waxbill *Brunhilda erythronotos*
- ☐ Common waxbill *Estrilda astrild*
- ☐ Quailfinch *Ortygospiza atricollis*
- ☐ Cut-throat *Amadina fasciata*
- ☐ Red-headed finch *Amadina erythrocephala*
- ☐ Violet-eared waxbill *Granatina granatina*
- ☐ Blue waxbill *Uraeginthus angolensis*
- ☐ Green-winged pytilia *Pytilia melba*

Indigobirds and whydahs
- ☐ Eastern paradise-whydah Vidua paradisaea
- ☐ Shaft-tailed whydah *Vidua regia*

Canaries and buntings
- ☐ Black-throated canary *Crithagra atrogularis*
- ☐ Yellow canary *Crithagra flaviventris*
- ☐ White-throated canary *Crithagra albogularis*
- ☐ Lark-like bunting *Emberiza impetuani*
- ☐ Cinnamon-breasted bunting *Emberiza tahapisi*
- ☐ Cape bunting *Emberiza capensis*
- ☐ Golden-breasted bunting *Emberiza flaviventris*

Mammals

Etosha currently hosts a substantial diversity of mammals, approximately 114 species. The larger and more visible mammals are well known, but over 75% of the park's mammals consist of the smaller, more secretive and often nocturnal species. The scientific status of many mammals, especially the smaller species, is frequently revised and reassessed, sometimes resulting in species being renamed or even reclassified as new species.

Mammals found in Etosha include the following.

Sengis (elephant shrews) Order Macroscelidea

The bushveld sengi *(Elephantulus intufi)* is an insectivorous species found in Etosha, occurring in areas with sandy soils.

Hedgehogs and shrews, Order Eulipotyphla

The southern African hedgehog *(Atelerix frontalis)* is the only species of the subregion and also occurs in Etosha. Shrews are tiny, long-snouted, short-legged mouse-like mammals, with the lesser-red musk shrew *(Crocidura hirta)* and the tiny musk shrew *(Crocidura fuscomarina)* measuring a mere 10 cm in body length, found in Etosha.

Bats, Order Chiroptera

Almost 20 species of bats occur in the park, notably the Mauritian tomb bat *(Taphozous mauritianus)*, found to be breeding in the Namutoni area and the giant Commerson's leaf-nosed bat *(Hipposideros vittatus)* with a wingspan of up to 60 cm, which roosts in considerable colonies in caves along the southern boundary.

Baboons, monkeys and bushbabies, Order primates

Only the chacma baboon *(Papio ursinus)* occurs in isolated parts of western Etosha. The nocturnal southern lesser galago or bushbaby *(Galago moholi)* occurs throughout the park but is rarely seen. Visitors have reported isolated sightings from Halali Camp.

Pangolin, Order Pholidota

Only the Temminck's ground pangolin *(Smutsia temmincki)* occurs in Etosha; sightings are rare.

Hares and rabbits, Order Lagomorpha

The scrub hare *(Lepus saxatilis)* is the most common, but the lesser-known Jameson's red rock rabbit *(Pronolagus randensis)* also occurs.

Rodents, Order Rodentia

Nearly 32 species occur in Etosha, with the most common species probably being the Cape ground squirrel *(Xerus inauris)*. Other rodents worth mentioning are the tree squirrels *(Paraxerus cepapi)*, frequently seen flitting around the camps; and the diurnal noki or dassie rat *(Petromus typicus)*, often seen perched on the granite rocks in western Etosha; also the sole member of the rodent family Petromuridae, a zoological distinction for Namibia. The acacia tree rat *(Thallomys paedulcus)* is arboreal and predominantly nocturnal, usually seen in trees near the Oakaukuejo waterhole at dusk. Another near-endemic in the western part of the park is the nocturnal and secretive Nambian rock mouse *(Petromyscus collinus)*. Springhares *(Pedetes capensis)* are part of the rodent family and are not seen during the day as they are nocturnal.

Carnivores, Order Carnivora

Of the large cats, the majestic lion *(Panthera leo)* is probably the flagship species of Etosha, a stronghold for lion in Namibia, as well as leopard *(Panthera pardus)* and cheetah *(Acinonyx jubatus)*. Leopard have become more habituated to cars in the last few years, and good sightings have been reported recently, with cheetah regularly observed, especially around the Namutoni area. Although most focus is on the larger, charismatic species, the park also hosts many medium-sized and smaller carnivores. The southern African wild cat *(Felis lybica)* occurs widely in the park, with regular sightings reported. The caracal *(Caracal caracal)* appears in a few isolated areas, preferring woodland habitats. Visitors have seen it around the Namutoni area. The nocturnal and timid black-footed cat *(Felis nigripes)* is classified as vulnerable, and scientists confirmed its presence in Etosha in 1991 and 2013 in the eastern and central regions of the park. A taxidermist specimen in the Museum of the Ecological Research Institute in Okaukuejo is a testament to that, but sightings are sporadic.

Both the spotted hyena *(Crocuta crocuta)* and brown hyena *(Parahyaena brunnea)* are at home in Etosha, with the spotted hyena frequently encountered but with few sightings of its shyer and predominantly nocturnal cousin.

Bushveld sengi

Slender mongoose

Banded mongoose

The charismatic Cape fox *(Vulpes chama)*, as well as the bat-eared fox *(Otocyon megalotis)*, have dens throughout the park, with the best areas to see the Cape fox in a wide radius on the plains en route to Okondeka and Adamax. There are regular reports of bat-eared foxes around the Okaukuejo and Gaseb areas, as well as Halali and Andoni. Both are partial to open areas with grassland and short scrub, primarily active in the hours of the early morning or late afternoon.

Of the two jackal species, only the wily and extremely adaptable black-backed jackal *(Canis mesomelas)* occurs in the park, always on the trot. The more nocturnal side-striped jackal *(Canis adustus)* prefers well-watered, wooded areas and occurs marginally in Namibia's northeastern regions.

The shy aardwolf *(Proteles crisatus)* is a medium-sized carnivore. It is primarily active at night but is sometimes seen foraging insects in the early morning or late afternoon. Visitors have seen them around Fischer's Pan and on the vast plains near Okondeka.

The feisty honey badger *(Mellivora capensis)* occurs widely throughout the park. It moves around in typical belligerent badger style, looking for tasty morsels. The Halali area produces the most frequent badger sightings, with some a permanent fixture in the rest camp.

The mongooses, family Herpestidae, deserve a special mention. Whole colonies of banded mongoose *(Mungos mungo)* often scuttle across the road, foraging for insects in the scrub lining the roadside or clambering up and around termite mounds. They are very social and their constant chattering and interaction are fascinating, especially when they have youngsters. Records show they occur in central and eastern Etosha, not the western parts.

The solitary slender mongoose *(Herpestes sanguineus)*, with its beautiful, lustrous reddish-brown coat and black tail tip, is frequently encountered. Still, it is more skittish and quick to beat a hasty retreat.

Yellow mongoose *(Cynictis penicillata)* is diurnal and frequently encountered. Look for them near the roadside, as they often have dens nearby.

The dwarf mongoose *(Helogale parvula)* is the most petite carnivore in southern Africa. They also occur in groups of up

Honey badger

Black-faced impala and springbok calves

to 10 members in the park, preferring open woodland and grassland savanna. They are shy but inquisitive, heading for cover when disturbed, but it is worthwhile to stand quietly and wait for them to reappear.

The near-endemic black mongoose *(Galerella nigrata)* is rare and found marginally in the granites and dolomites in the extreme western and southern Etosha.

Another nocturnal and very striking carnivore is the small-spotted genet *(Genetta genetta)*. Its distribution range is the southern and central regions of the park, and it often appears at night in the rest camps.

Aardvark, Order Tubulidentata

The aardvark is the only species of this order and is seldom seen in the park as it is predominantly nocturnal.

Elephant, Order Proboscidea

The elephant is the largest mammal found in Etosha and is the only species of this order.

Dassies (hyraxes), Order Hyracoidea

The Kaokoveld rock dassie *(Procavia capensis welwitschii)* is particularly interesting here. It is a Namibian near-endemic found in the western region of the park.

Odd-toed ungulates, Order Perissodactyla

Two species of zebra occur in the park: the near-endemic Hartmann's mountain zebra *(Equus zebra ssp. hartmannae)*, a sub-species of mountain zebra, and the Cape mountain zebra *(Equus zebra ssp. zebra)*, which, together with the latter, is listed as vulnerable in the IUCN red data list. The Hartmann's mountain zebra predominantly occurs in the park's western section, with the Burchell's zebra *(Equus quagga ssp. burchellii)* distributed widely throughout.

The other odd-toed ungulate family is the Rhinocerotidae, with both the southern white- or square-lipped rhino *(Ceratotherium simum)* and the southwestern subspecies of the black- or hook-lipped rhino *(Diceros bicornis ssp. bicornis)* occurring in the park.

Even-toed ungulates, Order Suiformes

There are two species, of which only the common warthog *(Phacochoerus africanus)* occurs in the park.

Even-toed ungulates, Order Ruminantia

The giraffe is a single species. A healthy population of giraffe occurs throughout the park, with the greatest concentration in the east.

Antelope family

The antelope family, with seven different tribes, is the most numerous. The larger antelope occurring in Etosha are the common eland *(Tragelaphus oryx)*, greater kudu (Tragelaphus strepsiceros), oryx *(Oryx gazella)* – which is also Namibia's national animal – blue wildebeest *(Connochaetes taurinus)* and red hartebeest *(Alcelaphus buselaphus)*, the medium-sized common impala *(Aepyceros melampus)*, as well as near-endemic black-faced impala *(Aepycerus melampus petersii)* and common duiker *(Sylvicapra grimmia)*. The near-endemic Damara dik-dik (Madoqua kirkii *damarensis)* belongs to the dwarf antelope family. It occurs throughout the park, with the best chance of spotting them in and around the Dik-Dik Drive near Namutoni.

The springbok *(Antidorcas marsupialis)* is a gazelle, along with the steenbok *(Raphicerus campestris)* and the klipspringer *(Oreotragus oreotragus)*. They prefer isolated rocky areas in western Etosha.

Checklist for mammals of Etosha

- ☐ Bushveld sengi *(Elephantulus intufi)*
- ☐ Southern African hedgehog *(Atelerix frontalis)*
- ☐ Lesser-red musk shrew *(Crocidura hirta)*
- ☐ Tiny musk shrew *(Crocidura fuscomurina*
- ☐ Mauritian tomb bat *(Taphozous mauritianus)*
- ☐ Commerson's leaf-nosed bat *(Hipposideros vittatus)*
- ☐ Chacma baboon *(Papio ursinus)*
- ☐ South African galago *(Galago moholi)*
- ☐ Temminck's ground pangolin *(Smutsia temmincki)*
- ☐ Scrub hare *(Lepus saxatilis)*
- ☐ Jameson's red rock rabbit *(Pronolagus randensis)*
- ☐ Cape ground squirrel *(Xerus inauris)*
- ☐ Tree squirrels *(Paraxerus cepapi)*
- ☐ Noki or dassie rat *(Petromus typicus)*
- ☐ Acacia tree rat *(Thallomys paedulcus)*
- ☐ Nambian rock mouse *(Petromyscus collinus)*
- ☐ Springhare *(Pedetes capensis)*
- ☐ Lion *(Panthera leo)*
- ☐ Leopard *(Panthera pardus)*
- ☐ Cheetah *(Acinonyx jubatus)*
- ☐ African wild cat *(Felis lybica)*
- ☐ Caracal *(Caracal caracal)*
- ☐ Black-footed cat *(Felis nigripes)*
- ☐ Spotted hyena *(Crocuta crocuta)*
- ☐ Brown hyena *(Parahyaena brunnea)*
- ☐ Cape fox *(Vulpes chama)*
- ☐ Bat-eared fox *(Otocyon megalotis)*
- ☐ Black-backed jackal *(Canis mesomelas)*
- ☐ Side-striped jackal (*Canis adustus)*
- ☐ Aardwolf *(Proteles cristatus)*
- ☐ Honey badger *(Mellivora capensis)*
- ☐ Banded mongoose *(Mungos mungo)*
- ☐ Slender mongoose *(Herpestes sanguineus)*
- ☐ Yellow mongoose *(Cynictis penicillata)*
- ☐ Dwarf mongoose *(Helogale parvula)*
- ☐ Black mongoose *(Galerella nigrata)*
- ☐ Small-spotted genet *(Genetta genetta)*
- ☐ Burchell's zebra (*Equus quagga burchellii*)
- ☐ Hartmann's mountain zebra (*Equus zebra hartmannae*)
- ☐ White rhinoceros, white rhino, or square-lipped rhinoceros (*Ceratotherium simum*)
- ☐ South-western black rhinoceros (*Diceros bicornis occidentalis*)
- ☐ Common warthog (*Phacochoerus africanus*)
- ☐ Giraffe (*Giraffa giraffa angolensis*)
- ☐ Red hartebeest (*Alcelaphus buselaphus caama*)
- ☐ Blue wildebeest (*Connochaetes taurinus*)
- ☐ Springbok or springbuck (*Antidorcas marsupialis*)
- ☐ Klipspringer (*Oreotragus oreotragus*)
- ☐ Steenbok (*Raphicerus campestris*)
- ☐ Common eland (*Taurotragus oryx*)
- ☐ Greater kudu (*Tragelaphus strepsiceros*)
- ☐ Common duiker (*Sylvicapra grimmia*)
- ☐ Gemsbok or South African oryx (*Oryx gazella*)
- ☐ Black-faced impala (*Aepyceros melampus petersi*)

Male leopard

Research: Etosha's large carnivores

The **Etosha Ecological Institute** was founded in 1974 in Okaukuejo and has always played a pivotal role in conducting research, such as studies of game diseases like anthrax, game-capture techniques, ecological surveys and analysis of problem animals.

The **Greater Etosha Carnivore Programme** investigates determinants of carnivore fitness and distribution in the Greater Etosha Landscape (GEL: including the area extending 40 km surrounding ENP). This programme aims to form long-term collaborations with research and academic institutions to answer carnivore ecology and persistence questions. The core elements investigated are carnivore natural history, prey guild composition and environmental variables under different human management regimes. **The aim** is to understand how these variables interact and influence carnivore distribution, abundance and human-carnivore coexistence.

At present, a collaboration with the Ministry and the University of Georgia Atlanta, USA, and Ongava Research Centre looks at human-carnivore interactions along the northern periphery of ENP (tagged livestock, and assessing livestock husbandry practices), **effects of land use on fence crossing behaviour** by wildlife (camera deployment at selected areas on the ENP boundary fence to cover different land use types), as well as the effect of anthropogenic activities on carnivore behaviour (this includes diet analysis within the GEL, and movement of lion and spotted hyena around tourist hotspots in ENP). They also investigated the **effect of the ENP boundary fence** on the lion and spotted hyena movement.

Another current collaboration with the Leibnitz Institute for Zoo and Wildlife Research (IZW), Germany, examines **lion home range sizes**, whether they overlap, and lion activity patterns (how far they move). Another aspect is to investigate spatial and temporal long-distance communication in lions.

Ruben Portas collaring male lion

Etosha ecological institute

A recently completed study in collaboration with the University of Witwatersrand, South Africa, investigated **thermoregulation and water conservation mechanisms** in free-ranging lions. The lions were GPS-collared and had an abdominal temperature and activity microbloggers implanted. The collars also had audio loggers to record sounds from feeding and drinking. The specific objectives were to assess:

- Body **water management**, as measured through water turnover rates, acoustic loggers, frequency of feeding and location to water sources.
- Thermoregulation about **macro- and micro-climate**.
- Thermoregulation about **activity levels and home range size**.

Although much current research focuses on lions and hyenas, the GECP aims to conduct studies that include all carnivore species within the GEL.

Etosha elephants

ELEPHANT HISTORY IN ETOSHA

1881: Elephants were absent from Etosha National Park for about 70 years, with reports of the last remaining elephants that were driven into a marsh near Namutoni in 1881 and wiped out. The stage seemed set for a bleak future for these giant pachyderms in the park.

1907: When Etosha was proclaimed Game Reserve No. 2 in 1907, there were no records of elephant, nor in 1934, when Captain GC Shortridge undertook his extensive survey of the mammals in former SWA.

1952: The year 1952 saw the return of the first elephants from the country's northwestern region, with an estimated number of 50 to 60 animals.

1955: An elephant commission recommended that Etosha expand westwards to include Otjovasandu in 1955.

1961–1961: Several boreholes were drilled along the 19th latitude to draw elephant back into the park and mitigate human-wildlife conflict between elephants and farmers in the Kamanjab district and Kowares settlement.

1967: After an aerial census, the estimated elephant population was 500 by 1967, which rose to 1 293 by September 1973.

1980: By 1980, the start of the prolonged drought period, the elephant population consisted of 2 300 individuals, resulting in the extreme opposite measure taken of drawing elephant back to the park; 525 elephants were culled in Olifantsrus in two separate operations, 1983 and 1985 respectively, owing to the persistent drought.

1982: Between November 1981 and January 1982, approximately 200 elephants perished from an outbreak of anthrax in western Etosha.

1989: Again, a few years later, an estimated 101 elephants succumbed to the disease in northwestern Etosha between October and December 1989.

2024: The estimate of the current population is at approximately 3 000 individuals.

African elephant tusk

ETOSHA ELEPHANT TUSKS

Etosha's elephants are known for their relatively small and brittle tusks, which could be attributed to a few factors:

- Nutritional deficiencies, possible mineral imbalances, intense competition when vying for access to the best drinking sites, and violent sparring between males, judging from the frequent incidence of ivory chips found at waterholes. The arid climate might also be a contributing factor, leading to the dehydration of the exposed parts of the tusks, thus the development of cracks.
- A study by Caitlin O'Connell-Rodwell in Etosha has demonstrated elephants not only communicate through low-frequency calls inaudible to the human ear – also known as 'infrasound' – but also a previously unknown system of seismic sensing of vibrations received through the bottom of their feet.
- People call Etosha's elephants the 'white' or 'ghost' elephants because they take mud baths and coat themselves with the predominantly white, calcareous soil to keep cool, lending them the imposing countenance of giant, white marble statues.

ELEPHANTS OF ETOSHA ARE AMONG THE TALLEST ELEPHANTS IN AFRICA

- Adult male shoulder heights from northwestern Namibia, including Etosha, at 3.5–4.2 m, exceeding the size of elephants from the eastern parts of southern Africa by 0.5 m. Adult females in Etosha often exceed adult males – for instance, in Kruger National Park – in shoulder height.
- Elephants in arid regions are said to be taller than those from humid regions. This opinion applies to Etosha's wildebeest, lion, impala and others, which are said to be larger than those in Kruger National Park.
- The 5th and 8th tallest elephants ever measured came from the Namutoni area, measuring 4.0 m and 3.86 m at the shoulder.
- The body size and shoulder height of elephants are determined by age, sex, genetics and environmental factors.

ARE ELEPHANTS EXCELLENT OR BAD FOR THE ECOSYSTEM?

The impact of these giant pachyderms is visible at the waterholes, as they have considerably opened the areas of trees and shrubs around them by their feeding habits. This impact is constricted to a two-kilometre radius, so their overall effect here is considered marginal. They also play a positive ecological role in the ecosystem by clearing thickets, thus opening areas for larger grasslands for herbivores like zebra and wildebeest, which favour open areas for grazing. The browsing and breaking of small trees make the foliage more accessible to black rhino and greater kudu, while their mud wallows create a microhabitat for other species like frogs, ducks and dragonflies. Elephant also distribute the seeds of the vegetation they eat in their dung, which fertilises the soil and is utilised by dung beetles and other invertebrates. The foliage of the mopane, the dominant vegetation of large parts of Etosha, is a staple in the elephants' diet.

Hybridisation between Hartmann's zebra and Burchell's zebra in Etosha

Since 2015, the Ministry of Environment, Forestry and Tourism (MEFT) has been conducting research in Etosha National Park on the two zebra species: **Hartmann's mountain zebra** and **Burchell's zebra**.

The species differ because the mountain zebra has a grid-iron pattern on its rump, a dewlap, and more prominent ears. It also has a white belly, lacks the 'shadow stripe', and has stripes down to the hooves.

Burchell's zebra lack the grid-iron pattern on the rump and have an additional shadow stripe superimposed on the white stripe, especially the hindquarters. The stripes also extend to the white underparts of the belly.

The **pertinent question** is the hybridisation factor: **is cross-breeding between the two species possible?**

According to Kenneth Uiseb, head of wildlife monitoring and research at MEFT, the project involves 16 000 Burchell's zebra and 1 000 mountain zebras in the park. Researchers collared seven mountain zebra and seven Burchell's zebra and collected tissue samples for analysis, but more sampling work needs to be done.

Mr Uiseb states that hybridisation between the two species will likely produce viable hybrid offspring and that male mountain zebras are suspected of driving this hybridisation. The research primarily aims to provide answers to these questions.

Hartmann's mountain zebra is a protected species in Namibia and of global conservation importance. It is listed as vulnerable on the IUCN Red List Category.

Interesting facts about rhino translocation and conservation in Etosha

Active rhino conservation in Namibia started in the mid-'60s with the translocation of black rhino. The successful adaptation of the species is one of Etosha's greatest conservation success stories.

Between 1967 and 1977, black rhinos were captured and successfully translocated to Etosha National Park to supplement the current small population. However, the operation was not without its challenges. The rhino's natural habitat was extremely rugged and the logistics of accessing that terrain with the right vehicles and capture gear was tricky, especially in the '60s and '70s. Rhinos are also shy and elusive and researchers needed to do extensive groundwork and surveys before any translocations could take place.

The animals had to be darted from a helicopter and transported by road to holding pens in the park. Later, the rhino were translocated within Etosha between 1978 and 1989, when they soon established themselves as a viable population.

Namibia's Black Rhino Custodianship Programme started in April 1993, when the first black rhino were translocated from national parks to freehold farms under a memorandum of understanding signed by the farmers and MEFT.

Today, Namibia holds the **largest unfenced population of black rhino**.

Before the turn of the century, rhino were extinct in Etosha because of relentless hunting. They were reintroduced in 1995 when a few animals were brought in from Kruger in exchange for the giraffe. In 1997, the population was further boosted when white rhino were translocated from Waterberg Plateau Park in the late 1990s, with more to follow in 2003.

Sadly, Etosha has not been exempted from the scourge of rhino poaching, necessitating the establishment of an anti-poaching unit in 1988. De-horning rhinos and the translocation of some to more secure areas in the country were also drastic measures implemented as a preventative measure against poaching.

The latest, innovative approach to curb poaching in the park saw the implementation of horse-mounted patrols intended to enhance the efficiency of current foot patrols in combatting illegal rhino poaching. The horse patrol unit will complement the K9 unit, which has already operated for a while. It is comprised of a special team of trained dogs and handlers stationed in Okaukuejo. The working dogs are trained to detect highly protected species, such as rhino, pangolin and elephant, as well as firearms, ammunition and other items.

Interesting facts about attempts to introduce African wild dogs into Etosha

Although Etosha's illustrated maps still indicate the presence of wild dog, none occur there.

Wild dogs are considered vermin by farmers and relentlessly persecuted. In 1962 alone, 81 wild dogs were destroyed on the southern boundary of the Etosha National Park after conflict with domestic livestock. The last resident pack of wild dogs in Etosha consisted of 16 individuals around Homob, on the southern edge of the pan until 1970. In western Etosha, one last wild dog was recorded in 1983. Small groups of dogs were sporadically recorded in the park, entering from the north or northeast, but they still needed to become residents. In 1986, staff recorded 13 wild dogs in the northeast.

Given the uncertain future of the dogs and to maintain species diversity, three attempts were made to reintroduce wild dogs into the park. In 1978, six wild dogs, raised from pups, were released at the age of one year on the southern edge of the pan. They all died within four months after release, mainly owing to starvation or predation by lions. In 1989, another attempt was made when the park introduced five adults at Okawao in western Etosha, but again, all of them died from unknown causes within three months.

In January 1990, the park made a final attempt when they captured 13 wild dogs – five adult males and eight females – between the ages of one and four years. During transport, one male allied with two domestic dogs and was recaptured three weeks later when hunting as a pack.

The researchers initially held the pack in an enclosure near Grootvlakte, and one male and one female were radio-collared. The pack killed the recaptured male as the

Black rhinos

researchers reintroduced him into captivity. The rest of the pack was released on Grootvlakte in early March 1990. During the following five and a half months, lions killed the dogs and, when only four of the pack remained, they were seen feeding on a black-backed jackal carcass. They subsequently perished two weeks later, the established cause being rabies.

No further attempts were made to introduce wild dogs into the park again.

Interesting facts about translocation of roan antelope from Khaudum to Etosha

In 1970, an ambitious project was launched by the Division of Nature Conservation and Tourism, namely that of attempting to relocate 74 roan antelope from Khaudum, located in the northeastern corner of Namibia, some 460 km by road from Grootfontein, all the way to Etosha National Park.

The aim was to conserve the dwindling roan population, estimated at only 400 animals in the northeasterly part of the country, excluding the Caprivi.

Transport by road was logistically impossible, so the only option was to consider airlifting the roans directly from the area of capture in the dry riverbed of the Khaudum Omuramba. The relocation plans involved building a 1.8 km landing strip five kilometres from the roans' boma. The roans recovered very well after their capture ordeal.

After successful experiments to determine the effects that prolonged immobilisation would have on the animals, the roan was re-immobilised on 20 October 1970 and airlifted in three separate flights to Otjovasandu, western Etosha, until all animals were successfully released into their new enclosure. Only four mortalities were suffered, and a remarkable event occurred when one cow gave birth merely a week after being translocated.

In August 1973, 159 roans were counted during a helicopter census. In the long run, though, the roans could have adapted better as the area where they were located fell below the 300 mm isohyet, and the roans needed more water to establish a viable population. However, the population flourished when 34 roans were again translocated from Etosha to the Waterberg Plateau Park in 1975, where the rainfall was above 400 mm. The DNCT could later sell the surplus animals to private game farms with higher rainfall.

You are not likely to see any roan in Etosha, except on an off-chance in the western part.

Interesting facts about the translocation of black-faced impala

Approximately 226 black-faced impala were translocated from their historic range in the Kunene region (then Kaokoland), northwest Namibia, between 1968 and 1971 to Etosha National Park by the Ministry of Forestry Environment and Tourism. This translocation aimed to increase the subspecies' range and abundance in Namibia following a severe decline in the population in the Kunene region because of poaching, competition with livestock and severe droughts. Securing a population within a protected area close to their natural range proved tremendously successful, with the black-faced impala thriving since their re-introduction and almost half its population in Namibia now found in Etosha (approximately 1 500 animals). In the early 1990s, the Ministry of Environment, Forestry and Tourism could translocate black-faced impala from Etosha to the Kunene.

A study was conducted on 127 black-faced impala from the five subpopulations in Etosha to determine their hybridisation with the common impala in the park. Still, no signs of hybridisation between the subspecies in Etosha could be established.

Interesting facts about anthrax in cheetahs

Anthrax is an infectious bacterial disease caused by *Bacillus anthracis*. It is endemic in Etosha and has been studied there since 1966.

While anthrax affects mostly herbivores, only a few suspected anthrax mortalities were reported from free-ranging large carnivores. Cheetah are a particular case, with a few confirmed mortalities in the park. Although cheetah can mount a response against the bacteria, infections typically lead to rapid disease progression and death.

Rutting behaviour of male black-faced impala

It is thought they have not built up immunity through exposure to anthrax carcasses because they are not scavengers and feed only on freshly killed meat. Their low or undetectable levels of antibodies to anthrax protective antigen supports this theory. They probably become exposed to it by catching and consuming prey, probably springbok, infected with anthrax and then die soon after. Because cheetah share their kills, such an event will probably kill entire cheetah families.

The cheetah population in Etosha is relatively low. Data from camera trap placements to determine cheetah movements in Etosha National Park and neighbouring southwestern farms estimated the cheetah density to be between 0.50 and 0.66 cheetah/100 km^2. The low numbers are generally attributed to competition from other predators, especially lion, but it confirms that anthrax may be a significant population limiting factor.

Salt-harvesting

Salt harvesting from some pans north of Etosha has been practised for centuries. As early as the 18th century, salt was one of the commodities exported by Owambo traders and gathered for domestic use.

Some of the pans rich in salt are the Ongandjera and Ongandjera East pans, Otjivalunda pans, and Ondangwa Pan. However, salt production was allowed in only some Ovambo communities, the **Ondonga**, **Ongandjera** and **Uukwambi**.

The salt collection occurred at a certain period of the year, usually from July to September after the harvest and before the sowing of the new crops, and was strictly controlled by the king.

Salt production was also classified as a handicraft because it was refined and usually shaped into blocks between 1–3 kg before the community sold them.

Salt gathering was culturally significant, marking the transition from boy- to manhood.

Damara dik-dik

Acknowledgements

This book would not have been possible without my husband, Heiko's, love, encouragement and support. I love and appreciate your unwavering support and help with this project.

I wish to thank the following people and institutions for their expertise in various fields, generous time, proofreading and help with plant identifications:

Hanjo Böhme for his valuable input regarding the blue cranes in Etosha and expertise in the field of birds, Prof. Gillian Maggs-Kölling, Hartmut Kölling, Leon Gerhard Lubbe and Coleen Mannheimer for their tireless effort in identifying various plant species and grasses; Nicole Grünert for her expertise in the field of geology; Ruben Portas for generously sharing and providing information and photos on various research projects; as well as the whole GAIA team, namely Ortwin Aschenborn, Joerg Melzheimer, Gabriel Shatumbu, Wanja Rast, Teja Curk, Miha Krofel and Douglas Branch for information on the vulture and lion research projects. Wilferd Versfeld, Martina Küsters and Werner Kilian for their time and expertise on all matters Etosha and Ute von Ludwiger for information regarding Twee Palms and finding the Etosha agama; Kerstin Engelking for her time, during which I peppered her with herpetofauna-related questions; Kenneth Uiseb, head of wildlife monitoring and research for information on hybridisation between the two zebra species; and to Nico Louw – pilot extraordinaire – for the many unforgettable hours in the 'Hoogtevreesvoël' and the privilege to observe Etosha from a bird's eye perspective!

All this would not be possible without the help of the Ministry of Environment, Forestry and Tourism (MEFT). I am profoundly grateful to the Hon. Pohamba Shifeta, Minister of the Ministry of Environment, Forestry and Tourism for having granted permission for aerial footage in the park, as well as Colgar Sikopo, Deputy Executive Director; Shayne Koetting for the logistics; Evaristo Nghilai, Control Warden for Directorate Parks and Wildlife Management ENP, for his co-operation and kind assistance in the park; as well as Bernd Brell, Wildlife Scene of Crime Investigator and K9 Handler; Claudine Cloete, Senior Conservation Scientist and current acting head of the Etosha Ecological Institute (EEI), for her help in providing information on the research on Etosha's large carnivores; Martin Hermann, former acting Chief Warden East; Elvis Mwilima, former Area Warden Central; George Masilo, former Deputy Director; Petrina Ndumbu, Area Warden Halali; and Gabriel Shatumbu, pilot and nature conservator.

Thank you also to the Namibian Film Commission, especially Shirley Kariange, for granting the permit for filming in the park.

Special thanks also to the Van den Berg family – Ingrid, Philip and Heinrich – for letting this book come to life under your guidance and expertise.

Photo credits: Ruben Portas, photos of collaring male lion, vulture ringing and tagging. Heiko Denker, photos of Kalkheuwel lion and zebra chase, and profile photo of author.

Aerial view of lion pride with Burchell's zebra kill on Etosha Pan

About the Author

Born, raised and schooled in Windhoek, Namibia, I have always had somewhat of an artistic nature, combined with an intense love for animals. Upon completing my studies in Cape Town in the field of office administration and fashion design, as well as working as a fashion designer for a few years, home beckoned. Earning a living as an office administrator in Windhoek proved to be pretty stifling and boring for my artistic soul and I started to illustrate school- and children's books from home after the birth of my daughter, as well as designing postage stamps for Namibia and other SADC countries.

In 2010, while on holiday in Australia, we bought our first DSLR – a Nikon D5000 – which was shared in the family. This set me on a new path, that of photography.

As a child I spent many hours in my uncle's dark room; enticed by the smell of chemicals, sheets of photographic paper bathing in their trays of chemical solutions, red light and the sense of excitement and wonder as images were slowly developing and hanging out to dry on a line… The first camera I held in my hand was my Dad's Minolta, which I was allowed to use, and I did – frequently!

It was thus just a natural extension of my artistic career, coupled with my love for nature and animals, combined with those early childhood memories and exposure to photography, that I have finally come full circle.

Published works include photo feature articles and online blogs for magazines and books, such as *Travel News Namibia*, *Africa Geographic* and the international very successful *Remembering Wildlife* series.

Selling fine art prints and calendars and doing the occasional stint as a specialist guide with the main emphasis on Etosha, puts the proverbial bread on the table every now and again.

I strive to convey emotion through my work, be it through photography, visual art or words and my happiest moments are those spent in the nature, camera close by.

Anja Denker

Selected bibliography/Sources

Auer, Claudia. 1997. *Chemical quality of water at waterholes in the Etosha National Park.* Madoqua, 1997 20(1) 121-128

Berry, Hu and Rocher 'Stoffel' and Paxton, Mark and Cooper, Tryg. Revised edition, 1995. *Origin and Meaning of Place Names in the Etosha National Park Namibia.* Windhoek: Instaprint.

Berry, HH, 1971. *Flamingo breeding on the Etosha Pan, South West Africa, during 197.,* Madoqua. Series 1, No. 5. 1972 (5-31)

Berry, Conny and Berry Hu and Brain, Conrad K and Böhlke, Immo and Burger, Helga and Burger, Pompie and Dieckmann, Ute and Ebedes, Hym and Friederich, Reinhard and Griffin, Mike and Hipondoka, Martin HT and L'Estrange, Piers and Lindeque, Pauline and Mauney, Ginger and Rack, Hans and Schoeman, Amy and Silvester, Jeremy and van Schalkwyk, Paul. 2007. *Etosha 100: Celebrating a hundred years of conservation.* Windhoek: Venture Publications. John Meinert (Pty) Ltd.

Berry, HH. 1997. *Historical reviews of the Etosha Region and its subsequent administration as a National Park.* Madoqua, 1997, 20(1): 3-12.

Berry, C and Loutit, B. 1982. *Trees and shrubs of the Etosha National Park.* Windhoek: Multi Services.

Bethune, Shirley (Editor) and Shaw, Danica and Roberts, Kevin S and the Wetland Working Group of Namibia, 2007. *Wetlands of Namibia.* Windhoek: John Meinert (Pty) Ltd.

Bridgeford, Peter. 2018. *Conservation pioneers in Namibia and stories by game rangers.* Windhoek: John Meinert (Pty) Ltd.

Beugler-Bell, H. and Buch, MW. 1997. Soils and soil erosion in the Etosha National Park, northern Namibia. Madoqua 1997, 20(1): 91-104.

Bro-Jørgensen J, Dabelsteen T. *Knee-clicks and visual traits indicate fighting ability in eland antelopes: multiple messages and back-up signals.* BMC Biol. 2008 5 November;6:47. doi: 10.1186/1741-7007-6-47. PMID: 18986518; PMCID: PMC2596769.

Curtis, BA. 1990. *Freshwater macro-invertebrates of Namibia.* Madoqua 1991, 17(2): 163-187.

Cunningham, Peter and Jankowitz, Willem. 2010. *A Review of Fauna and Flora Associated with Coastal and Inland Saline Flats from Namibia with Special Reference to the Etosha Pan.* 10.1007/978-90-481-9673-9_2.

Ebedes, Hym. 1976. Anthrax epizoötics in Etosha National Park. Madoqua 10(2): 99-118. 187.

Erb, Peter K. *Rhinoceros conservation in Namibia*. Namibia Environment, Vol. 1.

Simmons, Robert and Brown, Christopher and Kemper, Jessica. 2015. *Birds to watch in Namibia: red, rare and endemic species.*

Friederich, Reinhard, and Lempp, Horst. 2014. *Etosha: Hai//om Heartland, Ancient hunter-gatherers and their environment.* Windhoek: Namibia Publishing House.

Griffin, Michael. 2003. *Annotated checklist and provisional conservation status of Namibian reptiles.* Windhoek: Namibia Scientific Society.

Grünert, Nicole. 2013, 6th edition. Namibia – *Fascination of Geology: A Travel Handbook.* Göttingen-Windhoek: Klaus Hess Publishers.

Hipondoka, Martin HT and Kempf, J and Jousse, H. 2013. *Paleo and present ecological value of the Etosha Pan, Namibia: An integrative review.* Journal NWG/Journal NSS Band/Volume 61-2013.

Hipondoka, Martin HT. 2005. *The development and evolution of Etosha Pan, Namibia.* Dissertation, Würzburg 2005.

Hipondoka, Martin HT and Versfeld, Wilferd D. 2005. *The root system of Terminalia sericea shrubs across a rainfall gradient in a semi-arid environment of Etosha National Park, Namibia.* Ecological Indicators 6 (2006) 516-524.

Hofmeyr, JM and Ebedes, H and Fryer, REM and de Bruine JR. 1975. *The capture and translocation of the black rhinoceros Diceros bicornis Linn. in South West Africa.* Madoqua, Vol. 9, No.2, 1975 (35-44).

Hoffmann, LAC. 1988. *An annotated list of amphibian and reptile observations from the Etosha National Park.* Madoqua 1989, 16(2): 87-92.

Jensen, RAC and Clinning, CF. 1976. *Birds of the Etosha National Park. 1980.* Windhoek: John Meinert (Pty) Ltd., 2nd edition.

Kolberg, Holger and Kolberg, Claire. *Etosha Pan is a wetland of international importance.*

Lindeque, PM and Nowell, K Preisser, T and Brain, C and Turnbull, PCB. 1998. *Anthrax in wild cheetahs in the Etosha National Park, Namibia.* Madoqua. Series 1, No.8, 1974.

Le Roux, CJG and Grunow, JO and Morris, JW and Bredenkamp, GJ and Scheepers, JC. 1987. *A classification of the vegetation of the Etosha National Park.* South African Journal of Botany, 1988, 54(1): 1-10.

Lindeque, Malan and Archibald, TJ. 1990. *Seasonal wetlands in Owambo and the Etosha National Park.* Madoqua, 1991, 17(2): 129-133.

Nordenstam, Bertil. *Notes on the Flora and Vegetation of Etosha Pan, South West Africa.* Dinteria Nr. 5, Windhoek, S.W.A., July 1970.

Marais, Anna Louise and Marais Christine. 1995. *Etosha Experience.* Windhoek: Gamsberg Macmillan Publishers (Pty) Ltd.

Mendelsohn, John and El Obeid, Selma, and Roberts, Carole. 2000. A Profile of North-Central Namibia. Windhoek: Gamsberg Macmillan Publishers.

Mendelsohn, John, and Jarvis, Alice and Robertson, Tony. 2013. *A profile and atlas of the Cuvelai-Etosha Basin.* Windhoek: John Meinert (Pty) Ltd.

Miller, Roy McG. and Pickford, M. and Senut, B. 2010. *The geology, palaeontology and evolution of the Etosha Pan, Namibia: Implications for terminal Kalahari deposition.* South African Journal of Geology, 2010, vol. 113.3, pages 307-334.

Ministry of Environment, Forestry and Tourism, Large Carnivore Management Association of Namibia and Namibia Chamber of Environment. 2022. *Conservation Status and Red List of the Terrestrial Carnivores of Namibia.* Windhoek: John Meinert (Pty) Ltd.

Müller, Michiel AN. Revised edition 2007. *Grasses of Namibia.* Windhoek: John Meinert (Pty) Ltd.

Nature Conservation, S.W.A., 1982. *75 Etosha, 1907–1982.* Windhoek: Multi Services.

Osborne, Tim O and Versfeld Wilferd, D and van Schalkwyk, Paul. 2007. *Etosha National Park Centenary Edition: Guidebook to the Waterholes and Animals.* Windhoek: Venture Publications. John Meinert (Pty) Ltd.

Portas, R. 2023. *Density estimation of cheetah (Acinonyx jubatus) across Namibia's biomes using GPS movement data to inform camera trap placement.* The thesis is submitted to fulfil the requirements for the Master of Natural Resources Management degree at the Namibia University of Science and Technology. Windhoek, Namibia, February 2023.

Riddell, Edward S.; Kilian, Werner; Versfeld, Wilferd and Kosoana, Martin. Groundwater stable isotope profile of the Etosha National Park, Namibia. *Koedoe* [online]. 2016, vol.58, n.1 [cited 2024-02-29], pp.1-7

Scheepers, JL and Venzke, KAE. *Attempts to reintroduce African wild dogs Lycaon pictus into Etosha National Park, Namibia.* South African Journal of Wildlife Research 1995, 25(4)

Schleicher, Alfred. 2020. *Reptiles of Namibia.* Windhoek: Kuiseb Publishers.

Siiskonen, Harri. 1990. Trade and Socioeconomic Change in Ovamboland, 1850–1906.

SHS/Helsinki/1990.

Stuart, Chris and Tilde. 4th edition, 2007. *A field guide to mammals of southern Africa.* Singapore: Kyodo Printing Co (S'Pore) Pte Ltd.

Tinley, Ken L. 1971. The case for saving Etosha. African Wild Life, Vol. 25, No.1. Cape Town: Gothic Printing Co. Ltd.

Turner, Wendy C and Périquet, Stéphanie and Goelst, Claire E and Kimberlie, Vera B and Cameron, Elissa Z andAlexander, Kathleen A and Belant, Jerrold L and Cloete, Claudine C and du Preez, Pierre and Gertz, Wayne M and Hetem, Robyn, S and Kamath, Pauline, L and Kasaona, Marthin K and Mackenzie, Monique and Mendelsohn, John and Mfune, John KE and Muntifering, Jeff R and Portas, Ruben and Scott, Ann H and Strauss, Maartin W and Versfeld, Wilferd and Wachter, Bettina and Wittemyer, George and Kilian, Werner J. 2022. *Africa's drylands in a changing world: Challenges for wildlife conservation under climate and land-use changes in the Greater Etosha Landscape.* Global Ecology and Conservation 38 (2022) e02221.

Van Oudtshoorn, Frits. 2009, 2nd edition, 5th impression. *Guide to grasses of southern Africa.* Singapore: Tien Wah Press (Pte) Ltd.

Walters, Matthew. 2015. *A study of the distribution and diversity of small mammal species within the different habitats of Etosha National Park.* Research Report, Etosha National Park, 2015.

Wiggs, Giles and Baddock, Matthew and Thomas, David and Washington, Richard and Nield, Joanna and Engelstaedter, Sebastian and Bryant, Robert and Eckardt, Frank and Holdt, Johannah and

Kötting, Shayne. 2022. *Quantifying Mechanisms of Aeolian Dust Emission: Field Measurements at Etosha Pan, Namibia.* Journal of Geophysical Research: Earth Surface. 127. 10.1029/2022JF006675

Martin, Esmond B. *Rhino poaching in Namibia from 1980 to 1990 and the illegal trade in the horn.* Pachyderm No. 18, 1994?

Bushman's poison

(Adenium boehmianum)

A particularly striking summer-flowering plant to look out for is the Bushman's poison *(Adenium boehmianum)*, a Namibian near-endemic. It occurs in a few isolated spots, usually near the roadside, and is a few-stemmed shrub or tree growing up to one or two metres in height.

However, the plant is as beautiful as it is deadly. The striking, tubular, bright pink blooms are roughly 50 mm in diameter and flower from December to May.

When the Hai//om still resided in the park and practised their hunter/gatherer lifestyle, they used the tuber of this plant to prepare poison for their arrows. The milky-white sap was heated in a container over embers until it solidified into a sticky, tar-like substance. The hunter placed this around a stick for later use. The Hai//om used to refer to the plant as **ouzuwo**, meaning poison.

The hunter did not place the poison directly onto the arrowhead but immediately behind it, on the shaft of the arrow, to minimise the danger of cutting himself accidentally during handling. It is highly potent, with reports of even elephants hunted in this fashion.

Steenbok and common duiker reportedly browse on the leaves.

Bushman's poison

Index Waterholes

Leopard

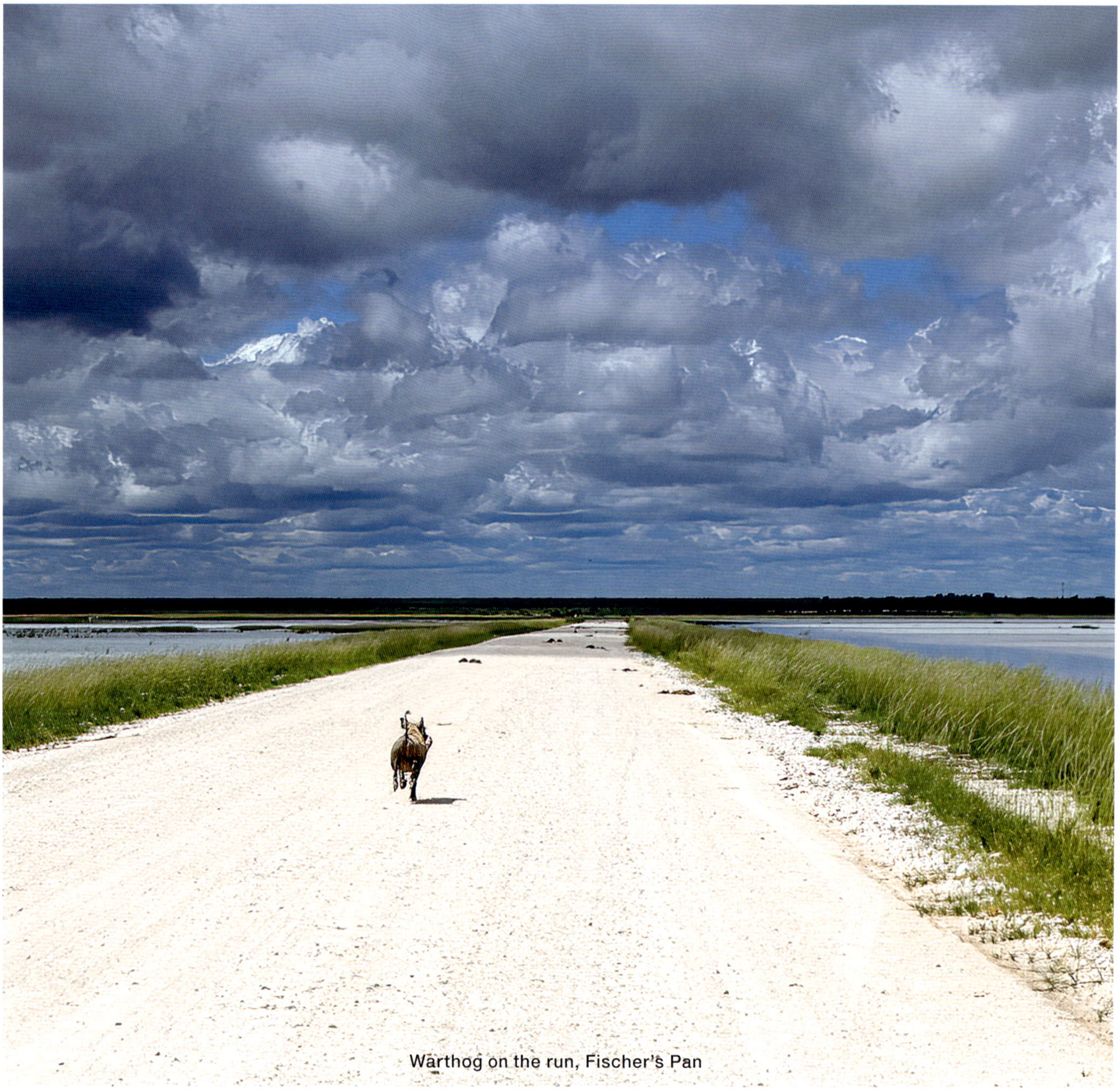

Warthog on the run, Fischer's Pan

First Edition
ISBN 978-1-7764332-5-4
Text and photography by Anja Denker
Publisher: Heinrich van den Berg
Edited and proofread by Margy Gibson
Design, typesetting and reproduction by
Heinrich van den Berg and Nicky Wenhold
Maps by Heinrich van den Berg and Nicky Wenhold
Printed in China

First edition, first impression 2024
Published by **HPH Publishing**
50A Sixth Street, Linden, Johannesburg, 2195, South Africa
www.hphpublishing.co.za
info@hphpublishing.co.za